The Well-Chosen Garden

Christopher Lloyd

The Well-Chosen Garden

Elm Tree Books · London

This book was designed and produced by
The Rainbird Publishing Group Ltd
40 Park Street, London W1Y 4DE.
First published in Great Britain 1984 by
Elm Tree Books/Hamish Hamilton Ltd
Garden House, 57–59 Long Acre
London WC2E 9JZ

Designed by Yvonne Dedman

British Library Cataloguing in Publication Data
Lloyd, Christopher
   The well-chosen garden
   1. Gardening
   I. Title
   635   SB450.97
ISBN 0–241–11144–7

Text set by Tradespools Ltd, Frome, Somerset
Colour originated by Bridge Graphics Ltd, Hull, Humberside
Printed and bound by New Interlitho SPA, Milan, Italy

Frontispiece: The red rose 'Florence May Morse'
with the diaphanous Mount Etna broom, *Genista aetnensis*,
in the Long Border at Great Dixter, July.

Contents

Preface

The origin of this book was an illustrated talk which I called 'Placing Your Plants'. It was not so much of the good health of garden plants that I was thinking, for this is the first consideration that enters most gardeners' minds, whether they are new to the game or old hands. It was rather the organization of plant material; considerations such as how plants look with their neighbours and in their setting and whether they are giving maximum value in the space available.

Myself I am a plantsman, not a landscape or garden architect, but I do appreciate the danger of becoming so excited about plants as individuals that we forget to stand back and evaluate them in their context. Is the context itself worthy? If it consists to a noticeable extent of gaps or dead plant material at a season when we want to be in the garden most and enjoying the best months of the year, then I think there is cause for concern.

In a very large garden with adequate staff there is always the option of treating it in sections, according to the season, and of personally avoiding an area such as the iris garden for ten or eleven months of the year. Let it look as dishevelled as it pleases during that period so long as it builds up to a great and glorious climax for a few weeks.

But most of us will want to husband and exploit our resources so that we can live amicably with them over a large part of the year. Then how about a self-supporting garden consisting largely of ground cover, heathers and conifers, which is permanently decent yet undemanding? There are plenty of writers, broadcasters and nurserymen promoting that sort of garden without my joining them. To me it spells Boredom with a capital B; all very well for those who don't much care about gardening anyway, but then I don't care much about them.

The readers I have in mind are passionately keen on plants but want to make the most of them in the limited space at their disposal (and even with a garden of five acres or more I find myself severely limited). They want to see and enjoy a garden that changes with the seasons and looks good at many seasons in different ways. Change *and* continuity. They must not keep on moaning, 'that's too much fiddle; I haven't the time.' If they're wholehearted about gardening, the time spent on it will be a pleasure.

But a knowledge and understanding of garden economy must be mastered. We need to know how to organize our plant material so as to reap the desired rewards. I don't pretend to have learnt all the answers. One never comes to the end of learning, thank goodness. But I have accumulated, by trial and error, quite a bit of experience on choosing the right plants to achieve, or at least approach, an ideal, a kind of harmony yet with excitement always near the surface.

As a yardstick for comparing their conditions with mine, it will be helpful to readers if I briefly indicate what soil and climate I'm working with. Great Dixter, where I live, is in East Sussex, that is to say in southeast England about ten miles inland from the English Channel coast. My garden lies near the top of a southwest facing slope and maritime winds are often very strong. Wind is the great enemy, here, and we have planted a good deal of shelter over the years. Blotting out a view matters so much less than being able to grow plants without having them battered to pulp or blown out of the ground.

The compensation for these winds is that frost and snow are comparatively minor problems. Perhaps every other winter, frosts are severe and prolonged enough for the ice on my horse pond to carry one's weight, but then only for a few days. There are exceptional winters, of course, like 1963, when the air temperature in our porch dropped to 10°F and frost was prolonged, but these aberrations are soon forgotten. I always believe in planting masses of semi-tender shrubs after a hard winter, backing the odds that there won't be another for some years to come! (The pessimist – and how many such there are vociferously around us – would predict the onset of a new ice age and be petrified into inactivity.) Spring radiation frosts are uncommon because the cold air drains away, and in autumn we seldom sustain an air frost before November.

Rainfall averages thirty inches a year, distributed fairly evenly. If I don't have to irrigate at some time between spring and autumn, it's a pretty poor summer. But our soil is clay-based with a good deal of badly draining silt included, so drainage is a recurring problem. One way and another I am pretty fortunate and there are always plenty of visitors to tell me so.

In no book that I have written to date (except for *Clematis*, where identifications were necessary) did I consider the illustrations to be of great importance. Word pictures of individual plants were, I considered, almost sufficient. But here the photographs are paramount because they are pinpointing relationships; showing how plants can be worked into a pattern and can help each other or the sites in various ways. Many of the pictures were taken, either by Pamla Toler or myself, at Great Dixter, where I live – for this is my workshop and I know the background story to what the photograph actually shows. Others were taken in friends' gardens but only a few where the garden was strange to me. A photograph, taken at just one instant in time, can be deceptive. Ideally I should like to be showing the same area at different times of the year in far more examples than I have, but colour printing is expensive. We've not done badly, I must hope you will agree.

Christopher Lloyd

1. Top of the Long Border at Great Dixter in early August with large patches of pink and mauve border phloxes. *Phlomis fruticosa* (Jerusalem sage), centre front, recently dead-headed. *Escallonia* 'Iveyi', back right, carrying white blossom.

Mixed Border

A garden must have beds and borders in which to grow the majority of its plants and the mixed border seems to me to be the ideal, rather than segregating your material into shrubberies, rose beds, herbaceous borders and bedding-out areas.

Different kinds of plants grown in juxtaposition, help each other. Shrubs often provide firmness and solidity of form and texture. Many can be used for foliage effect over a long season. Herbaceous plants are the great contributors of colour. By and large they need massing rather than speckling, while the foliage plants, including grasses, set them off. Bulbs extend a border's season and can often be worked in among other plants without demanding a special position for themselves. Annuals and bedding plants allow us to ring the changes. Certain self-sowing annuals, like opium poppies, which I grow in my Long Border near where phloxes are flaunting are half friends, half foes. Their seed heads are decorative and as plants they are nice for filling in but if allowed to seed into a group of shorter plants they would quickly weaken and maim them. Verbascums, whether biennial or perennial, are deceptive too. When growing they develop so quickly that, like a friendly lion laying its paw over a kitten, a single leaf can within days utterly swamp some smaller neighbour. We want our borders to look full but we have to guard against this kind of thuggery. Especially when practised against slow shrubs that are small in their early years. They cannot be expected to make strong, bushy growth if towered over by neighbours that grow feet tall within weeks.

In fact you need to take great care about choosing suitable shrubs for a mixed border. Let us say that the border's main season is between June and September, when plant growth is naturally at its peak. It would be a mistake to include a spring flowering shrub like *Spiraea × vanhouttei*, because it would become a complete passenger after May, of no interest for its shape or for its foliage.

The Jerusalem sage, *Phlomis fruticosa*, is another matter. It is evergreen and its grey leaves are an asset for much of the year. Also, it makes a show of old-fashioned looking, dusky yellow flowers in June, which comes into our season. My plant is a slight worry in that the end of its flowering season overlaps with the beginning of a shocking pink phlox's on its left, so the sage needs dead-heading fairly smartly, after which its foliage again resumes a helpful role of setting off its flowering neighbours as you see in the picture taken on my Long Border (**1**) in early August.

Too many evergreens in a garden can bring on heaviness in summer but a leavening in the mixed border is invaluable, especially if the border itself has no evergreen hedge as background. My Long Border has yew, but I still use a good many evergreens right to the front. Another that you see here (top right) is the July- to August-flowering *Escallonia* 'Iveyi', covered with panicles of white blossom. It is a sight (and a sound – bees adore it) for ten days but would I choose it if I were starting again? I sometimes wonder. Point in favour: it has a cheerfully glossy leaf. Point against: its dead flower heads make the shrub look rather awful in winter. Point against: it has reached tree-like proportions but (point for) by selectively removing a number of branches each year I can plant quite close to it. The area around its trunk is colonized by woodruff, *Asperula odorata*, which makes a carpet of white each spring. So the site occupied by the escallonia is doing more than one job and the extension of the border's flowering season with woodruff does not weaken the display in July–August. The escallonia has it.

Some evergreens are improved in appearance if they themselves have a dark evergreen background, notably those with coloured (usually yellow) or variegated foliage. In the top back corner of my Long Border I have a variegated holly, *Ilex × altaclarensis* 'Golden King', which is an abiding joy throughout the year. Given me as a tiny plant in 1954, it is desperately slow growing in its early years. One would be tempted to choose the variegated *Elaeagnus pungens* 'Maculata' instead, but wrongly, for this popular shrub has the inelegant habit of side shoots that grow at every sort of awkward angle away from its main branches, whereas the holly, especially if pruned a little every five to seven years to keep it from opening out, makes a shapely column and it carries marvellous crops of red berries in holly-berrying years. Another point in its favour is that it is virtually prickle-free. The shed leaves from prickly hollies persist for a long while and are distressing to the hand weeder.

Slow growers make the comeliest specimens in the long run but the fastest growing shrubs have advantages of quite another kind and most of them are suited to mixed border life. I mean such as tree mallows, tree lupins, buddleias, shrubby hypericums, Spanish broom, summer flowering tamarisk (*Tamarix pentandra*), indigo (*Indigofera heterantha*) and most hydrangeas. Many of them flower in the summer on their new wood and can consequently be pruned hard back in winter or early spring just as though they were herbaceous plants, except that you're pruning to a stump instead of to the ground.

And there are shrubs grown for their foliage that can be treated in the same way. Such is the golden cut-leaved elder, *Sambucus racemosa* 'Plumosa Aurea' which you see at the lower end of my border (**2**) with groups of a 5 ft herbaceous daisy *Buphthalmum* (*Telekia*) *speciosum*. The lime-green leaves of the elder go well with the bright yellow daisies of the plant. If I didn't prune the sambucus annually, it would make a larger, scruffier bush with smaller, less distinguished leaves, and it would flower. That is no help at all; the flowers are insignificant and dissipate the shrub's purpose of carrying gorgeous leaves.

When choosing herbaceous plants for a mixed border, two main considerations will be colour – slabs of it to offset all the foliage plants you'll be revelling in – and length of flowering season. I'm not greedy in the last respect. Three weeks for a group will satisfy me, but then mine is a big border. With less space you'll be seeking longer-flowering plants like

2. At the shady lower end of the Long Border, the golden cut-leaved elder, *Sambucus racemosa* 'Plumosa Aurea', with the yellow daisy, *Buphthalmum (Telekia) speciosum*; late July.

Japanese anemones, which go on from early August to mid-October, and you may also turn to tender perennials like dahlias or cannas, to annuals, or to long-flowering bedding plants like verbenas.

A really short-season perennial is not to be tolerated unless it is so exciting (like the yellow-flowered *Arum creticum*) that you concentrate on those few days so that they seem to have been as many weeks. The sort of perennial I would be shy of recommending is *Centaurea macrocephala*. It has large yellow thistle heads and a clump of it takes the eye. I first saw this in the Royal Horticultural Society's gardens at Wisley and was bowled over but it is hard to know, until you've grown it yourself, that its season is only a week or ten days long and it has absolutely nothing else to offer. Some plants on the other hand, can be coaxed into flowering a second time. The purple-spiked *Salvia nemorosa* 'Superba' is one of my favourites in this category and so is *Helenium* 'Moerheim Beauty', which I grow next to it.

Weeks Farm, in Kent, is in essence a cottage garden on a large scale with a *mêlée* of flowers (**3**) among which you must not be surprised or shocked to see mustard-yellow achilleas hobnobbing with brilliant pink phloxes. When you stand back, these violent incursions are totally absorbed and this is largely achieved by an abundance of foliage and also by the size of these double borders. They are some 12 ft across and the path between them 9 ft. These are very relaxed proportions, though the borders are quite short. It is far more satisfactory to have one large border in a small garden that will accommodate some big groups and units without looking top heavy, than to finnick around with a mass of incident, nothing large enough to make its mark.

At the Pollock Halls of Residence in Edinburgh University, you have the very different ambience of institutional gardening and yet because the superintendent, Geoffrey Brooks, really cares about what he is planting and where, any interested resident or visitor must be enormously stimulated by what he finds. In one courtyard you notice first that the gravel path is broad so that plants from either side can encroach upon it. Everything has elbow space and room to breathe. When you have to be content with a lawn frontage, there is nearly always an uncomfortable feeling of containment.

Polygonum affine has been allowed to flow out from their border and root into the gravel. Its pink spikes have a months-long season and the foliage colours in the autumn. If suited it gives splendid value – in fact we couldn't hit it off in my garden, but then it takes all sorts. You notice an isolated clump of blue leaved grass, *Helictotrichon sempervirens*. Although at the border's margin it rises feet above its surroundings. A too careful grading for height looks smug and bland.

Behind all this is a great bank of cotoneaster, which has two seasons: early, when flowering, and late, when in berry, but anything tending towards the fidgets in so large an expanse of tiny leaves is compensated for by its flowing habit and also by the strong vertical lines of the sword-like leaves of *Phormium tenax* behind it.

I am always surprised but try not to be resentful when I visit Scotland, by the number of plants that do better for them than they do for me. I've never had much growth from the bush willow, *Salix lanata*, but this is a native of Scotland and northwards to the Arctic. Here it makes a fine dome of grey-green foliage between flowering colonies of shrubby potentillas. When young, this willow's foliage is greyer still and even earlier, male bushes carry woolly pussies covered with yellow specks of pollen while the female's fruits develop into grey candles several inches long.

Wherever a border's contents consist of a fairly high proportion of herbaceous perennials, there will be a tendency for it to fall away in colour content after the second week in August (in the south of England). Even the phloxes will be ebbing and it becomes a challenge to maintain the interest without weakening the earlier display.

3. Double mixed borders at Weeks Farm, Egerton, Kent, with broad central path giving excellent proportions.

For late August and early September I have for several years been working at a grouping (4) based on *Aster sedifolius*, better known as *A. acris*, and *Crocosmia* (*Montbretia*) 'Citronella'. Behind them, the inestimable *Weigela florida* 'Variegata' whose May season of scented tubular pale pink blossom and young, white-edged leaves, merges without weakening into a months-long span when the leaves, now gold and green, become a lively background to whatever you may choose for companions. I once grew the waterlily decorative dahlia 'Scarlet Beauty', in front of it, and that was dramatically satisfying.

The crocosmia/aster link up was harder work than I had expected. In the first year the aster was crippled by rabbits nibbling its young shoots. In the second the crocosmias simply failed to flower at all. In the third, all went well until I had secured my photograph, but then the crocosmia suddenly died out in large chunks as it did in many other gardens, including the Wisley trial grounds, in that year. Easy plants, as we all know, can prove surprisingly difficult.

4. Late August planting at Great Dixter. *Aster sedifolius (A. acris)*, left, and *Crocosmia (Montbretia)* 'Citronella' with shrubby *Weigela florida* 'Variegata' behind.

One of the advantages of 'Citronella' is the fresh green of its spear leaves all through the summer. And *Aster sedifolius* has the advantage of flowering a month earlier than the general run of Michaelmas daisies and of keeping going for a couple of weeks longer than they do, too. In fact, Michaelmas daisies of the popular *A. novi-belgii* types are a liability in many ways and I have given them up. The plants look excessively stodgy in the long run-up, then they flower only for a fortnight so that you really need a special Michaelmas daisy border to make them worthwhile, and then they are liable to mildew and several other troubles which I need not dwell on.

Aster sedifolius is very old-fashioned because it needs a lavish framework of supporting twigs. It is usually sold in its dwarf form which nobody bothers to stake but that's not the same thing as the splendid eiderdown of colour from a well-managed colony of the type plant. (Mine is not yet all that wonderful.)

At the front is a late flowering pink, *Dianthus amurensis*, with single mauve flowers. It can be treated as an annual. And on its right, a Michaelmas daisy not yet in bloom, but this one looks fresh and contributes all through the summer with airy, much-branched stems and a bright green colouring. It is a form of *Aster ericoides* called 'Esther' and its flowers are nearer pink than mauve.

There's the fruit of *Rosa moyesii* peering in from the right and, behind that, a pale, grey-leaved willow, *Salix alba argentea* that is simply grown for foliage and pollarded annually. It also plays host to an early display of the parasite, *Lathraea clandestina*, which feeds on its roots and carries dense clumps of purple, hooded flowers (they look like crocuses from a distance) from March to May.

Roses need company

The vast majority of roses make ugly bushes. To herd them into borders and gardens on their own is merely to emphasize their defects. The only point in its favour is that a monoculture enables the grower to concentrate on a comprehensive spraying programme for the control of their numerous pests and diseases. It should, however, be remembered that the greater the numbers and density of any single crop or creature, the greater the field day for the parasites and disease organisms to which they are a prey. Your efforts to keep on top will be in a state of progressive escalation.

On the other hand the greater the variety of plants you grow, the fewer will be your problems with any one of them. It would be good if roses ceased to be big business and gardeners abandoned rose worship in favour of regarding them as just another shrub that it is nice, indeed necessary, to own, but in reasonable numbers. There will then cease to be any need to segregate them. Or, if you do fancy a rose garden, it could consist up to half of shrub roses having a reasonably pleasing habit and, for the rest, plants that extend the former's season and contrast with the round blobs which are the rose's typical shape. Clematis, delphiniums, lilies, campanulas, cranesbills, Japanese anemones and alchemillas all associate particularly well with roses but the possibilities are unlimited. I realize, of course, that it is intellectually far easier to settle for a garden of roses than to have to work out a scheme where they are only one among perhaps a dozen or twenty ingredients. But the more taxing approach is also the more stimulating and will give you greater pleasure in the long run.

Lloyd now has to confess that he has a rose garden himself; it was there before I was born, was designed as such and would be difficult to use in any other way. But my preference is for introducing roses into other parts of my garden by way of the mixed borders.

There are not many red-flowered hardy perennials and most of those have a short season so a red rose can be an invaluable supplier of this colour. At the lower end of my Long Border (*frontispiece*), 'Florence May Morse' can be seen in front of the Mount Etna broom, *Genista aetnensis*. The latter flowers in July and is an exceptionally long-lived tree/shrub compared with most brooms, which pack up after a few years. Furthermore it casts so little shade that you can plant right underneath it. The red and yellow combination could be a bit hot, but does not seem so because of the genista's flowers being so very small. They pile up like a luminous thunder cloud. 'Florence May Morse' is a straightforward shade of red without any blue or orange in it. The flowers are not endearingly shaped, but they show up and are borne in two big flushes, summer and autumn. It grows 8 ft or more tall, with me, and is pruned and tied once a year to a chestnut post. I should perhaps say that none of the roses in my borders are ever sprayed and they don't seem to need it, holding their leaves well into autumn. Any that needed treatment for ailments would be discarded.

'The Fairy', a small double pink polyantha pompon, bears long trusses of blossom from mid-July till November in a setting of glossy, healthy foliage.

The habit is arching rather than upright and at 2 ft it is well suited to the border front. The August-September-flowering Chinese chives, *Allium tuberosum*, seeds itself around the rose's crowns (**5**), and I like its white umbels showing through the pink rosettes. An apron of the prostrate, glaucous *Acaena affinis* laps over the paving in front of these two.

Rosa moyesii and *R. setipoda* are dual-purpose. Single flowers in May-June, long red hips in August-September. The former has a stiff, gaunt habit, readily absorbed by planting something bushy, like hydrangeas in front of it. Stiff stems also suggest the drapery of a clematis which will not bear them down with its weight. Any of the hybrids of *Clematis texensis* would be suitable.

The true rugosas (rather than the hybrids) with their rough-textured yet glossy leaves are always the picture of health and eminently suited to mixed border life (they go well with *Acanthus*), where they successively flower and fruit with a considerable overlap between the two. The fruits are globular, like small tomatoes, and can raise an eyebrow when conjoined to the magenta flowers of such as 'Scabrosa', but somehow it works. There's plenty of diluting greenery. Eventually the foliage turns pure yellow, so these roses are marvellous value. The double kinds don't fruit and my first preference would be for singles like 'Alba' and the soft pink 'Frau Dagmar Hastrup'.

The pink colouring of 'Zéphirine Drouhin', an almost thornless, perpetual-flowering pillar rose with a marvellous scent, is brash and quarrelsome. I had it near my yellow *Sambucus/Buphthalmum* set-up (**2**) and really only noticed the jangle when I saw the photograph. By framing a scene, a photograph forces you to focus on a small area. I ousted that plant but still enjoy another (**6**) which is surrounded by self-sown *Campanula persicifolia* in blue and white. No clashing here.

The campanulas also look good with the double pink 'Crested Moss', which I have in the middle of the Long Border. It is a charmer in flower but with a scrawny habit that makes concealment imperative. Here, with so many other kinds of plants around, it is entirely sublimated.

5. *(above left)* 'The Fairy', growing here at the front of a border, its pink flowers contrasting well with the white umbels of self-sown Chinese chives; mid-September.

6. Quarrelsome pink Bourbon rose 'Zéphirine Drouhin' offset by the cool blue and white of self-sown *Campanula persicifolia*.

'Perle d'Or' is stiff, angular and chunky, but a great flowerer and with a long repeat season. Its second flowering is particularly sweet on the air. The apricot flowers are miniature Hybrid Tea-type but on a large bush, and in most situations I'd rather have miniature roses on a large bush than miniature roses on a miniature bush. They achieve more individuality. Our original specimen is now nearly 50 years old and has oriental poppies growing around and through it, but that's in May-June before the rose has got going.

Two specimens of 'Grüss an Aachen' grow close together on adjacent poles at the back of the border; this is the climbing sport, which I rooted from cuttings. With its full, double, pearly pink flowers it looks old-fashioned but is not. It only flowers at midsummer and therefore shares with the purple clematis, 'Gipsy Queen', which is at its best in August.

There are, then, roses of all sizes and types to fit into your mixed border. A particularly stiff yet vigorous variety like 'Queen Elizabeth' might be hard to disguise. You could try running the pale blue clematis 'Perle d'Azur' through its legs.

Tulips as fixtures

When you grow tulips as spring bedders, they have to be lifted to make room for summer flowers. You harvest, store and then forget about them till the autumn, by which time mice have eaten the lot. In rough grass, tulips look delightful but slowly dwindle and vanish. The one way to keep them over the years is as permanencies in your mixed borders.

I have a patch of the Parrot tulip, 'Orange Favourite', which has been going for fifteen years at least. There were 100 bulbs at the start and I still enjoy 100 blooms in good years – tulips have their ups and their downs. They were, and still are, interplanted among clumps of *Rudbeckia* 'Gold-sturm', a perennial black-eyed Susan that starts rather late into growth. Its golden daisies open from early August and give fully two months' value; it is 2½ ft tall, shade-tolerant but moisture loving, and fully self-supporting. So that makes good use of one patch of ground.

You see the same treatment at Barnsley House, near Cirencester, Gloucestershire (7), where the border is backed by a Cotswold stone wall. Round about are rose, peony, oriental poppy, hebe, for the main display, but in the meantime a spring bonus: tulips and self-sown forget-me-nots. You have to be firm with the latter, weeding out the seedlings that would interfere with nearby perennials, but they are easily pulled out when dead. The tulips merely need dead-heading. By the time their foliage is dying the surrounding plants will have taken over.

In a newly planted border it is never difficult to find room for tulips but in an old border you should site them so that they will need only occasional disturbance, that is to say among perennials that do not themselves need frequent division but that are not so early and voluminously in growth (as lupins, for instance) as to swamp the bulbs. Japanese anemones, *Aster × frikartii* and any *Heliopsis* (a restrained perennial sunflower) are good hosts.

If you overhaul your border in autumn, you'll be able to make any desired new plantings or replantings as soon as the neighbouring perennials have themselves been dealt with, supposing they need anything more than cutting down and top dressing with manure. Often they won't. The only disadvantage in autumn work is that established tulip groups won't yet be showing through. There'll be no guidance sign, unless they were marked with short pieces of cane – an invaluable early warning system. Even if you can't remember what the cane meant, you'll investigate carefully near that spot before using your trowel or fork.

Nowadays I leave my borders till the spring which is not, I must confess, quite so good for the tulips. Admittedly you'll be able to see where they are and so they are easily bypassed, but if you wanted to move them on account of the plants they're among needing to be re-set, you'll not be able to do so without seriously upsetting their growth.

Tulips are rather good among foliage shrubs or sub-shrubs like santolinas, *Senecio cineraria* and certain hebes, that have to be, or at least can be, cut back in late winter or early spring, thus leaving open spaces between the plants in which the tulips can develop before the gaps close in again.

7. Tulips give early colour to the mixed borders at Barnsley House without interfering with or mitigating the main summer display.

More bulbs in borders

8. *Allium murrayanum* flowering at Great Dixter in early June. It is surrounded by the spreading young growth of *Geranium wallichianum* 'Buxton's Blue', which will flower July to November after the allium has withered.

Tulips are only one example of the use of bulbs in the mixed border context. Daffodils, by and large, die off much too obtrusively to be suitable; I shall come to them later, but a great many others can be used.

Hyacinths that were once grown for winter and early spring display in bowls should always be saved and planted out. If properly sited where disturbance will be unnecessary they will carry on indefinitely. We have a clump of 'l'Innocence' that was first given to my brother in hospital when he had an appendicitis – in 1929. Hyacinths are good among roses, if you don't feel obliged to be messing around with the ground over-busily, but by far their best position is among herbaceous June-flowering peonies (*Paeonia lactiflora* forms). The carmine shoots of these will already be a few inches high when the hyacinths are flowering in March–April, and they go awfully well together.

I have already mentioned *Allium tuberosum* (**5**) in connection with roses. That species is late flowering but between them the alliums (onions, in English, but that sounds as bathetic as paste for pâté: try House Paste for Pâté Maison) cover a flowering season of six months. Early kinds like *A. murrayanum* (**8**), which flowers in May–June, can be grown in gaps that exist only in the early part of the season. You see it here invested by the young shoots of a remarkable cranesbill, *Geranium wallichianum* 'Buxton's Blue'. This spreads as much as 2 ft in all directions from a central crown and will climb 18 in or 2 ft into any taller plant which it encounters on the way. But in autumn it dies back to the original very small crown from which it originated and much ground is vacated for early performers like snowdrops, crocuses, anemones – and alliums. By the time they are being swamped again, their seed has been set and they are ready for a long siesta.

A. aflatunense reaches a height of 3 ft and carries spherical heads of lavender stars in May that look uncommonly well behind any hosta with waxy blue leaves. The pale straw-coloured seed heads retain their shape and beauty through the summer. It is rather a bore that the leaves on most of these larger alliums are already dying off, obtrusively, by the time their flowers are coming out, but the hostas' own foliage will utterly conceal this defect. In the same way you need to place *A. giganteum* behind masking shrubs or plants so that only its dramatic, lilac-coloured heads are seen in its June flowering season. Light, well-draining soil is a great advantage for such as this. It tends to go down to fungal diseases on my clay if the early summer is wet.

Neither are lilies in general (though *Lilium pardalinum* is an exception) any too happy on clay soils where, also, they become a prey to the small black slugs that can live among their scales until no bulb remains. But lilies in mixed borders are an attractive proposition, and also among shrubs. In grand woodland gardens where rhododendrons and azaleas predominate, they are used to extend the season beyond rhododendron time.

The deliciously scented Madonna lily, *L. candidum*, flowers in early July and is no trouble if you start with virus-free stock and keep it that way. 'Broken' tulips (the stripy ones) carry a lily virus and are better kept in another part of the garden. The Madonna lily bulb should be planted only just below the soil surface and it will thrive in hot, exposed places, on chalk as well as other soils, but it looks better when among other plants – I have it with *Penstemon* 'Drinkstone Red' here. *L. henryi*, with apricot-coloured turkscaps, is easy going and flowers late in July, into August. I have it emerging from quite a tangle of low shrubs – daphne, hydrangea, nandina. Given good drainage and with the addition of humus in the form of peat or leaf mould, it is worth trying groups of some of the more captious lilies like the golden-rayed Japanese *L. auratum* among shrubs. But it is a sad fact in respect of lilies, as of roses, that the more kinds you grow together, the more liable they all are to pick up and succumb to one another's diseases. Madonna lilies traditionally thrive in cottage gardens better than any-where, and this is because they are the only lily on the scene. It is possible to be a happy gardener by doing really well with just that one.

The best-known galtonia is the Cape hyacinth, *Galtonia candicans*, whose 3 to 4 ft spikes of waxy white bells open in July and August. They look dreadfully stiff and artificial if massed in unrelieved colonies, but are delightful in a general mix-up. These, too, suffer from virus diseases, but they seed freely, and seedlings start with a clean bill of health. If you plant them at the back or in the middle of a border, they may find themselves too housed in but are then liable to seed themselves into the border's margin

and this is a happy arrangement, as I shall have occasion to say again of other plants. If rather tall yet sparse in their growth so that you can see through and past them, they look absolutely appropriate, rising above their neighbours. I had a pleasing arrangement at one time with Cape hyacinths among the self-sowing *Lychnis coronaria*, with magenta flowers, and *Fuchsia gracilis* 'Versicolor' in various shades of carmine, pink and ashen green.

I very much like colchicums as mixed-border inmates though many gardeners make a great fuss about their voluminous foliage which appears in spring. It is glossy and luxuriant, by no means to be despised. Admittedly it goes through a bad patch when dying off in late May and early June but by then it is safe to cut it down. These bulbs – or corms, rather – are often incorrectly known as autumn crocuses. Their blooms do have the shape of a crocus but much more substance, and they are normally suffused with pink, as no crocus ever is. I have put a group of 'The Giant' in front of an interesting and late-flowering herbaceous perennial called *Liriope muscari* (**9**). The liriope, itself like the colchicum a member of the lily family, bears spikes of shiny mauve flowers like little sugar balls over a long late summer and autumn season. Its evergreen strap leaves are often hideously dowdy at flowering time and spoil the display. This is easily prevented by cutting them all to the ground in late winter so that the leaves at flowering time are of the same year and in pristine condition.

I am quite pleased with my team but I must admit that the brilliance of the colchicum is rather subduing to the liriope. As a companion to the latter, Graham Thomas, formerly Garden Adviser to the National Trust,

10. *Zephyranthes candida*, the flower of the west wind, enlivening the front of the Long Border in early October. Blue *Ceratostigma willmottianum* to its left.

recommends *Nerine bowdenii*, which is even more brilliant than the colchicum. Indeed, the colour of this autumn flower is quite untypical of the season. I find it goes well with *Aster amellus* 'Violet Queen' ('Veilchenkönigin') and have interplanted them accordingly. In this way, too, you remain unaware of the nerine's foliage, which is moribund at flowering time, although there's nothing against cutting it all away in early September, and I do this where I have a colony whose leaves are exposed to the public gaze (my gaze, that is to say). To dot your bulbs evenly among the asters is unsubtle if just left at that. My planting is still in the formative stage. I shall have asters without nerines and a concentration of nerines without asters in outlying parts and I shall run a meandering grey-leaved plant – *Helichrysum petiolatum* or *Senecio leucostachys* – through the colony from one end.

These nerines are remarkably hardy and free-flowering in Britain, even in the north. This is just as well, because however deep you plant them, they will always rise to the surface, which is where they want to be. If zero degree frosts are a serious risk, you can cover with fern litter, but remember that the nerine's new growing season starts in February and the young leaves will need to see the light.

The flower of the west wind, *Zephyranthes candida*, is a close relation, and produces white crocus-like flowers from August to October (**10**). The freedom with which they flower is directly related to the heat of the previous summer. A good front-of-border plant, this. Its leaves are more or less evergreen, unless killed off by frost, and that is no serious matter. The bulbs increase quickly and soon build up a colony. Flowers like this having the freshness of spring are particularly welcome in autumn.

Two-tier gardening

Yet another member of the allium tribe provides an example of space-saving in what has been called two-tier gardening, that is to say the situation where one kind of plant grows underneath another. In this case (**11**) *Allium christophii* rises 18 in to 2 ft above a carpet of *Sedum* 'Ruby Glow'. Neither inhibits the other.

This allium is one of the most remarkable of its tribe. Its mauve flowers open in early June and the globe which they compose continues to enlarge as the colour fades until it is some 10 in across. Meantime the 'petals' (perianth segments) stiffen and lose nothing of their structure. Thus it remains until summer's end when the ball of now ripened seed pods becomes detached from the stem and is bowled around in the wind till it lodges among the stems of some other plant. There the seeds are shed and if you remove and look underneath any of these balls in the following March you will see the green, thread-like stems of its newly germinated seedlings. And so, if you're not too busy or tidy a gardener, in time you'll have this handsome plant growing at considerable distances from where you originally planted it.

The mauve of its summer colouring tones in with the purplish cast to the sedum's fleshy leaves. 'Ruby Glow' is a strong, not quite prostrate stonecrop whose purplish red flowers expand in late August and September. Bees love them. It is lucky that I never have to disturb *Sedum* 'Ruby Glow' for its well being, because, as well as *Allium christophii* it also has clumps of *A. neapolitanum* in among it.

Behind these two I have a wavy line of the hydrangea called 'Preziosa', whose colouring matches the sedum's flowers. It has small, hortensia-type (that is, bun-headed) inflorescences that open pale and rather disappointingly wan but steadily intensify in colour until they are deep red – or purple (according to the acidity of your soil). Its young stems and leaf stalks are reddish also and the leaves also take on similar autumn tints.

A. neapolitanum starts growing in the autumn and continues right through till April–May when its head of pearl-white flowers expand. As soon as these fade, at the end of May, I firmly grasp all the decaying leaves and stems and give a sharp tug, whereupon they break cleanly away from the bulbs below the soil's surface. This gives the sedums more light and a better chance to develop but it also prevents the alliums from seeding, which they are apt to do incontinently.

Another example of two-tier planting is under the Mount Etna broom, *Genista aetnensis*. I remarked that it casts very little shade – all its greenery is concentrated in thread-like stems; and actual leaves are short-lived and unimportant. Under it I grow clumps of a giant yellow daisy, *Inula magnifica*. It makes 8 ft in height and the fine-spun rays of its flowers are such as one imagines Van Gogh would have enjoyed painting. They are exactly the same colour and open at the same time as the broom's own flowers and look out from among them, so the two, very different in every other respect, make an intriguing comparison.

11. Performing on the same piece of ground but at different levels, the globes of *Allium christophii* above a carpet of *Sedum* 'Ruby Glow', which will flower six weeks later, in August–September. The background to this planting is *Hydrangea* 'Preziosa'.

Weavers and edge breakers

Some plants have the inestimable habit of infiltration. They push slender shoots through neighbouring plants and flower among them. As these shoots extend, so they open new flowers and thus their season tends to be a long one. These plants have a unifying quality. They knit your tapestry of flowers and foliage into a single piece of living fabric. This looks comfortable. 'How your plants do enjoy themselves', is a likely comment.

There is, as so often, another side to the picture. Infiltration is a term commonly used of one's enemies. Among plants, also, a competitive situation is set up and one plant, the infiltrator, may unless checked kill the infiltrated. It happened in my garden when a clump of aubrietia filtered into an old specimen of candytuft, *Iberis sempervirens*. This dark evergreen, mat-forming shrub has dead white flowers and I thought it much enlivened by the mauve of aubrietia in their April season. What I should have done was to pull out the invading strands after it had flowered. But I was inattentive and the iberis succumbed.

I am more careful where an aubrietia is growing through the double, salmon pink evergreen azalea called *Rhododendron indicum* 'Balsaminiflorum'. This does not flower till early June so the routine is to let the aubrietia make its contribution in April and May; then to pull out as many as I can of its long strands before the azalea takes over.

Aubrietia will climb into the lower reaches of shrubs – in our back drive it has utilized topiary yews and elsewhere we have a welcome and rather late flowering seedling in *Syringa* × *persica* 'Alba', whose growth is thin and thus allows enough light to penetrate for the aubrietia to climb from its basal mat about a foot into the lilac's lowest branches.

Those who confine their aubrietias to smug little blobs on rockeries, which they cut right back immediately after flowering, each year, have no idea what a jolly plant it can be when given its head and allowed to think up a few ideas for itself.

The interlocking and weaving of plants that you (I hope) and I think fun is absolutely *never* practised or indeed possible in a public garden and will rarely be met in the suburban front garden where orderliness is of the essence and every plant is allowed its allotted space but no more. Thus the hoe is kept busy round each border clump so that you are always aware of the canvas behind the tapestry. There has to be a line of demarcating soil between one clump and the next. 'Thou shalt not trespass' is the motto. This attitude allows no scope for the natural exuberance of plant growth and its expression. Plants should always appear to be enjoying themselves even though we are constantly under the necessity of restraining them. We can do this without appearing to.

Violas and cranesbills are two of the best hardy plant groups for the weaving habit. In a friend's Scottish garden on the Black Isle (north of Inverness), an edging of the old-fashioned mauve viola 'Maggie Mott', found itself at one point in front of the modern, lime-green-leaved form of *Spiraea* × *bumalda* called 'Goldflame' **(12)**. The viola climbed into the

12. *Viola* 'Maggie Mott' climbing into the lime green *Spiraea × bumalda* 'Goldflame' in a Scottish garden north of Inverness; July.

spiraea's lowest branches and had a look at the world from its vantage point. If the spiraea had been allowed to grow on unrestrained from year to year, the viola would soon have been overwhelmed, but in fact this shrub develops the best leaf colour, flowering less and later (the flowers are no asset whatsoever), if it is cut hard back every winter, so there's no reason why this team shouldn't remain in amicable balance over a long period.

Even violas planted in the first instance for bedding will survive a succession of winters if given the chance and perform their weaving trick when near to something taller than themselves.

But the best and most permanent of all violas for weaving among mixed border plants is *Viola cornuta* 'Alba'. It self-sows and if kept away from coloured strains remains white – pure white with very fresh green foliage. Its first burst of blossom comes in May and if the position is moist will continue, though somewhat abating, right into autumn. If the plants look tired you can cut them to the ground, say in June, water them well and off they'll go again, performing with renewed zest in September. But it is preferable where the weaving habit is to be encouraged, not to touch these

plants at all. The plants seen here (**13**) at the top of my Long Border are growing principally through a colony of the Scotch rose, *Rosa pimpinellifolia* 'William III' ('King' seems to have been shed), which is itself a colonizer and spreads by suckering. It has no great inclination to grow tall anyway but I make sure that it remains only 18 in high by pruning a good number of the oldest shoots back to ground level every winter.

You need bold plants for contrast somewhere near your intermeshers, so here you see *Hosta sieboldiana* 'Elegans' with waxy foliage, textured by longitudinal veining, with cross-ripples of puckered leafage in between.

In front, a hefty colony of *Alchemilla mollis* (not yet flowering, in May) which also grows and seeds itself into the cracks of the flagstone paving. This is an edge-breaker. It annihilates the hard line that would otherwise define the juncture of path (or lawn) and border.

Some lawn-and-neatness enthusiasts (they are never true plant lovers) take enormous pride in this discontinuity, and it is another inevitable mark of institutional gardening. Lawn; cliff edge; well-weeded border margin of clean earth; then your first border plants, neat things like annual alyssum and blue lobelia or, if perennials, plants of a predictable and easily restricted habit like London Pride or sea thrift.

It is, of course, a great advantage if your borders are next to a hard surface so that they can flow forwards on to it, as *Alchemilla mollis* will. If paving divides a border from a lawn, be as generous with its width as you can afford. A three-foot sandwich will not be excessive.

If there is no paved divide between lawn and border, I would still say, let some at least of the plants flow forwards from their official confines as you

13. At the top of my Long Border, photographed 7 June, the dazzling white *Viola cornuta* 'Alba' filters through the stems of *Rosa pimpinellifolia* 'William III'. The bold foliage of *Hosta sieboldiana* 'Elegans' is behind and an edge-breaking colony of *Alchemilla mollis* laps over the path.

14. *Senecio* 'Sunshine' flowing forwards over a lawn edge at Great Dixter. Not an example that will be found in any textbook on lawn management.

see my *Senecio* 'Sunshine' (*S. greyi* or *S. laxifolius*) bulging on to a lawn (**14**). When it has flowered – and I love its daisies which are bright without being brassy – I prune out all the flowered branches and a patch of bare lawn is revealed. Never mind, it'll soon recolonize or else be re-invaded. Grass growing into invading border plants that the motor mower cannot charge over isn't really difficult to deal with, as your lawn maintainers like to pretend.

Cranesbills, which I can now come back to, are both weavers and edge breakers, but you want to pick the right one for your purpose. Unless you have a death wish for anything smaller in your garden than a 6 ft shrub, avoid the beguiling *Geranium procurrens*, whose purple, blackcurrant-eyed flowers so much enliven the autumn scene. This species colonizes by rooting wherever it touches down and it is a great traveller with deep tap roots. It will also climb, given an obstacle, to 3 ft, choking its prey. It is a menace. Most cranesbill weavers, however, are only modest colonizers because their seasonal growth, however exuberant, dies back to the crown of the original plant in autumn.

G. endressii does gradually extend its range. Its bright mauve-pink flowers are specially useful for lighting shady places. The silvery pink 'A.T. Johnson' is more vigorous and can be a bit boring if overused as a filler, but it weaves with a will and so does the salmon pink 'Wargrave'. More interesting for general mixed border work is the brilliant magenta bloody cranesbill, *G. sanguineum*, and this has a number of colour variants, one of them bright pink. The albino is thin-textured and disappointing. On *G. wallichianum* 'Buxton's Blue' I have already expatiated (p.20). Its deeply cut

leaves are beautifully patterned. Flowering starts in July and reaches its peak in September, the flowers being blue saucers with a large white eye and purple stamens. In its more modest way, *G. wlassovianum* is pleasing with dusky purple flowers and a rambling habit.

But the pick of them all for border work is 'Russell Prichard', a hybrid. It has rather silvery foliage and begins to open a succession of rosy magenta flowers (a strong colour but not as blue as typical *G. sanguineum*) in May. They continue in full spate for the next six months. This, in a reliably hardy and perennial plant (or so I have found it though doubts on its hardiness have been voiced) is unique.

My photograph (**15**) shows it in the Long Border in late August and you can see how much of the path it has invaded. But it also climbs into the 'Preziosa' hydrangeas behind. Next to it is *Dimorphotheca (Osteospermum) ecklonis* 'Prostrata', a South African-type, mat-forming daisy with white rays and a blue eye and bluish reverse. It is another stalwart edge breaker but only moderately hardy. I lose it in as many winters as not but if it survives, it flowers abundantly in May, then grows a lot and flowers with greater or lesser freedom for the rest of the season. The pinky-mauve-flowered *D. barberae* with a yellow eye is somewhat hardier and if lucky with its winters a single plant can build into a vast mat, 7 ft across, but there are times when you wish it had more flowers and less leaf.

Most of the mat-forming acaenas, however, make a special virtue of their leaves, which are pinnate, like a small rose's, to which family they belong. For mixed-border work I particularly value *Acaena affinis* (its name is always changing, alas) with blue leaves and pinkish stems. It is an adept weaver.

15. Late August in the Long Border. *Geranium* 'Russell Prichard', flowering since May, now moves out on to the flagstone paving. *Dimorphotheca (Osteospermum) eklonis* 'Prostrata' to its left and *Hydrangea* 'Preziosa' behind. In the background can be seen the mauve *Aster sedifolius*, plumes of the tall flowering grass, *Miscanthus sinensis* 'Silver Feather', and the white 'pokers' of *Kniphofia* 'Little Maid'.

Following through

The gardener employs all sorts of devices for maintaining a succession of interest in important parts of his garden and some of them will be called cheating by those who can't be bothered, but that's from envy. Gertrude Jekyll used to drop pots of lilies and hydrangeas into her mixed border where some permanent ingredient had gone over. Fuchsias and hedychiums (particularly the yellow-flowered, canna-like *Hedychium gardnerianum*) lend themselves to this treatment, which has the added advantage of helping to empty your greenhouse just when you want to clean it out.

Some plants leave dreadful gaps after flowering, and yet we love and want to grow them. Such are lupins, whose gaudy ebullience and hot, airborne scent give us an early intimation of summer's arrival. But they are not good rent payers. A fortnight's flowering, no more, and then for the whole summer and autumn those derelict, mildewed plants have nothing more to offer.

My policy is to treat them as biennials. I sow a batch in a box in April, line them out in a spare plot for the summer, then plant a large patch in our High Garden, in the autumn. There they flower at the end of May and before June is out have been chucked on the rubbish heap to be replaced by annuals sown in April or May; China asters, perhaps, cosmos, lavatera or the mallow-like *Malope grandiflora*. This is not a difficult routine but you must have a spare bit of ground as a back-up area. Glass is not essential but growing-on space is. In this way a number of late-flowering perennials can be kept in the wings until needed.

Michaelmas daisies and chrysanthemums can be given a heavy watering, then lifted from the open ground (chrysanthemum shoots are brittle, so watch how you handle them) and brought on the scene in late July or August, when sweet Williams, Canterbury bells, anchusas or foxgloves have gone over, or some early flowering perennial. There's a place in my border where I grow the pale yellow yarrow (much paler than 'Moonshine') *Achillea taygetea*, with *Geranium sanguineum* to its left, *Santolina neapolitana*, cut back hard each spring, behind (**16**); and perhaps anchusas, perhaps delphiniums grown as biennials like the lupin, perhaps *Campanula persicifolia* grown similarly, behind all of these. Come July, the achilleas are fading. They can be cut back, watered and lined out in a spare plot from which they are replaced with, say, scarlet lobelias (**17**), these being interplanted with the grey foliage plant *Senecio leucostachys*, brought on in pots (their foliage is whiter if the roots are kept restricted, but I turn them out of the pots when planting out. Some gardeners don't.) And the anchusas (or whatever) are replaced by castor-oil plants, *Ricinus communis* 'Gibsonii', raised from seed, under cold glass to start with. This is a purple foliage plant with large palmate leaves and it grows at enormous speed in a warm July. Another good replacement would be the annual *Tithonia*, with bright orange flowers like a zinnia's, but growing to 5 or 6 ft.

Of course, it isn't *necessary* to do this sort of thing and some years I don't, but if the place is important and much seen, perhaps from your house windows, special efforts are warranted and anyway a switchover of this kind, successfully achieved, gives you the hell of a kick.

Oriental poppies, *Papaver orientale*, have a marvellous flamboyance and the brightest scarlet is rarely too bright because it can so easily, in its early season, be surrounded by masses of green foliage. The colour is very welcome. The poppy ·I most use, however, is the blood red 'Goliath', because its sturdy, upright habit to 4 ft is much easier to stake successfully than the average flopper. Now, poppies have thick, fleshy roots and they won't tolerate being moved around. Lupins are deep rooted too, but you can move them as first-year seedlings. Poppies are seldom raised from seed but from root cuttings. However, they have this great advantage, not shared by lupins, that you can cut them right to the ground as soon as flowering is completed. They'll need no light or air for the rest of the summer. So I space the plants some 2 or even 3 ft apart and interplant them in late June with cannas – actually a canna grown entirely for its purple foliage, but you could grow flowering kinds just as well if you preferred, or any other convenient gap filler.

The first picture (**18**), taken in mid-June, shows poppies, *Iris spuria* and, behind, the white lacecap flowers of the shrub, *Viburnum opulus* 'Compactum', which is a selected, not too large growing clone of the guelder rose. In the second picture (**19**), taken 27 August, I have moved in on the viburnum, now in fruit, so as to avoid showing the iris! But you can see some canna leaves where the poppies were, and still are, underground.

The viburnum itself, while we're thinking about it, is an example of the double season plant that makes two successive contributions. For reasons which I cannot fathom its berries, even in my bird-packed garden, are invariably left untouched, being eventually blown off by autumn gales.

The treament of alstroemerias offers unique follow-on opportunities to the enthusiast. The Ligtu Hybrids are the most popular strain, having azalea-like flowers at the turn of June–July in shades of buff, flame and pink but never orange. On the other hand, 'Dover Orange' is a worthwhile strain of the once popular *Alstroemeria aurantiaca*, with the only disadvantage of being somewhat invasive. And there are other promising South American species and hybrids coming along that are proving themselves to be hardier than had at first been feared.

All have deep, tuberous roots whose main spheres of action, once established, are some 6 in below the soil surface (a habit that conveniently protects them from frost damage). When they have finished flowering, in mid-July, you can simply yank out all the dying stems and they will break cleanly away from the tubers, leaving 6 in of vacant top soil into which you can now bed anything that you have handy: tender perennials like *Helichrysum petiolatum*, for instance, or seedlings just coming into flower of *Salvia patens*, or any late-sown annual you may fancy.

Alstroemeria Ligtu Hybrids being one of the lines that I, as a nurseryman, sell, I have to save all the seed I can muster, which means leaving their

16. *(above left)* Mixed border in June from which pale yellow *Achillea taygetea* and anchusas behind can later be removed and replaced. Grey *Santolina neapolitana* in the centre with *Geranium sanguineum* in front and *Phlox* 'Elizabeth', left.

17. *(above right)* The same piece of border in October, *Geranium sanguineum* flowering on young growth after being cut back. The santolina has bulked out and become paler. *Senecio leucostachys* and *Lobelia cardinalis* replace the achillea; *Ricinus communis* 'Gibsonii', grown as an annual, replaces anchusas.

18. *(centre)* Oriental poppy 'Goliath' sandwiched between *Iris spuria* (front) and the white blossom of *Viburnum opulus* 'Compactum'; mid-June.

19. *(right)* By late August the viburnum is fruiting; the poppies have been cut down and interplanted with *Canna indica* 'Purpurea'.

dying remains on the plants until the autumn. But there are ways of masking derelict early flowerers such as this. In Pamla Toler's earlier picture (**20**) taken on 6 July when the alstroemerias were in full bloom, you can already see the stems and early, flowering heads of *Verbena bonariensis* rising in front of them. By 10 September (**21**), when she took the second photograph, they have gone up to 5 or 6 ft and now have *Senecio leucostachys* weaving among their stems (*Sedum spectabile* is in front). This went out as a small pot-grown plant in the late spring. It is an arch-weaver and works its way upwards and backwards into the alstroemerias' stems and supporting pea sticks.

The verbena is a see-through plant that lends itself to front-of-border siting. Most of its photosynthesis is performed by thick green stems, square in section, while the leaves are much reduced. Thus it claims your attention, flowering from July to November, but you can see past it if you wish, to other parts of the border. Not one hundred per cent hardy, but when established it seeds itself and you'll never be without.

Plants that give a long season of interest of one kind or another, and without fuss, are the most valuable of all. I have a northwest-facing border

20. *(far left) Alstroemeria* Ligtu Hybrids in their July season; the stems of *Verbena bonariensis* beginning to rise in front of them.

21. *(left)* By September *Verbena bonariensis* and the interplanted *Senecio leucostachys* entirely mask the alstroemerias' dying stems; *Sedum spectabile* in front.

22. *(below left)* Late May in a wet and heavy border. *Euonymus* 'Emerald 'n' Gold' in front; the glaucous *Hosta* 'Buckshaw Blue' and purple-leaved *Rodgersia pinnata* 'Superba' with *Euphorbia palustris* flowering lime green on the right.

23. *(below right)* By late June the rodgersias are in flower and last in beauty right through to autumn, their colour deepening and intensifying.

with very heavy soil and thus inclined to lie wet, whose contents, for the moment anyway, seem to have worked out just right, at last.

In May, everything is fresh and by the end of the month the ground is fully covered and obscured (**22**). Beyond the stripy *Hosta undulata* 'Univittata' (bottom right of the picture) is a bush of the low evergreen *Euonymus* 'Emerald 'n' Gold', round which I have clustered the heavy purple-leaved *Viola labradorica*, since I find this sombre violet needs a lift from some lighter-coloured neighbour. Both have a long season. Then, in front, a particularly glaucous hosta, 'Buckshaw Blue' (it does look rather tired later in the summer), and behind it the young foliage, purple in colour and deeply pleated before expanding fully, of *Rodgersia pinnata* 'Superba'. There is another, taller and more vigorous but less pigmented form (unnamed) of *R. pinnata* behind this and at the back of the border, top right, two large clumps of *Euphorbia palustris*, which revels in this gooey soil. It is my favourite spurge, so fresh and sparkling in the spring; literally sparkling, because there are droplets of moisture, nectar perhaps, in the flowers which catch the light like tiny bits of crystal. At the border's end is a large specimen of that popular variegated evergreen, *Elaeagnus pungens* 'Maculata'.

At the end of June (**23**), the rodgersias, which are really the backbone in this piece of planting, are flowering, in light and deeper pink. Still later, their flowering heads darken to a sulky shade of red but retain their shape and freshness right into October.

There's another, somewhat larger-growing bush *Euonymus*, *E. fortunei* 'Silver Queen', on my Long Border that I dearly love, but it has taken years and years to achieve its present size and still I long for it to be larger. In

24. The variegated *Euonymus fortunei* 'Silver Queen' in spring, pierced by spears of gladiolus foliage.

25. By June the variegation on the young euonymus foliage has whitened and *Gladiolus byzantinus* is in flower, but easily cut away on fading. *Geranium* 'Ballerina' in foreground.

spring its young greenery (**24**) is yellow margined and you can see gladiolus leaves spearing through it. By early summer (**25**) the variegation has settled down to its characteristic silver-white, and *Gladiolus byzantinus* is in full flower. It has a short season but is easily fitted into a succession in this way. All its growth is made in winter and spring. By the time its flowers have faded the leaves can be cut away, even as they begin to turn brown.

There are other June-flowering gladioli of the same growth cycle, starting in winter, that can be used in the same way. If there is a bit of shelter from nearby shrubs, this compensates for any deficiency in hardiness in some of them. They're usually listed as G. × *colvillei* and G. *nanus*. 'Robinette', with cherry red flowers, is one of my favourites and you can soon build up a large stock of its freely multiplying corms.

Eremurus, the foxtail lilies, are dramatic in flower but leave a complete hole afterwards. With a voluminous species like E. *robustus*, which grows 8 ft tall in as many or fewer weeks, that can be a large hole. I have this flanking the exit through a yew archway from the Long Border to the next enclosed garden and the gap is filled by nasturtiums which self-sow from year to year. They also climb the hedge, which is fun, and not too damaging, as their growth has to be removed when the hedge is clipped. Their only trouble is that they can take over an entire border, so you have to prevent their long, questing shoots from exploring too far.

One of the most astonishing examples of follow-through technique that I know is in a friend's garden on the chalky South Downs. In summer it is a mass of Californian tree poppies, *Romneya*, with floppy white blooms crowded with yellow stamens, above glaucous foliage. If you returned in February you would exclaim 'What has happened to the poppies?' It is a shrubby species but by far the best cultural treatment is to cut it absolutely flush with the ground in winter so that it has to behave like any herbaceous plant. This leaves the area (a large area, for these poppies are great colonizers once established and spread by suckering) free for early bulbs. My friend has sheets of winter aconites and the early mauve *Crocus tomasinianus*. It's a marvellous feature and they've all set and shed their seeds by early May, when the poppies are just taking over again.

The subject of successions has so many by-paths and ramifications that I shall return to it again under other headings, but I'll close this chapter with a delightful example photographed in Beth Chatto's garden, near Elmstead Market, Essex, on the last day of August (**26**). Among a ground-covering community of such as lungworts and columbines was a gaily coloured assemblage of orange berries by *Arum italicum* 'Pictum'. This arum's main display is in winter and spring. Its beautifully marbled and veined leaves begin to appear in early autumn and build up in luxuriance over the next six months when such as columbine and lungwort are resting. Then, as these return to life, the arum flowers and itself goes to rest, with only its developing seed heads to betray its whereabouts.

26. The clubs of orange berries from *Arum italicum* 'Pictum' in late summer. This is a bonus to the main feast of the marbled foliage, carried throughout the winter and spring.

Contrasts of colour and form

Bright colours and violent contrasts appeal to us when we are young. The spikes of royal blue delphiniums rising behind mustard yellow *Achillea filipendulina* 'Gold Plate' would epitomize a youthful zest for the bright and the brash. Some people never get any further than that, but given an awareness of and curiosity towards our environment, we shall always be reassessing and before long we shall find ourselves preferring our blue delphiniums with double pink and carmine peonies. Their spherical forms are still in sharp contrast to the delphinium spikes but there is also a blue element in the pink and carmine flowers which accords with blue more easily than yellow. And we shall further soften the colour impact with grey-green cardoon (*Cynara cardunculus*) leaves, themselves, however, with a strong personality by dint of their size and jagged foliage outline. The yellows will look better, as I shall try to convince in the next chapter, with flowers like scarlet crocosmias nearer to their own end of the spectrum.

Violent and unassimilated colour contrasts are terribly easy to perpetrate. One autumn I planted a *Rhododendron* 'Tessa' where I thought it would do well. Only when its mauve-pink flowers came out in late February did I realize that the border contained a carpet of bright orange *Crocus aureus* just in front of the new bush. This crocus has a marvellously vital and cheering colour, much richer than the Dutch yellow which derives from it. Furthermore it sets seeds and spreads freely by self-sowing. The only thing to be said in favour of this excruciating colour contrast was that there's so little colour in the garden at that time of the year anyway and so much bare earth that it doesn't hurt as it would in summer. Anyway, I transferred the crocuses to turf – they look charming with the mauve *Crocus tomasinianus*. But inevitably I left some seedlings behind and they're building up again. I'm not even very fond of 'Tessa', now I have her, such is the fickleness of love. But she does flower bravely at an awkward season and when frost threatens to turn her flowers into brown pulp, they're nice to pick and bring indoors.

You often see violent contrasts in people's rockeries in spring. The brilliant yellow *Alyssum saxatile* with magenta *Phlox* 'Temiscaming' or with similarly coloured aubrietias, very commonly, yet all are good plants in their way when used with tact. A clever alpine gardener had a lovely clump of salmon-coloured poppies, *Papaver alpinum*, with nothing around to set it off except grit and a dumpy plant that was all flower, no leaf or shape to it, of the bright yellow flax, *Linum flavum* (**27**). That didn't help.

Contrasts in both colour and flower form were present in a pairing that I photographed somewhere in mid-July; a domed bush of *Hebe* 'Midsummer Beauty' covered with long lavender spikes and the round yellow saucers, also on a domed bush, of *Hypericum* 'Hidcote' (**28**). There are not so many colourful shrubs blooming in July, roses and hydrangeas apart, and these two were doing their level best but it was a flop. The colour contrast was obvious and unalleviated while the rounded shrubs were too similar in lacking personality.

27. Two flowering plants, *Papaver alpinum* and *Linum flavum* on a rock scree that do not help one another, and there are no surrounding or intervening plants to help them either.

28. *(right)* Summer-flowering shrubs: *Hebe* 'Midsummer Beauty' (left) and *Hypericum* 'Hidcote'. There is monotony in the similarly rounded forms of these two shrubs juxtaposed. Neither helps its neighbour.

29. *(below)* A better mauve and yellow planting wherein the level group of *Hemerocallis* 'Marion Vaughan' contrasts with the loose spikes of bells on *Hosta ventricosa* 'Variegata'.

I have a mauve and yellow planting in my Long Border that I think works (**29**) of *Hosta ventricosa* 'Variegata' in front of the slightly taller, 3½ ft *Hemerocallis* 'Marion Vaughan' (it is ironical to reflect that the recently formed Hosta and Hemerocallis Society would never have linked these two flowers but for the accident of their alliterative names). Both are liliaceous, it is true, and both hardy perennials, but the day lily bears pale yellow, upward-slanted trumpets while the plantain lily carries a carillon of mauve bells in a loose spike. The one has strap leaves the other, rounded hearts. And I might add that I see no point in growing *H. ventricosa* itself, whose plain green leaves become ultra-solemn in summer, now that we have this far jollier, yet by no means fussy variegated form with a broad cream margin.

Contrasts are necessary, at times. A border entirely of blue flowers is a very dull affair and looks worse rather than better if you mix in mauves.

How are agapanthus to be used? There are some lovely hardy, blue-flowered hybrids around these days and they come at a useful time, in August, when the season of perennials is on the wane and yet too often, as you see them, they seem wasted, neither self-sufficient nor being helped by neighbours. I think kniphofia companionship is one excellent solution. Their rod-like spikes are just the thing next to round and flattened agapanthus spikes. I have the deep blue 'Isis' with the pale, August-flowering *Kniphofia* 'Modesta' which is salmon in the bud. Their leaves don't help each other, it is true. In John Treasure's garden at Burford House (Shropshire) there were white kniphofias (it becomes rather ridiculous, incidentally, as well as confusing, to speak of red-hot-pokers when so many of them are white, yellow or orange) at two heights with his agapanthus and some white Mexican poppies (*Argemone*) in front whose glaucous foliage made the desired contrast in this department. The dwarf, 18 in kniphofia was the very freely August- and September-flowering 'Little Maid' and the taller one at 3 ft was 'Snow Maiden'.

Although it is an aggressive plant, the serried spikes of *Lysimachia punctata*, a yellow loosestrife from Asia Minor, have great panache in the July garden and I shall always remember (helped by an underexposed photograph) how well they looked with pale hydrangeas under trees at the Northern Horticultural Society's gardens at Harlow Car, near Harrogate, North Yorkshire before the site was turned into a car park. The hydrangeas were hardy lacecaps and the white *Hydrangea arborescens* 'Sterilis' (better known as *H. cinerea* 'Sterilis'). In the northeast Scottish garden of Geanies, the loosestrife was growing behind and into a patch of *Astrantia major*, and this looked charming although one knew that the arrangement could not last without frequent interference otherwise the loosestrife would take over.

Now let us take a look at a piece of herbaceous planting at Inverewe, the famous National Trust of Scotland gardens way up in the northwest (**30**). Pyramids of red astilbes in front backed by flat corymbs of the brilliant yellow *Achillea* 'Coronation Gold', itself bolstered by a mound of magenta cranesbills, *Geranium psilostemon*. All beautifully grown and trained but a somewhat indigestible bellyful. If that were all, it would be insufferable, but when you stand back your eye can take in the supporting cast on either flank and this was all emollient. Tall panicles of soft *Campanula lactiflora*, spikes of dark blue aconites and the pale grey mounds of lavender cotton, *Santolina chamaecyparissus*. It's not something I should want to do myself; I

30. Red astilbes backed by bright yellow *Achillea* 'Coronation Gold' and this by magenta *Geranium psilostemon*. Violent contrasts but softened by neighbouring groups of grey santolina, purple and blue aconites and campanulas. A welcoming display for the public in the cool, wet north.

31. The solid domes of *Sedum* 'Autumn Joy' flanked by the drooping plumes of a grass, *Pennisetum villosum*, beyond, and the rambling grey *Senecio leucostachys* in front. The restful lines of flagstone paving play their part.

should take the hard edges off my bright colours with more foliage, but on its own terms *it works*. Display is a part of public gardening and it must be remembered that most of the rest of Inverewe Gardens is woodland and that woodland gardens have ceased to be very colourful by July. By and large, it is a grey climate and a short summer up there. All this adds up.

Yet the style and spirit of my last picture is much more relaxing (**31**) and the flagstone paving plays its part. The central feature, *Sedum* 'Autumn Joy' is a worthy plant. All summer it is pale but promising. Late in August the flowers begin to open but only very gradually, as they age, does the colour intensify to what you see here on 5 October, later becoming darker still and eventually warm brown. It is no disgrace to leave its heads on through the winter and see them capped with snow from time to time.

But on its own this is a too solid plant and you may find yourself irrepressibly yawning when you meet it. It needs the right neighbours. What better than the grass beyond, the soft and fluffy *Pennisetum villosum*, which you will treat as an annual if you believe the seedsmen or as a hardy perennial when you find that it is one? A spiky plant, but with upside down spikes on arching stems. Grasses, as I shall point out later, need the contrast of more solid plants. Each here helps the other and our old friend *Senecio leucostachys* of the grey comb leaves and easy rambling habit, helps all.

Colour contrasts are a challenge (that great and glorious word). Many gardeners of refined tastes but timid outlook are afraid to take them on because it's easy to put a foot wrong, both feet, in fact. They fall back on white gardens and single or two-colour borders. A border that contains every colour in the rainbow can be totally satisfying and very exciting but it'll take years to get it absolutely right, if you ever do, and you should certainly make generous use of foliage and other softening elements. Also you need space. Within a small area it'll be impossible to work out more than a few ideas. Always make your borders as large as you can. They're more important, much more fun and no more work than lawns.

Colour harmonies

32. Colour harmony but
contrasts in form from
Hydrangea 'Générale
Vicomtesse de Vibraye',
Astilbe tacquetti 'Superba' and
Geranium pratense 'Coeruleum
Plenum' with *Rosa glauca (R.
rubrifolia)* behind.

Your original plans for a garden's planting will be very different from what actually evolves. There was one corner in our Barn Garden where, soon after the war's end, I had a bank of pink dahlias. There was the 6 to 7 ft 'Jersey Beauty' at the back, a large but not giant decorative called 'Bonanza' in the middle reaches and a lower, anemone-centred in front. As it happens, and as I was not long in discovering, this sheltered-seeming nook is just about the draughtiest in the whole garden. The wind hits the barn at the back and comes off it with reinforced ferocity. Each dahlia had a strong chestnut post but this did not prevent disastrous smashing sessions of their brittle shoots.

In moving on to more solid, wind-resistent plants I indulged in an essay in contrasts, with the tall, bright yellow *Ligularia clivorum* 'Hessei' at the back, the penetrating mauve *Astilbe tacquetii* 'Superba' in front, and another *Ligularia clivorum* group, this time the shorter 'Desdemona' to one side.

I don't think I admitted, at the time, that the yellow/mauve syndrome was, even for one who loves yellows and mauves, a bit much. I dropped the ligularias (daisies that used to be called senecio) because although their growth suited the heavy, wet soil for which this border is notorious, yet for the same reason, the area is riddled with slugs. If slugs attack a leaf like an astilbe's that is already divided into many segments, you hardly notice the difference, but in a big smooth surface like a ligularia or hosta leaf, the visible carnage is appalling. I changed the tall ligularias for *Rosa glauca* (then *R. rubrifolia*), whose foliage has a purplish cast, and the other for a delightful *Monarda* called 'Beauty of Cobham', with pink flowers and purple bracts. As there was still plenty of space I also included one of the double 'blue' (campanula blue) cranesbills, *Geranium pratense* 'Coeruleum Plenum' and *Hydrangea* 'Générale Vicomtesse de Vibraye', an old hortensia

33. *Achillea filipendulina* 'Coronation Gold' and *Crocosmia masonorum* in John Treasure's garden. The bright green lawn surround harmonizes with these flower colours.

that blues very readily and is then a light powder blue that I find much more attractive than some of the deeper, electric blues which seem artificial, even though they are not. As you can see in the photograph (**32**), Vibraye decided that pink was to be her colour at Dixter and so pink she is and I can't say I mind, though it's a puzzle that my soil doesn't produce a blue hydrangea anywhere and yet is sufficiently acid to grow rhododendrons, camellias and other calcifuge plants.

My point, however, is that I've settled in the long run for a colour harmony of pinks and mauves rather than a contrasty set-up. I take this as a sign of advancing years, which is not necessarily synonymous with maturity.

Pink is a difficult flower colour that often goes a bit wrong. Either it turns to simpering salmon, as in *Dianthus* 'Doris'; or an element of harshness creeps in with a touch of blue as in the 'Queen Elizabeth' rose. When you find a really good pink flower like rose 'The Fairy' or the dandelion-like *Crepis incana*, or a *Sidalcea* like 'Sussex Beauty', you should seize it. *Schizostylis coccinea* 'Viscountess Byng' is one such, unlike the recently acclaimed 'Sunrise' which is tainted salmon. 'Viscountess Byng' mixes charmingly with a late flowering perennial, a kind of knapweed, really, and one would expect it to be a *Centaurea*, but it is *Serratula seoanei* (better known as *S. shawii*), with cut-leaves of a purplish cast, and masses of small mauve thistle heads on a densely branching intertwangled plant, 2 ft tall. This couple flowers over a long, late season – into November, in fact, which is generally considered purely as an overhaul, work month. It tends to be overlooked that we don't have to give up enjoying plants in November, just because the season is late.

34. A warm grouping of herbaceous perennials with the scarlet domes of *Lychnis chalcedonica*, the bronze daisies of *Helenium* 'Moerheim Beauty' and the purple spikes of *Salvia nemorosa* 'Superba'.

Many gardeners are so put off orange and red flowers by the excesses wallowed in by public parks and gardens with their blocks of scarlet tulips, bedding 'geraniums', marigolds and salvias, that they fear to handle these colours themselves. Colour harmonies can be found in strong colours and I had to admire one such (**33**) in John Treasure's garden (Tenbury Wells, Worcestershire) although, having lived with it for a number of years, he feels the need for a change. Near the river bank he has grouped *Achillea filipendulina* 'Coronation Gold' behind the hard orange-red *Crocosmia masonorum*. This is in a lawn setting, which is ideal for the purpose and better, for once, than stone. The bright green of turf is by no means a neutral colour and can easily be at odds with adjacent flower beds, but it harmonizes with crocosmias.

All the same, the individual shades of achillea and crocosmia are too brash to make life-long companions and I am not surprised that John wants a change. The pale yellow *Achillea taygetea* is a far more restful plant and there are now some warm red crocosmias that glow without scorching. I have raised one, and Bloom's offer such as 'Lucifer' and 'Emberglow'.

It is useful to have additions to the red range among hardy perennials. So many red flowers are contributed by annuals, tender perennials or roses. The truly scarlet *Lychnis chalcedonica* remains an outstanding relic of the past – a 3½ ft perennial that merely needs sympathetic handling. Last summer I saw it with *Achillea filipendulina* (that's not outrageous) and a stop-gap bush of the mallow-pink *Lavatera olbia*. It was, of course, an accident. Yet the lychnis harmonizes sumptuously with the brownish orange of *Helenium* 'Moerheim Beauty', while the purple spikes of *Salvia nemorosa* 'Superba' tune in well (**34**). The one disadvantage of this lychnis is

that its July season is irretrievably over in a fortnight. If you plan a red border you had better have recourse to dahlias, cannas, repeat-flowering roses and bedding verbenas after all. Work them in with purple or glaucous foliage as from barberries, castor oil (*Ricinus communis* 'Gibsonii'), cannas themselves, *Rosa glauca*, *Melianthus major*, *Corylus maxima* 'Purpurea' and purple or less purple-leaved forms of *Cotinus coggygria*, the smoke bush. Excellent ideas have been worked out in the red borders at Hidcote, in Gloucestershire.

Orange is particularly pleasing to handle when it comes in a warm, burnt shade though it looks good also in the deeper African marigolds, which you might combine with acid yellows in the same flower, and with green nicotianas – *Nicotiana langsdorffii* is particularly elegant with its pendent bells. One tends to be put off by the congested dumpiness of so many modern marigold (*Tagetes*) strains, but a widely branching three-footer is a noble plant.

In the May garden I have a satisfying burnt orange harmony with *Ozothamnus ledifolius* and *Euphorbia griffithii* 'Dixter' (**35**). The latter clone has much more richly pigmented foliage then the well-known 'Fireglow'. Its flowers are less fiery, but quite bright enough, given a sunny position. (In shade the colouring in any clone of *E. griffithii* becomes weakened with green.)

Ozothamnus ledifolius (*Helichrysum ledifolium*) is a marvellous evergreen shrub – from Tasmania, yet remarkably hardy. Its leaves are warm green, almost yellow on the undersides, which show up on the shoot tips. In late April a forest of flower-bud clusters becomes evident and their colour develops into this remarkable orange shade which intensifies for several weeks until the tiny white flowers mantle all, like hoar frost.

35. Burnt shades of orange in the High Garden at Great Dixter with *Euphorbia griffithii* 'Dixter' backed by the solid Tasmanian shrub, *Ozothamnus ledifolius*, covered in May with colourful bud clusters.

Yellow and white is soothing, particularly as so many white flowers carry a central boss of yellow stamens. The inestimable white Japanese anemone is one such. I have a large, permanent colony of it in front of the house with variable bedding in front and a backing of the grey-leaved *Artemisia arborescens* (**36**), which I should like to be more permanent than it is. Not only does it tend to get killed in the winter but young plants up to three or at most four years of age have greater vitality and vigour than old. Another snag with this, as with other aromatic grey-leaved plants is that house sparrows develop a passion for their foliage in the nesting season, and will quickly strip a plant to the bone unless it is protected with black cotton. Still, this wormwood is such a good plant that I persist with it and its paleness makes a remarkably telling background to the anemone's own. The difference is slight but it is enough.

I have tried a number of bedding plants in front. None was more effective than the pale yellow *Anthemis tinctoria* 'Wargrave', seen here. The deeper yellow of an annual black-eyed Susan, *Rudbeckia* 'Monplaisir', was also good, but the pale yellow harmonizes more closely. There are a great many deep yellow perennials, particularly among the daisies, but pale is comparatively rare and the more valuable for that.

To grow this anthemis as an annual, you take cuttings of its mossy, green shoots, only a couple of inches long, in February. Cold frame protection is all they need. Pot them up individually in 3½ in pots in April in John Innes No. 2 (potting soil) or a peat-based compost of similar strength and plant them out in early June to follow the spring bedding. Each plant will require one shortish cane and a single tie. Spacing can be 2 ft apart, which is economical. Flowering will run from the last days of June till well into October and a single dead-heading operation is all that's needed to make the display continuous.

36. Pale yellow *Anthemis tinctoria* 'Wargrave' bedded-out, but backed with a permanent planting of white Japanese anemones and these by grey-leaved *Artemisia arborescens*.

37. Harmony in yellow and white, the white helianthemum having yellow stamens. Top left, the self-sowing hardy annual, *Omphalodes linifolia*, with white gypsophila-like flowers.

Treated as a border perennial, *Anthemis tinctoria* grows inconveniently tall at 6 ft (instead of 3 ft here) and requires considerable support. It becomes liable to powdery mildew and doesn't flower for half as long. There is much to be said for the young plant.

On the small scale I enjoyed the yellow and white motif in paving (an East Anglian garden), where white and yellow sun roses (*Helianthemum*) grew side by side (37). A transitional link between them is created by the yellow stamens in the white-flowered plant. Top left you can see the white spikelets of a gypsophila-like annual (only it has more personality than any gypsophila), *Omphalodes linifolia*, whose leaves are glaucous. In light soils and a sunny position it will sow itself from year to year and flower at the end of May.

The diamond-sharp sparkle of such flowers is a far cry from the mellowness of autumn, but autumn tints suit my home whose tiling has that kind of warmth. Unless your house needs to be entirely obliterated with creepers, it is as well to reckon with its colouring when you're planting in that area so that the plants blend rather than quarrel. Yellow forsythia against pinkish terracotta bricks or tiles is not a happy conjunction. Here (38) you can see the climbing *Hydrangea petiolaris* against the house. Its leaves turn clear yellow in autumn. This self clinger is often recommended for north walls where, indeed, it will grow and flower very well, but its autumn colour will make twice the impression if it is touched by sunlight.

In the foreground is a green-and-white-variegated bush ivy, just coming into flower. I love this plant, especially in autumn, but it doesn't jump at you. It is *Hedera canariensis* 'Variegata', really, but grown from a mature, non-clinging shoot with unlobed leaves. Plants raised this way retain a bushy instead of a climbing habit and flower freely.

38. The warmth of autumn colours is matched by Dixter's weather tiling. *Hydrangea petiolaris*, with clear yellow foliage, grows up this. The bush form of the ivy *Hedera canariensis* 'Variegata' is in the foreground; *Skimmia japonica* in berry behind that, while faded hydrangea heads and the crimson dying foliage of *Aronia arbutifolia* 'Erecta' complete the picture.

Behind it are the crimson berries on a female *Skimmia japonica*. Faded pinkish flower heads on a lacecap hydrangea also tone in well with the general mood of autumn and a touch of more brilliant colour is provided by the dying leaves of *Aronia arbutifolia* 'Erecta', a neatly fastigiate shrub, quietly pleasing at most times but to be relied upon for a lively curtain call before retiring to its winter's rest.

For another house-side planting, you should see how the white window frames at Saling Hall (near Braintree, Essex), a little hard and uncompromising on their own, are diffused and scattered into an exhalation of white spots by the anemones growing in front of them. This seems to me to be a perfect marriage between natural and man-made material.

Foliage contrasts and effects

In *The Damp Garden*, Beth Chatto wrote 'I hope it is not becoming monotonous, my obsession with leaves, but if a plant has beautiful leaves it is, I think, the best reason for growing it. If it has good flowers as well, that makes two good reasons.' Is this undoubted obsession with leaves, which I share, a fashion, I sometimes wonder? A reaction against the tasteless blocks of colour that have, since Victorian times, been at the core of so much gardening? A little bit of that, I think, but for the most part an appreciation of the role of foliage is genuine.

Leaves tend to be larger than flowers and they create patterns in a way that flowers cannot. What flower could compete with the presence of a *Fatsia japonica* in a small town courtyard? Tulips, 'geraniums' and petunias will be jolly in their seasons but they cannot match those magnificent, glossy leaves, which will be replicated in shadows on wall and paving whenever the sun or moon or any artificial illumination we may supply in lieu, are shining on it.

There it stands the year round, and yet it is a living plant with changing moods, a time for flowering, a time for the unfolding of young leaves and the yellowing and shedding of old ones. In its more graceful way, a bamboo would be no less impressive or, indeed, a yucca, though far from cuddly.

Leaves sustain. Even the deciduous kinds are with us for far longer than most flowers. Evergreens can look pretty shabby at winter's end but throughout the darkest days they give us courage.

The freshness of leaves in spring is a miracle of renewal. Not just the trees and shrubs, either. Think how beautiful delphinium leaves are in spring, and lupins, each with a quicksilver drop of water at the centre of those unfurling spokes. There's still a lot of bare earth in my Long Border in April and May and not much colour, but the young foliage is a feast in itself as where young oriental poppy leaves (**39**) are backed by the splendid blue-grey jags of cardoon (*Cynara cardunculus*).

There are even roses that make a worthwhile contribution before they flower. The hybrid musk 'Moonlight' surprises by the richness of its purple foliage before its white flowers expand. 'Rosemary Rose', alas, is all too susceptible to mildew but its young leaves, purple again, are really good. I specially admired them in a friend's mixed border in spring when the wands of *Tellima grandiflora*'s little green bells above its own scalloped leaves were thrown up against a background of 'Rosemary Rose' in leaf (**40**).

Purple and lime green or purple and yellow often make striking effects in foliage. At Kew, in the Royal Botanic Gardens, the grassy sedge leaves of *Carex stricta* 'Aurea' – a plant generally grown in water but perfectly happy under moist border conditions – made a background to the round-leaved ground cover bugle, *Ajuga reptans*, in a purple-leaved form (**41**). Dark against light is just as telling as the more often used reverse combination. If you see the young foliage of a purple beech against the lime green of the red oak's (*Quercus rubra*) unfolding leaves, that looks good in the same way

39. *(above left)* Jagged grey cardoon leaves with the brighter green of oriental poppy. Self-sown forget-me-nots fill out gaps in the border's early May days.

40. *(above right)* A mixed border in May wherein the purple leaves of rose 'Rosemary Rose' act as a background foil to the green flower wands of *Tellima grandiflora*, itself an evergreen foliage plant.

41. Foliage contrasts at a low level. The sedge, *Carex stricta* 'Aurea' behind a bugle, *Ajuga reptans*, in a purple-leaved form.

but on a large scale. The same oak has a golden-leaved form, 'Aurea', which would look even more striking and is itself a marvel silhouetted against a blue sky.

Robinia pseudacacia 'Frisia' is being overplanted, these days, and it often makes a poorly shaped specimen, but it does look stunning against the purple of Norway maple, *Acer platanoides* 'Crimson King' or 'Goldsworth Purple' (usually one and the same) and the reverse effect of maple against false acacia is equally eye-catching.

The smoke bush, *Cotinus coggygria*, in its purple-leaved forms offers great scope to the gardener. The darkest kinds like 'Royal Purple' and 'Notcutt's Variety' do not make the haze of 'smoke' that can be expected from lightly pruned or unpruned bushes of some other strains. So it is often most satisfactory to go all out for the richest foliage effect by pruning them quite hard each winter. *Eucalyptus gunnii*, treated the same way, will then make a startling contrast as a companion, and its own juvenile leaves will be seen at their roundest and bluest.

But the greenish purple forms of *Cotinus* like 'Foliis Purpureis' have their own charm and are none the worse for not being heavily pigmented. Here (**42**) in a friend's garden you see it matched against the yellow form of *Lonicera nitida* called 'Baggesen's Gold'. Both shrubs can be given a light pruning in late winter to improve foliage quality as well as plant shape, for neither of them has a natural shapeliness and thus there is no point in allowing them to go untrimmed. But this *Cotinus* will carry lovely puffs of pink smoke if you allow some of its previous season's strongest shoots to remain unpruned.

Another stalwart shrub of the purple-leaved brigade is the barberry. Both the deciduous *Berberis vulgaris* and *B. thunbergii* have a number of purple-leaved clones (as well as those like 'Rose Glow' and 'Harlequin' in which the young shoots are pink or pink and white). I grow the hybrid between these two species, *B.* × *ottawensis* 'Purpurea', as a foil against the silver leaves of a pollarded willow, *Salix alba* 'Argentea'. The same colour juxtaposition can be produced at a lower level with *B. thunbergii* 'Atropurpurea Nana', a dumpy purple bush given character by intermingling glaucous shoots of *Acaena affinis*. At the season's end you would need to cut the acaena hard back so as to prevent progressive strangulation of the barberry.

From what I have already written it will be apparent that the pruning back of foliage shrubs not only restricts the space they occupy (which may be an essential consideration in small gardens, and even in large gardens where a vigorous tree or shrub is required to play a foliage role within the confines of a border) but also improves the quality of their leaves. They'll grow larger, more luxuriantly and be more intensely coloured. I should perhaps add that too severe and frequent pruning can weaken a shrub and predispose it to diseases like coral spot and silver leaf. If it is easily replaced by young stock (as are the willows) you may not mind too much about this.

42. Purple and yellow in 3 to 4ft shrubs: *Lonicera nitida* 'Baggesen's Gold' and the smoke bush, *Cotinus coggygria* 'Foliis Purpureis'.

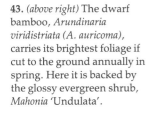

43. *(above right)* The dwarf bamboo, *Arundinaria viridistriata (A. auricoma)*, carries its brightest foliage if cut to the ground annually in spring. Here it is backed by the glossy evergreen shrub, *Mahonia* 'Undulata'.

Bamboo foliage is much improved by pruning. In the larger species, you can thin out the oldest canes. But the best policy with low growing, ground covering kinds is to cut the entire colony right down to the ground each April. I do this with *Arundinaria viridistriata* (*A. auricoma*) which is non-invasive and grows at the front of my Long Border (**43**). Its height is thus restricted to 2 ft and the green and yellow variegation in its young foliage is far fresher and more intense than if I let it alone.

The glossy, crimped leaves of *Mahonia* 'Undulata' make a nice background. Had I appreciated its vigour, I should probably not have planted this shrub so near the border front. As it is I have to cut it hard back into old wood every four or five years so as to give the bamboo breathing space. The mahonia will grow 6 ft high with ease if given the chance. Its yellow flowers are cheerful in the spring and are followed by tender copper shades in the young foliage. In cold winter weather the leaves turn deep bronze, which is handsome also and never gloomy because of the shine on them.

Foliage in winter will be noticed, for good or ill, more than at any other season. There's not much else to look at. Grey skies don't suit the grey-leaved evergreens. We'll need them at other seasons but must not count on their support now. Nor on some shrubs which are half-heartedly ever-green, and retain only a proportion of their leaves. There are privets like that and shrubs such as *Eucryphia* 'Nymansay', *Piptanthus laburnifolius*, *Viburnum* × *burkwoodii*, *Stranvaesia davidiana*.

Garrya elliptica is evergreen and furthermore its long grey catkins expand in January. Even so, I'd not call it a cheerful bush and its scarred leaves after a winter's battering are spitefully nasty. But you can hide a plant like this behind another that is more prominently placed. The foliage of *Daphniphyllum macropodum* never looks tired. Its leaves are shaped very like a rhododendron's but are brighter, quite pale on the undersides. Furthermore, leaf stalks and veins and dormant buds are all warmly suffused with coral pink. Its style, too, with rosettes of leaves that hang almost vertically, is entirely its own. Provided it is protected from the coldest winds, this is a remarkably hardy shrub yet seldom seen.

As for the flare-up of colour that some deciduous foliage briefly takes on in autumn, I think it is generally unwise to plant for this deliberately but rather to accept it gratefully as a bonus where other benefits such as tree form, leaf shape or a floral display are the major considerations. It is so easy to be let down by an expectation of leaf colour. Liquidambars, nyssas and scarlet oaks may regularly fail to do their stuff at all. Either your soil's wrong or you've got hold of a poor strain. Colour also varies greatly with the season. Small gardens cannot afford these failures. It is better by far to make a trip to one of the great gardens, famed for their colour, on a glorious autumn day and take your fill there. Or even to walk or drive about our countryside when the oaks and beeches and bracken are warm and rusty, and the birches and field maples shining yellow.

But there are some ways in which we should all pay attention to autumn colour. For instance in choosing one vine rather than another to creep over a wall or garage. The usual self-clinging choice, *Parthenocissus tricuspidata*, long known as *Ampelopsis veitchii*, from Japan, but inevitably dubbed Virginia creeper or Boston ivy, is a coarse plant. Admittedly it keeps close into a wall and does its job well, but it has little personality and its autumn colour is raw magenta. In the true Virginia creeper, *Parthenocissus quinquefolia* (**44**), the autumn colour is in warm shades of red. The divided leaf is much more attractive and sprays of growth are flung out from its main support so that it looks a freer plant. It makes a splendid background to a clump of pampas grass, where the sun can strike them both.

44. The finger-leaved Virginia creeper, *Parthenocissus quinquefolia*, turns to warm crimson shades in early autumn, and is seen here with bindweed, which also colours nicely.

Lighting

The kind of light in which you see a garden makes all the difference to its enjoyment. It seems a pity, though inevitable, that gardens which are opened to the public during the summer months are seen in the flat and unflattering noontide light. Shadows are minimal, the glare is crude, the flowers (roses in particular) are limp. After a few scorching days it is a relief to be capped by cloud again.

And yet, in our northern latitudes, we yearn for the sun and the times when we can most enjoy it is on summer mornings and evenings; in other seasons, at any time of the day. The shadows will be long enough and the contrast of shadows is a great help, even though they are the photographer's bane.

So you should always place certain plants where you know that the sun's slanting rays will flatter them. Particularly is this true of autumn and winter sunlight, whose quality is yellow. Place your variegated elaeagnus bush so that it is sunlit then. It will look bright as a glade of daffodils.

Dark backgrounds to side-lit plants look good, as when the late afternoon sun reaches a northwest-facing border that's backed by trees or a building. On a visit to the Savill Gardens (near Windsor) in late May, I caught their planting of ornamental rhubarb (they called it *Rheum australe* but I think it was a good strain of the variable *R. palmatum*) at the right moment. Its plumes of white flowers were highlighted by a dark background of trees in shadow. The jagged, blackish purple leaves are held obliquely for weeks after they unfold, so that the sun, particularly early and late, catches their under-surfaces which are dusky plum red. What a plant. But it's as well to have other plants that will grow up in front of it in later summer, to mask its latter days. The stately 6 ft *Nicotiana sylvestris* would be my choice.

Back lighting is even more dramatic. We have an 8 ft wall behind a north-facing border, but by early May the sun's declination allows it to illuminate much of the border's contents from behind while the actual wall face appears blacker than ever by contrast. It makes a setting for *Philadelphus coronarius* 'Aureus', the golden-leaved form of the common mock orange, whose translucent young leaves the sun illuminates like bits of glass in a medieval church window.

Purple foliage like that of the darkest sumachs (*Cotinus*) can seem almost glum with the sun behind you, but see it the other way and it is transfigured into ruby jewels.

A German photographer visited me recently and showed me enlarged colour prints of some of his work. He had only recently taken to photographing plants and I was particularly intrigued by one picture of *Acer palmatum* 'Dissectum Purpureum' taken against the light. This cut-leaved Japanese maple normally makes a very low, hummocky specimen with the tips of its branches trailing on the ground. I asked him whether he had had to crawl inside the bush in order to get his back-lighted picture, and he had done precisely that! But there are plenty of purple-leaved *Acer*

45. A purple-leaved form of the Japanese maple, *Acer palmatum*, shot through by spring sunshine in Sheffield Park Garden (East Sussex).

*palmatum*s that grow into decent sized trees and allow you to admire a curtain of back-lit foliage, like the one I photographed in Sheffield Park Garden, East Sussex (45), in physical comfort.

The greater the size of a leaf, the greater the scope for lighting effects, especially when the leaf has an interesting shape and casts shadows on itself. *Melianthus major* has a big glaucous, pinnate leaf. The deep marginal serrations are replicated in shadow on the smooth leaf surfaces and this is particularly noticeable early and late in the day.

The largest leaf we can grow on a hardy plant is that of *Gunnera manicata* (46), from the Brazilian highlands. Young leaves point upwards and are readily transfused by sunlight. And since this is a waterside plant, you will often see the golden lines of sun-reflected ripples moving across a gunnera leaf's lower surface.

Flowers respond to lighting in many different ways. Sometimes it drains them of colour; at others they seem to have their own inner source of light. so intensely do they glow. This is oftenest true of red and orange flowers. Towards sunset and sometimes even more so afterwards, they burn with a volcanic glow, only to turn quite black as night falls.

Some of the best flower lighting effects come from within an arbour. It is wonderful to be within a flowering laburnum tunnel (47) when all the sun's light is transmitted through the blossom above and around. You are bathed in this light and in the flowers' sweet scent, which is scarcely noticed from a tree in the open.

46. The young foliage on the moisture-loving *Gunnera manicata* has its structure dramatically highlighted when seen against the sun.

47. *(opposite)* The laburnum tunnel at Dundonnell House in northwest Scotland, transfused by June sunshine.

Around-the-clock duties

Flowers open at different times of the day and some remain open for different periods in the day. Thus they impinge on our own work schedules and recreational habits. Someone regularly going out to work at 8 a.m. and not returning till afternoon, will miss a whole range of the freshest and most cheering flowers, but if you were at home at this time you could create a 'good morning!' garden.

Flowers that behave like the common daisy must on this account be omitted. They stay shut not only at night but also in wet daytime weather and as this is unpredictable we have no control. But assuming the right weather to open them we can make certain dispositions.

A garden that's for enjoyment in the morning should include lots of poppies. They will flower all day, perhaps for several days, but first open in the morning. One of the most delightful summer's sunrise pleasures is to see the green boat-shaped calyx halves perched on top of a still crumpled but fast expanding bloom. Soon the calyx is pushed right off, the flower's petals are ironed smooth (a remarkable feat, considering that no iron is used) and the central boss of stamen – bluish purple and very dark in an oriental poppy – are revealed.

Cistuses and the related sun roses (*Helianthemum*) make a more dramatic sortie on to bushes which the previous night were completely destitute of blossom. By 9.0 a.m., they can cover a bush so completely with their discs that scarcely a leaf remains visible. By midday or soon after, the petals have all shattered like limp confetti. It is the same with flax, *Linum narbonense*, but here the blue colouring touches us nearest our hearts as it does in the miraculous blue convolvulus trumpets of *Pharbitis* (*Ipomoea*) *tricolor*. They should be sown rather late in spring and grown throughout in pots to climb over the walls of the warmest spot you have. By noon its flowers are tainted with mauve and pink; they crumple up soon after.

Convolvulus are close relations and *Convolvulus mauritanicus* can be treated as a hardy plant once established in a warm, well-drained spot. Or it can be used to tumble out of ornamental pots and window boxes, for it is a trailer, not a climber. Its flowers are campanula blue, and they remain open till mid-afternoon. *C. althaeoides* climbs and travels. It has silver leaves and pink flowers; a most beguiling villain.

Tigridia pavonia, of roughly triangular outline, comes in gaudy colours and spotted at the centre like silk handkerchiefs. Belonging to the iris family its corms are usually lifted in the autumn, but they can last indefinitely in a well-drained, sheltered spot where the sun reaches them, until found by mice or voles. Each flower lasts for the greater part of one day, from about 9 a.m. till 4 p.m.

Verbascums, the mulleins, are morning flowers unless the weather is dull or cool. They go limp in the midday heat and barely recover in the evening. Tradescantias and the related *Commelina coelestis*, which is peacock blue, are morning flowers that fold at lunchtime or soon after. No use to those who visit your garden in the afternoon.

48. *Osteospermum (Tripteris) hyoseroides*, an annual South African daisy, is brilliant each morning, even when it rains, but virtually disappears from sight in the afternoons when its ray petals roll back on themselves.

Some daisies are sensitive to the time of day as well as to the weather, especially those hailing from South Africa. Gazanias are very fussy about the weather and won't open on a dull morning but they must open in the morning if at all. A wet morning followed by a fine afternoon will see them shut all day. But if the day starts and continues fine they'll open around 10 a.m. (no earlier) and remain so till about 4 p.m.

I am delighted with an annual daisy with bright orange flowers and a dark centre which opens in the mornings even in wet weather (**48**). This is *Osteospermum (Tripteris) hyoseroides*. At noon its rays begin to roll back from the tips in an outward direction so that by 2 p.m. there's scarcely anything left to see. The kingfisher daisy, *Felicia bergeriana*, behaves like this too, but is open for so short a time as hardly to be worth growing. Better its relation *F. amelloides*, which is open for most of the day and keeps up a long succession of blossom. Both are blue with yellow discs.

The annual *Mesembryanthemum criniflorum*, with its glittering daisy-like flowers in many colours, flowers only for a month but gives you a good part of each day, sunshine permitting, until about 4 p.m.

A few flowers behave rather unexpectedly by opening at noon or soon after. I remember sitting out on our terrace with Beth Chatto having a drink before lunch on a sunny day at the end of May, and our observing what sulky flowers the sisyrinchiums are, that swarm between the paving cracks. The flowers were there, but unopened. By the time we returned with our coffee after lunch they were all open. It is the dusky blue, iris-like *Sisyrinchium angustifolium*. In Mediterranean countries in spring and early summer you'll find the even more iris-like and bluer *Gynandiris sisyrinchium* opening at the same time, but this is not an easy corm to flower in our climate.

At 4 p.m., we have, of course, the four o'clock plant, *Mirabilis jalapa*, expanding. It is scented and remains open all night. Although tender it can be treated as an annual but I find it a slightly horrid plant with disagreeable foliage. In quite another class is an elegant, 3 ft asphodel (**49**) with grassy leaves; a perfectly hardy perennial. Its flowering is based on July and for most of the day it looks nothing at all but at 4 p.m. it comes to life with yellow stars bursting wide open up and down its spiky inflorescence. They remain open till dusk and then close again. I call this the tired businessman's plant. It looks nice, as seen here, with the spiky blue sea-holly, *Eryngium oliverianum*.

Finally the night brigade, always scented but some opening earlier, some later. On shrubs like honeysuckle and summer jasmine, you hardly notice the new flowers, apart from their scent, because the old ones have remained open all day. It is not so with the night-scented stock, *Matthiola bicornis*, which is in a complete state of collapse by day as are the more old-fashioned and best scented tobacco flowers, *Nicotiana alata* and *N. sylvestris*.

It is deceptive to call all the *Oenothera* genus 'evening primroses' when none of them are related to or smell of primroses and many, like *O. tetragona*, open by day and close at night. The best for scent are the biennials, *O. biennis* and *O. lamarckiana* which is a larger plant in all its parts and less weedy looking. Their flowers open several hours after the nicotianas, not till dark, in fact, and in a series of jerks. You can hurry them by spraying with fine droplets of water at the vital moment.

49. The yellow stars of *Asphodeline liburnica* only open quite late in the afternoon and then contrast nicely with the blue sea-holly, *Eryngium oliverianum*.

Bold is beautiful

The cottage garden image is all very well in its charmingly informal way but it is largely a sham. Its appeal smacks of the granny's bonnets brand of sentimentality that goes with home-brewed mead and bowls of overspiced punch and potpourri. It is also an excuse for legitimized messiness with flopping masses of uncontrolled vegetation. Itsy-bitsy-ness is boring really. Many flowers are small and it's not their fault if they grow on plants of no particular or obvious structure, as do forget-me-nots or columbines themselves (it's only in the last twenty years that I've heard them called granny's bonnets, but now incessantly). Such flowers invite close inspection but in the mass they dissolve. That's why we put tulips among the forget-me-nots.

A group of boldly structured leaves, a stately inflorescence or a few imposing flowers, make all the difference.

I have always had mixed feelings about those bog garden primulas, such as *Primula florindae* with dangling, scented bells, and *P. bulleyana* with tiered whorls of flowers which we call candelabras (**50**). They do have structure and they are all the better for being massed and yet when they seed themselves around and the candelabras start lolling this way and that, they become weedy, especially if their leaves have nothing extra to contribute. But just set a clump of June-flowering arums among them and see what a difference it makes.

The arum flower is a beautiful shape, like a piece of sculpture. Botanists have invented two words to describe its special attributes: the club-like spadix and the sheathing spathe, yellow and white respectively in this, the florist's arum, familiar in church decorations at Easter time. *Zantedeschia aethiopica* is its awkward official name and it is widely regarded as a tender plant but can, in fact, be treated as a hardy perennial in many parts of Britain. Then it will flower, with the primulas, in June and July. Like them, too, it is happiest where the soil is moist; indeed it will grow under water. I have had a colony on a submerged island in my pond for many years. The glossy arrow-shaped leaves are entirely appropriate to its swaggering style.

Lilies, oriental poppies and peonies are examples of other bold flowers. But often it is the aggregate inflorescence that makes the impact; spikes of hollyhocks and delphiniums, for instance. Even the gladiolus; but this has been so top-heavily developed by the breeders that the hybrids are hard to accommodate in a mixed border.

The cones of lilacs, the tresses of laburnum have personality, while in hydrangeas you find, according to type, buns, lacecaps and cones. Pruning for quality and size can accentuate their impact. One of the most eye-catching features on Battleston Hill at Wisley in August is the white cones of *Hydrangea paniculata* 'Floribunda'. The plants are cut hard back each winter so that they make comparatively few but extra large inflorescences, each at least a foot long, cone shaped, and composed of a delicate creamy mixture of tiny white flowers and larger sterile florets. The size of these

flower heads is artificial but well balanced and not in the least vulgar in the general context of a flower garden.

Crambe cordifolia is a bold plant while *Genista cinerea* is not. They flower at the same time and look super together. The broom contributes with its rush of yellow blossom. The crambe (first cousin to our seakale) is white, its flowers no larger than the broom's, but spangled in a controlled galaxy, the spaces as important as the structure, above large, rounded, dark green leaves.

The crambe is a herbaceous perennial (it loves light soil and tends to rot on my clay) reaching 6 or 8 ft in a few weeks, while the broom might grow rather taller. Their season starts at the end of May and lasts for three weeks, no more.

Veratrums go on and on. I think *Veratrum album* (**51**) makes the strongest impression, because its paleness shows up at a distance, in shadow or in sun. I have the variegated *Hosta ventricosa* in front of it and the leaves of both plants are good value from May till slug-dinner-time. The hosta flowers elegantly for a couple of weeks in July. *Veratrum nigrum* is exciting at close range. Its deep maroon flowers lurk with sinister intent but it is scarcely a bold garden feature unless seen in silhouette against the sky. Its leaves make a ravishing, pleated bouquet in spring but go down to slugs and scorch quicker than any, so it is sensible to plant a late-developing masking plant in front. A third species, *V. viride*, flowers earliest, in May–June and its green colouring is of the liveliest. I've seen it standing out remarkably against a background of purple *Prunus* 'Pissardii' leaves. Individually, veratrum flowers are quite small stars but their arrangement and display are theatrical.

50. Bold flowers such as those of the florist's arum, *Zantedeschia aethiopica*, will pull any garden scene together. Here in the company of other moisture lovers: the giant cowslip, *Primula florindae*, and the candelabra-type *P. bulleyana*.

51. Not only is *Veratrum album* boldly constructed but its pale flowers show up at a distance better than other veratrum species. I have *Hosta ventricosa* 'Variegata' in front of it.

Foliage is the dominant feature in many bold effects. I have mentioned such as gunnera, rheum and fatsia. Bergenias are almost overworked as salient evergreen features on projecting corners or border bulges. Gertrude Jekyll was extremely fond of *Bergenia* (*Megasea* in her day) *cordifolia*. I wonder how she would react now that it is everywhere. It is true that you can't have enough of a good thing but if you see it a great deal you begin to appreciate its faults as well as its virtues. There is a gloomy leatheriness about those over-persistent leaves. I far prefer the less grown (is that the reason? I hope not) *B. ciliata* whose leaves, being deciduous, have a softer, more kindly texture. They are, furthermore, covered with soft hairs which have a light-reflecting sheen. Theirs are the biggest bergenia leaves I have yet seen and if you can make the plant happy on a ledge over which it can project a little, it becomes marvellously imposing. You may need to water it, in such a position. Moisture is necessary for the leaves to develop their full size and impact.

Hedges and topiary can be trained into bold shapes and architectural masses. I am sorry that topiary nowadays so seldom features in cottage gardens as it did when they were tended by genuine cottagers. Of course topiary takes time to assume the desired bulk and outline and most people are in a hurry because they don't expect to stay long. But the actual care of topiary is by no means time consuming, if you do it in reasonably slow growing material like yew or box.

My father loved topiary. There was a free-growing yew tree at Dixter when he came. He cut this back, almost to the trunk – which deters yew not in the least – and trained the resulting growth into a clipped topiary specimen which marries well with the hedges, yew archway and buildings around it. And I think it makes a fine contrasting background (**52**) to a willow that I have planted nearby. It is *Salix daphnoides* 'Aglaia' and it shows its large, silky white pussies as early as January (my photograph was taken on 1 February). By March they are covered in yellow pollen for which the bees forage enthusiastically.

52. The architectural quality of yew topiary condones a misty contrasting haze of willow pussies from *Salix daphnoides* 'Aglaia'. This was photographed at Dixter on 1 February.

Infillers

Here I have in mind those bare places underneath shrubs where the unimaginative gardener might not think of growing anything at all. Nature often lends a hand, however, and gives the necessary hint by sowing something there which your plans had allotted to quite another position.

On heavy soils *Campanula persicifolia*, whether in blue or in white, is the archetypal infiller. On light soils it never really takes off, but on heavy it seeds itself like mad and as its seeds are very small and light, they get blown around. *C. persicifolia* seems equally happy in sun or in shade. Where I found it in Eastern Europe it was following coppiced woodland as foxgloves do with us, but never in drifts.

More than half the time you'll have to weed its seedlings out. They are a menace, as are Welsh poppies, when they seed into a carpet of low ferns like *Adiantum venustum* or the oak fern *Gymnocarpium dryopteris*. But at other times they poke out from inside a hedge bottom or an olearia or some other shrub, deciduous or evergreen where you'd never have dreamt of positioning them. My favourite memory is of a white campanula that had pushed through *Olearia macrodonta*. The shrub's grey-green holly leaves were then covered in clusters of white daisies.

Welsh poppies (*Meconopsis cambrica*) are splendid associates with hydrangeas. They'll grow right into the centre of the bush and as the hydrangeas' leaves are still only half developed in May, when the poppies' main burst of blossom is in full swing, the latter show up well among all the surrounding greenery. Both the orange (a soft orange) and the yellow are equally pleasing and seed themselves in roughly equal quantities when grown together. If you can remember, after flowering, to grab and tug at all the poppies' top growth before they have seeded, they'll break away cleanly at soil level above the fleshy roots, and you'll be saved a lot of trouble with badly placed seedlings in the following spring.

Violets are delightful self-sowing infillers. Dog violets make clumps. The sweet-scented *Viola odorata* has a stoloniferous habit which enables it to spread over the ground into large patches. It flowers in March, just ahead of other kinds, but in fact there's seldom a time when you cannot pick a few. We have white, apricot, violet, pink and some bastard in-between colours. There's a white colony (self-appointed, I need hardly say) among the stems of a thirty-five-year-old Jerusalem sage, *Phlomis fruticosa*, and I particularly value them for the long stems which the shrub forces them to develop. It's easier to pick a bunch with stems that can be held. Elsewhere they are a great asset among shrub roses. We treat the ground with a simazine weedkiller (in the U.S.A. use any approved selective pre-emergent herbicide) each February. This deters the violets not at all and the absence of competing weeds allows them a free run.

All violets love to grow out of hedge bottoms. What better place? They can do no harm. Much as I love the purple-leaved, purple-flowered *Viola labradorica*, it is a sombre plant and shows up badly at the bottom of a sombre evergreen hedge like yew. But as I mentioned in my 'Following

53. The purple-leaved violet, *Viola labradorica*, can be tucked in under all sorts of shrubs and hedges but shows up more flatteringly in the company of a brighter partner, as here, *Euonymus* 'Emerald 'n' Gold'.

Through' chapter, I have it growing with a dwarf, variegated euonymus (**53**), which is lively enough for two, and they do blend well.

I would never have known how to make the best use of snowdrops if I had not seen how my mother would go round the garden with a trugful of flowered bulbs (some that needed splitting) and a narrow, sharp-pointed trowel, just looking out for bare spots into which to poke one here, one there. It's amazing what a lot of empty spaces you can find in March. Never mind that they'll have filled in later with other vegetation. The snowdrops will be resting by then. But you might just as well enjoy them first. Any place where they'll remain undisturbed will do for snowdrops. Among the deciduous crowns of *Bergenia ciliata*, for instance; at the bottom of a fig tree; under a lilac; between paving and a hedge. They should also come into the 'Making Use of Shade' chapter, because they often associate with trees and there are so many examples of snowdrop woods in Britain that some authorities think they must be native. I do not.

Girth control

We do not always choose our shrubs wisely for the positions we allot them and for the space which, within a few years, they would like to occupy. There is not necessarily cause, here, for despair. Pruning or cutting-back techniques can frequently save the day – for a while, at least.

Cutting back demands a temperament that is both sympathetic and resolute; an androgynous approach. It helps, for a start, to know whether a shrub will respond to a hard cutting back and make new shoots from old wood. I have written a long chapter on this subject in *The Adventurous Gardener* (Allen Lane, 1983), but the evidence, or at any rate its setting forth, is still full of holes.

Hedges are often planted too close to a path alongside which they run. Or a path may cut through a hedge at right angles and the gap becomes continuously narrower. Fairly drastic action needs to be taken, otherwise the same problem will be upon you within a few years. Cutting back into old yew or thuja wood is always successful. Within three years the surface will have completely recovered and you'd hardly believe it had been bare wood and stump ends so recently. And yet the cries of horror from family, friends and visitors when the job has first been tackled, and they see the results, are astonishing.

It also constantly happens that shrubs overgrow paths. Sometimes you can move the path but if not, then girth control must be imposed. In Pamla Toler's picture (**54**) there is an encroaching *Hebe* (*H. recurva*) on the right. I planted it much too close to the path. It had already been cut back once and has been again, since the photograph was taken. It makes fresh growth, either from the truncated stumps or, when these die (as old hebe wood sometimes will), from the base. If a hebe is likely to respond half-heartedly or in a piecemeal way to cutting back, you had much better replace it. Cuttings root easily and grow apace.

The shrub on the left is the evergreen *Bupleurum fruticosum* a member of the Umbelliferae, which includes parsley, carrot, celery, parsnip; also many garden plants and weeds but none of them woody like this. I had no idea how it would grow when I planted it, nor how it would respond to cutting back. In fact, it reacts perfectly. I cut it each spring and it immediately sets about making lots of new shoots on which it carries its green flower heads in summer and autumn. But this repeated cutting back has made the shrub round and dumpy. Its personality has been overlaid by middle-age spread. I'm not very clever at rooting it from cuttings but a few from a large batch will strike and I shall one day plant it where it can stretch and loll and behave as it pleases, for thus is character developed – unpredictably yet satisfyingly.

Between this and the castellated yew archway is a most delectable bamboo, *Arundinaria falconeri*. It is a rather tender species but probably less tender than nervous gardeners suspect. Given a sheltered position it will soon recover from a winter's maiming, but in ten years mine has not yet suffered in that way.

54. Shrubs and a bamboo (*Arundinaria falconeri*) whose exuberance has to be controlled when they encroach on a none-too-wide path.

Its wands are very slender and graceful, green and beautifully polished in youth. They shoot up from zero to 10 ft or so in one season, and in that year they scarcely make a leaf. But the following April they start to foliate luxuriantly and this added weight, especially after rain, sways the canes into parabolic curves. They hang over the path and administer a shower bath to anyone attempting to push through.

I have two ways of countering this unpopular behaviour. Every spring, just before growth is renewed, I cut out all the old, leafy canes, right to the ground leaving not even half an inch of stump. Those that remain are the unleafed, upright rods of the previous year's making. Thus the clump is entirely renewed every other year, no cane remaining in it for longer than two seasons.

Second, I loosely tie each of the remaining canes in a loop of string that passes from cane to cane and eventually returns to the stake from which it started, at the back of the clump. This tie is made at about 5 ft. It is not a truss, bunching the shoots together, but simply holds them, at that height. It is a great improvement but, alas, is still not enough to prevent the top 5 ft from swaying over and administering the statutory baptism.

This is a demurely clump-forming bamboo which increases its circumference at the base only very slowly but, inevitably, the plant has come nearer to the path in the course of ten years. Next spring I plan to dig out – correction – I plan to ask a friendly and cooperative gardener to dig out the front half of the clump. It will not be easy but it can hardly call for the setting of high explosives.

Did I hear someone whisper that it might be easier for everyone concerned if the bamboo were grown elsewhere? Yes it might; but I love the bamboo *there*, where it is, and while I am *here* and *compos mentis*, there it will remain. Unless it flowers, in which event it will die!

The thinning I have described can be applied to other shrubs throwing freely from low down or from ground level, and will reduce their overall bulk. It works particularly well on hydrangeas. If, having become impatient with a hydrangea's obesity near a path or passageway, you cut the whole shrub back, it will flower little or not at all in the following year. But if, every March, you get into the heart of that shrub with secateurs and saw and remove all the oldest, which are also the longest and lankiest, branches, you will reduce its overall circumference and at the same time renew your bush. Take out a quarter of its branches and it will be completely renewed in four years and it will be the more productive of high-quality blossom. Of course, for best results, you must feed and water it well too.

Grasses for ornament

Grasses have had their own little vogue, of recent years. Gardeners and, even more, perhaps, flower arrangers have looked beyond the pampas on the front lawn and have found much interesting material. In some it is the leaf colouring and arrangement that attracts, in others the panicle of flowers, sometimes whiskery and bristling, sometimes plume-like, sometimes a gauze. There is nothing brazen or brilliant about grasses. Their colouring is soft but their structure and bearing can be proudly individual – when given the chance, that is.

For it must be admitted that grasses are often misused. The collecting and categorizing instinct leads enthusiasts to pen them up together with similar unfortunate results to those seen in rose beds, ferneries, heather gardens, herbaceous borders etc. Few grasses set each other off. Seen in a mass they become confused and messy. The eye longs for a group of broad leaves to offset all those needles and straps. Colour harmonies are all very well but shapes needs contrasting.

The most effective use for many of the taller grasses is as single clumps soaring above much lower things in a mixed planting. This might entail bringing them almost to a border's margin, where most of the low growers will be congregated. *Arundo donax* is a super grass with broader, bolder leaves than most and well spaced on stems that rise to 8 ft in a single (warm) season. The colouring is blue. At Wisley (at the time of writing) they have this in the corner at the back of one of the mixed borders leading up to Battleston Hill. With an even taller evergreen hedge behind, it is lost, wasted. If a clump here, another there and a third elsewhere was brought close to the border's front you would, once past the stage of exclaiming 'What a curious place to put a tall plant; I wonder if they knew how big it would grow', be thrilled to see it standing proudly forward to be counted. Neither would it block your view of other nearby groupings.

There is an excellent German book on grasses and ferns by the late Karl Foerster (*Einzug der Gräser und Farne in die Gärten*. Verlag J. Neumann – Neudamm. Berlin, Basel, Vienna, 4th edn, 1978) and one of the most often illustrated grasses in this is the 6 ft clump-forming *Calamagrostis × acutiflora* 'Stricta'. This is apt to be listed in Britain (when listed at all) as *C. epigejos*, which is a native species but the plant in question has been shown to be a natural hybrid and the cultivar name 'Stricta' clearly indicates the stiffly erect habit of its flowering stems. The narrow flower panicles are each up to a foot long and flower at midsummer but become more conspicuous as they ripen to warm beige. A clump will grow very large, taking up almost as much space as a pampas grass. The illustration that most flatteringly presents it shows several widely separated clumps with big drifts of bedding plants in single colours – purple, rust red, white – in between, but none of these are more than 18 in tall. In a small garden, one clump would suffice. It would do much to pull together a bed of summer-flowering heathers.

There are many good things in the genus *Miscanthus*, which are stately grasses whose foliage arches outwards as though a living fountain. It was

55. Ornamental grasses often look messy if associated one with another, showing too little differentiation in habit. But the two here contrast markedly: *Miscanthus floridulus*, a leafy fountain behind, the shimmering flower heads of *Achnatherum calamagrostis* in front.

some time before I realized that single clumps displayed themselves so much more distinctly than when several were planted together. Each then grew into its neighbour and the fountain outline was blurred.

Most miscanthus are grown for their foliage. The flowers open so late in the autumn that they often fail to develop at all. Two cultivars shelter under the name of zebra grass and both, in this country, are interchangeably known as 'Zebrinus'. The true 'Zebrinus' is neither as hardy nor as impressive, with a rather lax habit, as the stiffly upright 'Strictus'. This develops the brighter yellow crossbanding, also, and the colour distinction between yellow and green is most marked in a sunny position. 'Variegatus', like the last, grows about 5 ft tall and makes a beautiful specimen clump. Its leaves, striped in cream along the margins, contrast strikingly with the broad purple paddles of *Canna indica* 'Purpurea' but there should

56. *Stipa gigantea* has a splendid presence when flowering and in seed. Two plants flank shallow steps in the chalk garden at Folkington Place in Sussex.

be a gap between the two of them filled by some 1 to 2 ft-tall plant. A shrub like the pale grey *Helichrysum splendidum* would do.

Miscanthus 'Gracillimus' usually grows to 5 ft and has very narrow leaves with a pale midrib. It is well named. Its colouring fades attractively to straw in late autumn and it needs cutting down only when leaf moult becomes tiresome in the new year. The one reliable flowerer in this group is the 6 ft 'Silver Feather', starting in August and continuing as its flowers gradually bleach until torn to pieces by wind. As with the others, it should be allowed to stand head and shoulders above nearby plantings.

Miscanthus floridulus (**55**) (usually known as *M. sacchariflorus* in Britain) is the giant of the family and in the reasonably warm climate of southern England, makes 10 ft of growth in a single season. Although it needs to stand well above its surroundings, it is not a bad idea to grow a 5 ft plant in front of it which will conceal its naked legs when stripped of leaves, as they are towards the end of the season. In front of mine I have, in fact, planted another (2 ft) grass because it is sufficiently different to make a contrast with the miscanthus. This is *Achnatherum calamagrostis* but in Britain it is nearly always known as *Stipa calamagrostis*, which is needlessly confusing since its inflorescence doesn't remotely resemble any stipa's. At flowering, in July, it is bushed out and shimmering, then closes up as it begins to ripen and slowly fades to beige. Thus its season of beauty is three or four months long. Grouping is worthwhile in this case and it is also worth lifting and resetting the clumps every third year because this makes for sturdy, self-supporting growth – otherwise the stems become floppy.

Of the true stipas the most inspiring is the 5 to 6 ft *S. gigantea* which looks so diaphanous, with a pink sheen on it in the evening light and is tellingly placed in a chalk garden on either side of shallow steps (**56**).

If I say little of the pampas grass, *Cortaderia selloana*, it is because it deserves a whole chapter to itself. Do choose carefully, here, for it is a variable species both in height and quality. The ideal is to choose a plant propagated from one that you have seen and liked in flower. Seedlings are sometimes offered and are considerably cheaper than vegetatively propagated stock, but they are a complete toss up. Nowhere does pampas look more exciting than by the waterside, marvellous in late autumn with red-stemmed dogwoods (*Cornus alba*), which shed their leaves quite early.

The smaller grasses are just as effective. It is only a matter of scale. *Molinia caerulea* 'Variegata' has a six-months-long season; first with its pale yellow variegated leaves on foot-tall clumps, then, at 2 ft, when its brown flowers come out in autumn and contrast with the now fading foliage. A good plant, this, for a promontory; a group of three or five would not spoil each other, where there was space, but one would be enough in a small setting, so long as it did not have to compete, in height, with neighbours.

Some of the hummocky fescues look well when massed, especially the grey-blue-leaved *Festuca cinerea* (*F. glauca*). This colouring is improved by fairly frequent division, in spring. If you want to pull your grasses to bits, always do it in spring or summer, when they are active. Autumn or winter divisions are frequently lethal.

Also illustrated here is a New Zealand grass, *Chionochloa conspicua* (**57**) which I grow behind *Grindelia chiloensis*, with yellow daisies on a shrubby plant. The grass is too housed in but it is sometimes easier to tell others what not to allow than to act on one's own advice. The grass hates being moved so I leave it.

57. The New Zealand grass, *Chionochloa conspicua*, flowering behind a yellow daisy shrub, *Grindelia chiloensis* from South America.

Conifers without gnomery

Those squat little figures sitting on rockeries are not always gnomes. Some of them are conifers, doing duty. Most such are man-selected, not known in the wild, and doubtless they reflect man's hopes and aspirations in some kinky way. 'They provide full stops and vertical accents', you will be told by those sufficiently articulate to put such claptrap into words (I do it myself, but then it's different). The time I begin to find them interesting is just when their owners are made uneasy by the size they are attaining (not what they'd been led to expect of a 'dwarf' conifer) or by their loss of symmetry; the way, for instance, that an Irish juniper in old age will take on a lean and splay open in places.

I was rather alarmed, it must be twenty years ago or more, when a friend gave me a small plant of *Chamaecyparis lawsoniana* 'Ellwood's Gold' – one of the many mutants of Lawson's cypress. What could I be expected to do with one of these wretched little things in my sort of garden? However, he'd raised it himself from a cutting and it looked forlorn and in need of mothering, so I planted it, with the result you see (**58**). It has developed, with the years, into a specimen of a sensible size and I like the contrast with the rounded hebes ('Pewter Dome') that cuddle up to it on one side. (They became too big and I've just had to replace them.)

This, I may say, is at the intersection of four straight paths opening out into a paved square in our High Garden. The place suggests that reasonably durable and important-looking plants should be presiding, so on an opposite corner, I have planted two *Chamaecyparis thyoides* 'Ericoides', a conifer of soft texture with juvenile foliage (**59**) which is sea green in summer, purple in winter when it develops the vegetable equivalent of a bottle nose.

I shouldn't like them on their own at all, but to one side there are the spiky evergreen leaves of the dwarf *Yucca flaccida*, and in front three plants of the inestimable South African *Helichrysum splendidum*, which I cut hard back every spring in order to prevent them from flowering and so as to stimulate production of the freshest grey foliage. Unpruned specimens quickly become shabby but this is an excellent substitute to santolina where low grey hedging is required and the santolina is insufficiently hardy.

I now call this conifer corner, for on the next corner round I have planted (six years ago, at a guess) *Thuja occidentalis* 'Rheingold' and this is surrounded on its visible sides by the grey-leaved *Dorycnium hirsutum*, a shrub which constantly renews itself by self-sowing (unless you employ a residual weedkiller, which I'm afraid I do, rather than become engulfed in a sea of weeds). It has clusters of white pea flowers with a faint blush to them, followed by shining bronze seed pods, shaped like little clogs.

The conifer turns such a deep shade of old gold in winter that it looks dead but quickly livens up in spring and summer, when I like it best.

A few yards further along the path, past the yuccas, I have *Abies koreana*, which is an odd ingredient, perhaps, even in a mixed border and friends

tell me, ironically, that I have a nice Christmas tree. It is a tree species, but not a big one and when it becomes too large for its position I shall get rid of it and plant another. All the abies, which are the silver firs, have fascinating cones. They develop like tubby candles on the top sides of their branches and with *A. koreana* this happens at an early age, which enables you to enjoy them at close quarters without binoculars and without getting a crick in your neck.

59. Another part of conifer corner at Great Dixter, with a pair of *Chamaecyparis thyoides* 'Ericoides'. Sea green in summer, they turn purple in cold weather. *Helichrysum splendidum*, a grey-leaved shrub, in front, and dwarf yuccas, left.

I have several more conifers in my garden; three are young developing trees and another bushy type, *Chamaecyparis obtusa* 'Tetragona Aurea', has young branches on which the gold-green foliage is encrusted like lichens – splendid to pick for winter flower arrangements but good in the garden at all times with other kinds of foliage, to wit *Arundo donax*, a pittosporum and some bedded-out plants of the tender *Geranium maderense* with enormous spikily cut palmate leaves.

Most successful, however, are two plants of the prostrate (but not too ground hugging) *Juniperus sabina tamariscifolia*, which proceeds, as it were, in a series of tiny crested wavelets – just enough movement to give it a lovely texture and personality. I planted one on either side of our sunk garden on the retaining wall that frames it, and they have cascaded 3 ft downwards and are now advancing across the garden's floor.

And here I suppose I have to make the confession that I have a passion for conifers, trees, shrubs and grovellers, but I do see that more than a few would look unsuitable in my (and probably also in your) garden. It isn't like Bedgebury Pinetum (the British national collection in Kent) where the conifers create a landscape of their own without any reference being necessary to the landscape of deciduous woodland that would be natural.

In a garden, conifers need handling with restraint but they can be mixed satisfactorily with other plants. All-conifer gardens are generally a nightmare and bring on the usual indigestion arising from monocultures. Even at Bedgebury, care has been taken to mix in deciduous trees.

There is one bed entirely of conifers in the late Robin Spencer's garden near Leeds in Yorkshire which I thought peculiarly successful, in which the shrubs were set against a floor of shingle. Very peculiar and individualistic and you would come to hate it if you began to meet it everywhere, but it worked for him.

Conifers have been pushed of late. They have become fashionable, which is bad for any plant. I think we should try and learn to admire them in situations where they look suitable and to suppress the urge to grow too many ourselves.

Are your heathers really necessary?

Heathers have suffered like conifers from becoming a cult. Entire suburban front gardens can be devoted to these two types of plants and there are plenty of nurseries geared to promoting and supplying them.

Heathers belong to heath and moorland, of which we have plenty in our islands. They look entirely appropriate there and I enjoy the sight of them when taking my summer holidays. I won't next say: 'Why bring them into the garden?' It's nice to have a few plants of some form of *Erica carnea* from which to pick sprigs for the house in winter. And, not surprisingly, there are Scottish gardens where heathers look right. There was one I visited recently where cultivated heathers on a rocky bank behind the house simply merged into wild heathers a little further on. You couldn't say where garden ended and heath began. And another, at Pitlochry, had a large expanse of lawn in which self-sown heathers took the place of grass in several areas. Heathers don't look their best when mown, and I should have been tempted to leave the lawn (or part of it) uncut through the summer months so that the heathers, bedstraws, harebells and other wild plants could flower. Grass does not grow rankly in those parts, so it would have looked charming.

Even in parts of Surrey, heather has its place. If I lived at the edge of a Surrey common I should be strongly inclined to plant my garden with birches, gorse, heather and a few conifers.

But in the generally lush setting of most lowland gardens, heathers look as out of place as rocks. There is monotony in their tiny leaves when often repeated. True there are many kinds, of callunas especially, with interestingly coloured leaves, grey, yellow, bronze, but the bittiness and the haphazard growth remain. And if you try, in a small space, to fit in a lot of different colours and varieties, see how fidgety is the result (**60**). The one restful area in the picture is that created by the grey shrub, *Euryops acraeus*, on the left.

As just one element in a mixed planting of many other kinds of plants, a generous patch of heather, grown either for its flowers or for its leaf colour but keeping the varieties down to one or at most two, can look very well. The yellow ling with the blue prostrate Colorado spruce in a friend's Scottish garden, was striking, I thought (**61**), and the soft grey one nearby fitted in, but any more heathers would have been superfluous.

Some gardeners treat them as convenience plants, and a way of covering difficult ground instead of turf. But even then the area would look far more interesting and be no more awkward to look after if you included other shrubs for variety; cistuses and low-growing rhododendrons, hypericums, periwinkles, some phormiums for height, and brooms. Tree heaths have more character as plants than the lowly kinds and a heather bed is much improved by their inclusion, but their hardiness cannot everywhere be depended upon.

Do at least give the matter thought and consider a range of alternatives before wading with both feet into the heather market.

60. Heathers, being flimsy-textured, should not be spotted around, as here. The different varieties need massing in a landscape setting. The grey *Euryops acraeus*, on the left, is a firmer, more reposeful plant.

61. A yellow-leaved ling (*Calluna*) contrasts strikingly with the blue, young foliage of a prostrate Colorado spruce (*Picea pungens* 'Glauca Prostrata').

Making use of shade

If you had a garden without shade you would very quickly want to create some. 'I can't grow sanguinarias or primulas or lilies-of-the-valley or Solomon's seal or anything like that', you'd be moaning: 'You see I have no shade. They all detest me.' Just as many gardeners, especially town dwellers, will lament their lack of sun. Shade, as often as not, is a blessing. A garden that was half in shade half in sun, taking a summer's day through from morn till eve, would be ideal.

I realize that the truth of that claim depends on various factors. Where you live, for instance. A honeysuckle like *Lonicera tragophylla* that is happiest in shade in the south of England will thrive in 'full sun' in the north of Scotland (where this commodity needs the protection of inverted commas). Then there is a difference between heavy shade, under an umbrageous tree, and light shade, under a Mount Etna broom. And there is the difference between dry shade and moist. I shall leave dry shade to the next chapter and assume that the moisture is present or suppliable or that it can be retained with mulches of organic matter, these being invaluable in every part of the garden.

One of the odd things about shade is the contradictory evidence and advice regarding what should be grown in it. Many of the plants habitually recommended for shade, such as periwinkles, the rose of Sharon, skimmias and snowberries will actually flower and fruit far more freely in the sun. The fact is that they will *tolerate* shade, which is not the same as to say they need it. But there are others which will scorch in an over-sunny position, none more so than plants with yellow foliage. In too deep shade their leaves will be too green for interest so light shade and moisture at the roots is the general recipe for such as the golden cut-leaved elder (*Sambucus racemosa* 'Plumosa Aurea'), the golden Japanese maple (*Acer japonicum* 'Aureum') and the golden marjoram (*Origanum vulgare* 'Aureum'). They're all lime green, really, but gold sounds good.

Shade flatters variegated plants like my *Hosta undulata* (**62**) which is presided over by an enormous fatsia (I have just cut a third of this away, to give the plants under it more light, but it will soon grow again). The white variegation here provides its own 'sunlight'. To have real sun on it confuses the pattern. Of course you don't have to wait for many hours to have the whole garden in the shade of a cloud umbrella, but the hosta is more vital for there being sunshine around while itself reflecting the sky and any other light source reaching it. There are ferns around it and interplanted snowdrops for the winter.

Another of my favourite light reflecting shade plants is the variegated honesty, biennial *Lunaria annua*, which colonizes under a big old 'Souvenir de Louis Spaeth' lilac. It is at its prettiest in spring and the mauve flowers go well with the pale leaves (I think they do with the variegated *Phlox* 'Norah Leigh' also, but I'm usually shouted down on this one and told that the flowers are worthless). Honesty is followed, in this area, by purple martagon lilies in June and by *Cyclamen hederifolium* in the autumn.

62. Variegation lights up shady places as shown here by *Hosta undulata* beneath the huge-leaved evergreen *Fatsia japonica*.

White flowers gleam out of shade with added lustre, too. There's a pure white honesty, which never looks quite so impressive out in the sun. These different kinds of honesty, incidentally, need to be kept separate from one another in the garden, otherwise they cross. They're all subject to virus diseases, so don't grow them, as I do, near wallflowers that you treat as perennials. These always become virus-ridden, as you can tell from their broken flower colouring, and they pass it on to their honesty relations.

The double-flowered form of Canadian bloodroot, *Sanguinaria canadensis* 'Flore Pleno', is a delicious shade plant, opening when the sun warms the surrounding air but not needing to be touched by it. If you allow forget-me-nots to sow themselves near it, make sure you pull them out before they swamp the bloodroot and it's the same with candelabra primulas (*Primula japonica*, here) which I have around this part of the border. They'll seed themselves into anything. The bloodroot flowers for only a week in April but it is so exciting as to seem longer. The double kind does last a little longer than the single and being in shade helps.

Tiarella cordifolia makes a carpet of its foaming white flowers in May and loves a cool leaf soil whereas *Saxifraga stolonifera*, one of several mothers of thousands, doesn't mind what soil it's given. Its sprays of white blossom come above scalloped evergreen foliage in June. Even better is a form of this masquerading as *S. cuscutiformis*, with more emphatically patterned leaves and stronger flower panicles. Whilst in the saxifrage family I must bring in *S. fortunei*, which carries great clumps of white blossom in October. Here again the leaves are good and there are cultivars in which the undersides are reddish purple. You usually see only one plant here, another there, but it is exciting in a mass, if you can find the space.

Many spring flowers can be grown in shade that becomes quite dense later on but if trees are the shade makers they'll need to be thinned to allow plenty of summer light to penetrate between them. This will enable shrubs like camellias, rhododendrons and hydrangeas to flourish underneath them and will also cater for summer-flowering perennials like astilbes, japanese anemones, lilies and hardy orchids.

In the shade both of our house and of a morello cherry I have (**63**) white martagon lilies (more telling, really, than the purple, because their yellow stamens show up so well against the white petals), the rich reddish purple orchid, *Dactylorhiza foliosa*, *Hosta ventricosa* 'Variegata' and the form of the soft shield fern, *Polystichum setiferum*, called 'Acutilobum', with sharply pointed pinnules and fronds that often take on a seductive twist as though they were rotating on a turntable. The orchid is hardy and showy with a flowering season that lasts through June into July, and its tubers multiply quite quickly so that from small (and expensive) beginnings you can soon build up a stock. This area is lit up only when the setting sun northwesters at the end of the longest days.

The sort of plant that I should like to get next to my hardy orchids is *Paris polyphylla* (**64**). All right, it's only green but what a marvellously structured

63. A shady area by Great Dixter, lit by sunshine only on summer's evenings. Filigree shield fern, *Polystichum setiferum* 'Acutilobum', contrasts with our old friend *Hosta ventricosa* 'Variegata' and spikes of the hardy orchid, *Dactylorhiza foliosa*. Buds of *Lilium martagon* 'Album' behind.

64. A most exciting newcomer to our gardens from the Himalayas, *Paris polyphylla*. What need is there of bright colour in a plant like this?

creature and with quite enough colour to emphasize its shape. And it retains this from the time it starts in June until its berry is ripe in the autumn. Our native paris of limy woodland is *P. quadrifolia* and that's a plant one enjoys finding, often in the company of butterfly orchis, but this *P. polyphylla* beats everything. It is getting around a little now though not mentioned in the Hardy Plant Directory to which I keep turning as I write, for it tells you where rarer hardy perennials may be tracked down. (The name and address of the Hon. Branch Secretary of the Hardy Plant Society to whom you should write is given on p.172.)

There's another large shady area in my garden under some *Magnolia denudata* and on the north side of a mulberry, into which I have packed many favourite plants. *Choisya ternata*, the Mexican orange, needs sun in the north to make it flower, but the ambient temperature is sufficiently high to ripen its wood and enable it to flower profusely in a shady position in the south, and here the leaf colour will be a much richer shade of green than the jaundiced complexion induced by a hot spot. Mahonias are excellent shade shrubs. I have here the rather tender *Mahonia lomariifolia* and the winter flowering, lily-of-the-valley-scented *M. japonica*. Right under the magnolias is a colony of *Danaë racemosa*, grown for its lustrous foliage which picks well to arrange with daffodils in spring. You can cut away all its old, 2½ to 3 ft-tall shoots at that season and allow them to be replaced by the asparagus-like young spears from the base. This is indeed a relation of asparagus but I've never had enough of it to try eating its succulent young shoots.

In the deepest depths behind, I have the shade-loving *Aster divaricatus* (*corymbosus*) given me by Margery Fish. It flowers at the usual Michaelmas daisy time and being almost white shows up well in the shadows. And so, even better, does *Rudbeckia* 'Goldsturm', which makes a large colony to one side. On 2½ ft stems its deep yellow, black-centred daisies impart wonderful richness and warmth to a shady position and they flower non-stop from early August to October. There is quite a bit of light under the magnolias when the hellebores are flowering in winter and early spring; *H. foetidus*, *H. lividus corsicus* and the Lenten roses (*H. orientalis*) which are in a range of soft colours.

65. All shade lovers, though seen in sunshine at the day's end. Yellow-flowered creeping Jenny on the near corner with pinky-mauve *Geranium endressii* to the right, *Campanula poscharskyana* to the left and a heavily spotted laurel, *Aucuba japonica* 'Crotonifolia', behind.

The plants in this area that actually come into Pamla Toler's picture (65) are *Aucuba japonica, Campanula poscharskyana,* creeping Jenny (*Lysimachia nummularia*) on the corner and *Geranium endressii* to the right. You either see the point of aucubas or you don't. Disorganized, unzoned variegation disgusts many people, males especially. If you can take a spotted aucuba, make sure it's really heavily spotted and splashed and proud of its spots. Mine, obtained from Hillier's Nurseries, is 'Crotonifolia', a male. It is the most cheerful of shrubs at every season except briefly in spring when changing old foliage for new. And it's excellent picking material, especially useful in winter. Behind it (out of sight here) I have planted a female called, simply, 'Lance Leaf' (also from Hillier's) with a narrow, elegantly tapering, glossy plain green leaf. Pollinated by its scorbutic husband, it makes large berries which ripen to red in late winter, at a most welcome time.

The campanula is a ground covering-thug and has to be restrained, but its wands of pale mauve stars are charming. Were I starting again I should probably grow its cultivar 'Stella' instead, for this is less invasive and its colour is a more definite campanula blue.

Creeping Jenny is a cheerful plant whose neighbours (there are cyclamen here also) may need protecting from its embraces. I got my stock from a doodlebug crater on the marsh nearby, which it was colonizing just after the war. I also have its yellow-leaved form but for best colour I grow that in the sun. In dry summer's weather it scorches but by then it needs cutting back anyway. Of *Geranium endressii* I have already sung the praises. Any crudity in its pink/mauve colouring is softened by shade.

There are innumerable other shade plants but I hope I have said enough to show that it should not be shunned. Even humans sometimes welcome it during the occasional torrid spell.

Dark, dry and rooty

It is the dry shade beneath dense trees that is the dread and despair of so many gardeners and their question 'What can I grow in it?' is the one most frequently put to the expert.

Dry shade under a north wall isn't so bad, as long as you realize that it *is* dry there, that the wall makes the soil doubly dry near to it first by itself lapping up moisture and second by physically preventing the rain, which in Britain is nearly all carried on southwest winds, from falling here. Appreciate that plants in the summer need an inch of rain in every ten days and you can make good the deficiency, which is roughly equivalent to four gallons of water to every square yard.

But few plants – few anyway that are worth growing – can grow healthily underneath the dense shade, which is far deeper than that cast by a wall, beneath a beech, lime, sycamore or plane, to name four of the worst offenders. Furthermore their roots reach right to the surface and mop up any moisture or food that's going before the intended beneficiary has had the chance to partake. Oaks are less villainous because they root deeply and therefore surface mulches will be of some benefit to surface vegetation. Ash trees cast much less shade than many. So do birches, but their roots are particularly superficial and greedy. Ornamental cherries have very boring foliage all through the summer which is scant compensation for one week of blossom in the spring. Consider whether it would not be more sensible to enjoy your neighbour's blossom and all that which lines suburban roads and forego it in your own plot.

However, your trees are there with, perhaps, a preservation order on them. One of the best things to do in this situation is nothing. Simply accept that bare ground is no more of a disgrace than a balding head. That saves no end of worry. Bare ground in a border that should be full of plants in summer *is* shaming, in my opinion, but under trees, certainly not. It's the tree and its trunk that should be looked at and admired in that situation, not a lot of trumpery nonsense under its feet. Because, remember what I said in the last chapter: you may possibly persuade things like ivy and variegated deadnettle and periwinkles to *grow*, but they won't do themselves or you justice. At worst they'll be scruffy, dusty, covered with sooty moulds and bird droppings; at best inoffensive.

Bare ground is cleaner and easier to keep clean. If you live in the country, it will be colonized by mosses in winter and spring. Let them come; you don't have to plant them any more than you have to plant moss in your lawns. One of the most satisfying features in the Savill Gardens at Windsor in spring is the undulating carpet of white fork moss, *Leucobryum glaucum*, underneath the beech trees as you enter (66). A wealth of colour and business awaits the visitor, but those mosses under those smooth grey trunks have a simplicity and dignity which are, in their own way, matchless.

You can colonize early-flowering bulbs even under a beech. Any plant that can flower, grow and die off in the first four months of the year is

sitting pretty. At that season the necessary moisture is there and so is the light. I know a huge purple beech in a chalk garden under which self-sowing *Crocus tomasinianus* and winter aconites have spread thickly. You also see this crocus with the winter-flowering *Cyclamen coum* at the foot of a tree where mosses also play their part, in a photograph (**67**) I took in the late Collingwood Ingram's garden shortly before he reached his century.

Whether they flower in autumn, winter or spring, cyclamen time their growth cycle so as to dovetail in with a deciduous tree's. They all rest and disappear from sight in summer and do their growing between winter and spring. *Cyclamen hederifolium* enlivens the autumn months by flowering from August to October or even later if there has been a drought. It will then bide its time until the autumn rains arrive and start up when they do. Its marbled leaves are particularly decorative and vary from plant to plant, so they are always a pleasure.

C. coum has a wide geographic distribution in the Middle East and hence varies, itself, a great deal. Most typically its flowers are vivid magenta

66. The white fork moss, *Leucobryum glaucum*, beneath the dry shade of beeches in the Savill Gardens, Windsor. At its best in spring before the ground dries out.

67. *Crocus tomasinianus, Cyclamen coum* and mosses give winter and early spring colour beneath a tree where dry summer conditions will later make it sensible to be content with bare ground for half the year.

which is a cheering colour in winter and goes with practically anything at that season. There is also an excellent near-white form often called 'Atkinsii'. In *C. hederifolium*, whose colour is normally some shade of cyclamen pink, the albino form is pure white all through and comes true from seed.

There are shrubs that will survive in deep dry shade but the only one that I would wholeheartedly recommend (and there is also a fern I shall come to) is *Euphorbia robbiae*. It makes dark, shining rosettes of evergreen leaves on foot-tall stems and spreads by suckering. In April it more than doubles its height and carries its lime-green inflorescences. These are a long time fading, and if grown in a hot, sunny position they take on beautiful coppery tints. When finally dead and unsightly, it is essential to cut flowered stems right down to the ground and to remove them. Not only does this keep your colony looking sightly but it prevents it from dying out in patches, as it otherwise will. It is surprising how seldom this small task is attended to.

Fitting in ferns

Like ornamental grasses, ferns look better in the company of other types of plant when mixed up with each other. The one exception to this general rule is the plain-leaved hart's tongue, which looks so different from all the rest that it contrasts distinctly with any of them. But if you plant a lot of pinnate-fronded ferns, together, confusion reigns.

Generally speaking, moist shade with plenty of humus in the soil is the recipe for making the majority of ferns happy, but you have only to see them in a range of wildly differing natural habitats to realize how misleading a generalization this is. Also, plants are often more adaptable than you'd expect. Few of the specialized ferns are suitable for garden cultivation anyway; the rest are pretty amenable.

If I will not allow you your fernery or mixed fern border, how are you to work in many kinds without which you would eke out a miserable existence? The male, lady and shield ferns – *Dryopteris*, *Athyrium* and *Polystichum* – are certainly good in damp shade. Where a fern makes a great shuttlecock of fronds about a central crown, as does *Dryopteris wallichianum*, it should not be interfered with by planting anything of its own height nearby. Better to underplant it with low bulbs (snowdrops are ideal) or shade-loving perennials like *Omphalodes cappadocica*, *Brunnera macrophylla* 'Variegata', pulmonarias or *Arum italicum* 'Pictum', which dies away as the fern fronds unfold. These are covered, in youth, with dark brown scales and they look immensely exciting as they unfurl, more like an animal than a plant. I cannot recommend this fern too highly and although it is hard to come by at the moment there is already plenty of young stock available in Holland, raised from spores. I cannot but think that, with the ever increasing demand for hardy ferns that we have in this country, it will soon be available here. *D. wallichianum* grows a good 3 ft tall and it seldom makes offsets, which is frustrating for the amateur propagator but does mean that it never spoils itself by one crown growing into another. This often happens with other kinds, however, such as the coveted *Polystichum aculeatum* 'Bevis', in which the pinnae at the frond's tips close in to form a kind of tail. So you should lift and divide clumps of such as these at not too infrequent intervals. Spring, just as growth commences, is the best time.

Fern fronds always look well near hosta leaves. I said I had them under my big *Fatsia japonica* behind the illustrated clump of *Hosta undulata* (**62**).

I also like them with hardy fuchsias and would here add that fuchsias are themselves improved by not being in beds on their own but allowed to join the throng. They like moist conditions and are as happy in shade as in sun. On either side of *Fuchsia* 'Tom Thumb' I have a form of *Polypodium vulgare*. On its left, 'Cornubiense' (**68**), whose typical fronds are much divided but firm of texture and a brilliant shade of green. This cultivar is unstable and often reverts to plain polypody or something near it. Such fronds should be removed as they appear. On the fuchsia's other side is a crested polypody. I don't know which one but the crests are well balanced and do not look abnormal.

68. An elegant mutant, 'Cornubiense', of the European polypody, *Polypodium vulgare*. Ferns and fuchsias – 'Tom Thumb' is seen here – like the same moist, partly shaded conditions.

Once you have introduced hart's tongue ferns, *Asplenium scolopendrium*, they will sow themselves wherever they think they ought to be, and often they'll be right: into dry walls or making a fringe along the bottom of a wall or into the risers of garden steps. They show up particularly well in winter, when other plants have died back, but it is wise to cut their old fronds away in early March, because it is difficult to do neatly once the young crop is growing and the old ones become unsightly at that time.

In the risers of steps is one of the most charming places to see ferns and particularly good, in sun or in shade, are the maidenhair and black spleenworts, *Asplenium trichomanes* and *A. adiantum-nigrum*; also the rustyback, *Ceterach officinarum*, with scalloped leaf margins. It crumples up in dry weather but returns with the moisture and rains. The very air we breath is thick with fern spores, awaiting the right spot to alight; four natives that I never introduced, grow luxuriantly under my cold green-house staging. If you have an old wall in which the mortar is crumbly, wall rue, *Asplenium ruta-muraria*, will turn up of its own accord. You'll not want to go in for any busybody repointing, once that happens.

Rather than forming clumps which keep more or less to themselves, some ferns spread by under- or overground runners or rhizomes, and thus make carpets or colonies. *Matteuccia struthiopteris*, the ostrich feather fern, is one of the strongest colonizers and makes beautiful shuttlecocks of fresh greenery up to 3 ft tall each spring. It scorches readily if at all parched, but is admirable for rambling among azaleas in partial shade. Or, like the regal fern, *Osmunda regalis* (**69**), it will revel in a bog or by the waterside, so long as the water is not merely within sight but within reach of its roots. *Onoclea sensibilis*, the sensitive fern, is another travelling species for such a position and these two are sufficiently different from the osmundas (of which there are several more worthwhile species) to look well in their company. My photograph shows the osmunda's unfurling croziers in May. It will grow 4 or 5 ft tall when happy and takes on warm autumn colouring before it finally withers.

But this is a clump former (which also sows itself into new positions) and I have more to say on those that make carpets and mats of foliage. *Blechnum chilense* (*B. tabulare*) from southern South America, is typical of the plant that is normally grown in shade but gives a far livelier account of itself out in the open. In shade it will grow sparsely, making 3 to 4 ft fronds but in sun it forms a dense thicket, 18 in high, and with new fronds being unfurled from spring to autumn, you get patterns of colour from copper through pale to dark green (coppery tints never develop in shade). Mature fronds have a satisfying harshness of texture that makes them pleasing to grasp. Evergreen, like all the blechnums (and likewise calcifuge, be warned) but hard frosts blacken the fronds and snow breaks them. Whatever the winter, you should cut them down in March and encourage them to start afresh from square one. This looks well with the purple-leaved *Hebe* 'Mrs. Winder'.

Our native *Blechnum spicant* will run around in paving cracks or can be perched on a rock ledge or slightly raised edge, where its foot-tall fertile fronds will be well displayed. The diminutive New Zealander, *B. penna-marina*, is ideal for running in and out of *Cyclamen hederifolium* clumps. The cyclamen's main season of activity is between autumn and spring; the fern's between spring and autumn.

A fine display position for many ferns is perched on a rock or low dry wall ledge or edge; always provided they are moist enough to grow healthily. They make a stunning contrast with bergenias. One that will creep about over mossy rocks and root in their interstices is the hare's foot fern, *Davallia mariesii*, whose forked rhizomes are covered in brown, hairy scales. Its deciduous fronds grow only 6 in tall and are most delicately divided. So are those of *Adiantum venustum*, a low, carpeting maidenhair fern that is perfectly hardy. Its leaves are held through the winter and bronze attractively (even if killed) in cold weather.

69. The unfurling croziers of the royal fern, *Osmunda regalis*, in the kind of setting that enables it to develop its greatest luxuriance.

Our native polypodies, *Polypodium vulgare* and other nearly related species will colonize a wall top and face, even if dry, and they are excellent in the dry shade of a tree, or indeed on a tree stump or branch, if there is enough moss and detritus to give them the wherewithal to live.

On the tiles

That brings me apropos to the gardening that can be indulged in on a tiled roof, provided you don't suffer from a mania for keeping it clean of mosses and all other vegetation. Mosses will grow on shaded roof slopes and polypodies (**70**) will sow themselves here as well as on a tree branch. It's all the same to them whether there is wood or tile under the moss. Although the owner of the lean-to roof in my photograph answered roundly 'yes' when I asked if she'd started the fern herself, I know very well that she didn't – I just wanted to hear what she would say. It isn't an easy thing to achieve from a ready-made root. A spore alighting on the right spot at the right time has the best chance, but that might be hard to organize. You could shake the contents of a ripe frond over the area you wanted to colonize and just keep your fingers crossed. It'd be worth trying.

Houseleeks and stonecrops are more easily managed. We have a huge old lump of a houseleek on one outhouse roof at Dixter that was established before my parents came on the scene, and it must be getting on for a century old. My Dutch gardening friend, Romke van de Kaa, who was with me here for a few years, started several more colonies on this roof, of *Sempervivum* and *Jovibarba*. He collected some pats from our neighbour's pedigree Sussex cows (I mention the pedigree in case it has significance) mixed them with clay (our natural subsoil) and water into a dough and slapped this tasty mixture here and there where the succulents were next pinned on, once the mixture had set a little. A hairpin is suitable for this purpose. They all took but in some cases shrinkage of the matrix caused it to be blown off in a gale. Others have stuck and survived.

70. Polypody colonizing a mossy, penthouse roof.

71. Stonecrops, both yellow- and white-flowered, colonize the stone tiling on this porch at Gravetye Manor, Sussex, once the home of William Robinson.

At Gravetye Manor in Sussex, now a hotel but once William Robinson's home, I was fascinated by the assortment of white and yellow-flowered sedums thickly established on the stone-tiled roof of a porch (**71**). Most of the display when I was there in August was from the white clusters of *Sedum album*, a rampant species, every one of whose detached leaves will make a new plant, but perfectly suitable on a roof.

For an earlier display, *S. dasyphyllum* starts at the beginning of June and is blush white with leaves that flush pink under dry conditions. *S. anglicum* is not unlike, and *S. acre*, flowering in June-July, is the brilliant yellow stonecrop that you find on shingle and in other hungry, sun-baked soils. The cowpat technique would work to get any of these started and they would only need the friendly company of mosses and lichens in order to seed themselves over the remaining area.

Porch and patio

The patio or (as at Dixter) terrace, or courtyard – the enclosed area where we sit out and relax when the weather permits – is immensely important. I shall come to its olfactory aspects in a later chapter. Here I am concerned with appearances. When you're not looking at your companions or the swallows or staring balefully at the wasp or fruit flies in your drink, you're looking appreciatively but critically (the critical faculty never sleeps) at the plants. I don't think they matter tuppence in the winter and I would sooner then see empty containers or nothing at all than evergreens brought in to cheer things up. Those sort of evergreens never do.

But courtyards are, or should be, sheltered (our sitting-out terrace is open to howling southwest gales but it's lovely when the wind's in the north) and wherever the sun strikes one of its enclosed walls it'll be roasting hot and just the place to grow something like angels' trumpets (*Datura sauveolens*) – moving it out and then back to a greenhouse for the winter. Or that marvellous sky blue convolvulus (*Pharbitis tricolor*), which is popularly known as ipomaea or morning glory. They crumple at noon, but that's a good excuse for cracking a mid-morning bottle of champagne – no better hour (especially if it's Sunday and the pious are at church).

Those floppy Grandiflora petunias that get smashed to pulp under normal British conditions (how lucky they are in Switzerland and Bavaria), may stand a chance; hibiscus, even oleanders, though in my experience their buds begin to drop the moment they leave the greenhouse.

The blue ipomaea is not the only sort of pot-grown climber you should train up a sunny courtyard wall (a couple of nails and a string between is all the apparatus that's necessary). The early-flowering form of *Tropaeolum tuberosum* called 'Ken Aslet' (**72**), in two shades of orange, is excellent. At the end of the season you just collect up its tubers and store them in a cool but frost-free place. Pot them up again in the spring (a large pot or tub for a dramatic show) and away you go again. The spring-bulb lists include all sorts of odd corms and tubers, among them *Gloriosa superba* or an even more plutocratic number called *G. rothschildiana*. They're like waxy turk's-cap lilies, orange or scarlet, on a tendril climbing plant. It also looks good to have a light blue plumbago with these. The gloriosas make tubers which you can store like the tropaeolum's.

You'll have 'geraniums' (they are pelargoniums, really) in your tubs; I always think the trailing ivy-leaved kinds give best value and it's amazing how well their vivid colours all mix together, though you'd expect them to clash. I rather draw the line at the crude pink 'Galilee'. The one you see most on the European continent and a little more than we used to, here, is 'Ville de Paris'. It has quite narrow-petalled salmony flowers and particularly fresh green foliage. There are red flowered forms (I brought a cutting of one such back with me from Hungary and then found it here) which make a change.

The shrubby *Mimulus glutinosus* is a very nice tub plant with a semi-recumbent habit and a non-stop flowering season. Typically an apricot

72. *(right)* Pot-grown tubers of the climbing *Tropaeolum tuberosum* 'Ken Aslet' are moved in summer to a position outside our porch at Dixter, where they can ramble up a cotoneaster.

73. *(far right)* The grey-leaved *Helichrysum petiolatum*, grown in a tub, has one shoot trained up a cane, giving it a tree-like habit. With it, the orange *Cuphea cyanea*, whose flowers are brighter orange when given a restricted root run. An autumn-flowering pampas grass, *Cortaderia argentea* 'Pumila', in the background.

orange shade, 'Puniceus' is deep bronze red. This is not always an easy plant to locate. Particularly suited to pot or tub culture because a spot of root containment and starvation improves the intensity of its orange colouring, is *Cuphea cyanea*. It is, in fact, hardy. My picture (**73**) taken in late October (a dwarf pampas is flowering in the background) shows it tubbed up with a plant of *Helichrysum petiolatum*, which is the ideal summer foliage plant for tubs, troughs and window boxes. Its felted grey heart-leaves are borne on sprays which normally grow horizontally or downwards. However, by training one shoot to a vertical cane, as I have in this instance, it will make a miniature tree in the course of the summer, with horizontal branches. Sometimes the first shoot that you choose for this purpose starts flowering and you have to begin again with another.

One of the prettiest courtyard plantings I've seen is Beth Chatto's at White Barn House. Most high-powered nurserymen can't be bothered with such uncommerical refinements, but Beth Chatto can. It makes all the difference to the looks and enjoyment of the place. There's a delightful flower arrangement for all-round viewing in her office; a famous garden in which the plants she loves – and most of which she also sells – are displayed, and then this courtyard which is pure fun (**74**).

In the centre you see another way to grow sempervivums – in a 'stone' trough. Real stone troughs are rare and expensive these days but an old china kitchen skin can be coverted into a life-like imitation. The Alpine Garden Society has a pamphlet with instructions.

Of course it's nice to have several varieties of house leek in contrasting colours and sizes in such a trough but if your garden is much visited by the public and the trough is not immediately under your eye (at White Barn House it is), its contents will quickly disappear. The light fingered will only be satisfied with a rosette of each variety. Safer to have only one and safer still, as they have at Kew, to grow a ferociously prickly plant like *Cnicus* (a sort of thistle), which won't tempt anyone.

On the wall by Beth Chatto's seat is the ornamental vine, *Vitis coignetiae*. Its leaves are particularly large and well textured and turn to brilliant colours in early autumn. At its feet a heap – but carefully arranged – of plants in pots: succulent crassulas, variegated agaves, ivy-leaved 'Ville de Paris' and other 'geraniums', *Helichrysum petiolatum*. Elsewhere in this patio were cannas in pots, the angels' trumpets and an ipomaea with seventeen newly opened blooms when I arrived at 8.15 one morning. It all looks luxuriant and contented. We can do with a bit of that in summer. I don't think a spring display matters so much.

However, outside my porch, where one is constantly passing without pausing for long, I start with pots and pans of spring bulbs in March and keep up an exchange of plants in season till October. Early on there are anemones. The form of *Anemone blanda* called 'White Splendour' is particularly showy. And I have the pinky mauve *A. hortensis* which grows wild in Tuscany. Various daffodils and narcissi follow, *Iris reticulata* and then a very nice iris, from Turkestan, bulbous but with thick perennial roots, called *I. bucharica*. Its leaves are glossy; the flowers, several to a stem, yellow and white.

In April–May there is at least one pot of the white *Spiraea × vanhouttei*. I said what a bore it would be to include a shrub like this in a mixed border, but if you grow a plant in a spare patch, lift and pot it in the winter and bring it into the greenhouse or not, according to when you want it to flower, it makes a useful decoration in or out of the house. After flowering you prune away all its flowered shoots, turn it out of its pot and plant it out for the growing season. *Kerria japonica* (I like the single yellow kind) can be treated in the same way. When a plant becomes too big to pot you simply split it in half.

74. In the courtyard outside Beth Chatto's Essex home, groups of sempervivums (houseleeks) occupy the 'stone' trough. Behind a seat, the ornamental vine, *Vitis coignetiae*, and in front of this an assemblage of tender ornamentals in pots.

Another pot shrub for Easter flowering but with a long season is the florists' genista (it used to be seen far more frequently in the shops than nowadays). This is a rather tender broom from the Canary Islands, with long racemes of deliciously scented yellow blossom. Plunge your pots outside in the summer (they are liable to red spider damage under glass at that season) but house them in the cold months. They'll take a degree or two of frost. Plants that grow over-large should be replaced by rooted cuttings.

Summer is the season for lilies. In many ways they're easier to grow in pots than in the ground. You have so much more control over slugs. The most exciting to pass as you walk in and out are the scented kinds: *Lilium regale* and hybrids derived from it like the apricot-coloured 'African Queen'; then *L. auratum*, *L. speciosum* in late summer and early autumn and the long white-trumpeted *L. formosanum*, seen here (75), of which I grow batches from seed every year, so there are always plenty coming on and replacements for those that go down to virus diseases, which they easily do. As soon as you see a plant with twisted leaves and distorted flower buds, whip it out. This particular photograph, in which there are four or five pots of *L. formosanum*, was taken on 10 September but they often flower on into October. I pot three bulbs to a 7 in pot. Seedlings can be flowered in their first year, if sown early, but are really good in their second and third.

At the front of the group is an oblong, trough-shaped pot with the fern *Davallia mariesii* in occupation (see p.90). It spends six months here and takes on autumn tints in early October before moulting.

Another good pot plant for late summer and autumn displays is the ginger plant, *Hedychium*. The only species readily available is *H. gardnerianum*, with canna-like leaves (they all have that) and short spikes at 3 ft of yellow flowers with red stamens. Very striking and individual, especially at night when it wafts a powerful scent, pleasanter at a distance than close to.

75. Outside the porch at Great Dixter I change pots around from March to October so that there is always a greeting as one goes into or out from the house.

Plants for paving

How you deal with the cracks in your paving reveals quite a lot about the sort of person you are. If they are cemented in and the slabs are all square, that's the sort of person you are too, square and cemented in, no cracks showing.

But cracks that have merely been finished with sand or grit will allow plants to take a hold. A more relaxed outlook immediately becomes evident. There'll be weeds, however, and weeds mean work. The best course will be to treat paths with weedkillers but to use the larger areas – where you sit or the surrounds to a formal pool, for instance – as a projection of your gardening activities.

Awkwardly placed weeds that are growing through the plants you cherish can either be pulled out (after a thunderstorm is the ideal moment for extracting them root and all) or dabbed with glyphosate (in the U.S.A. use, for example, 'Roundup' – a non-selective translocated herbicide), from a small, moist, but not dripping brush. This systemic killer has brought new hope into many hitherto hopeless situations.

The obvious choice of plants for paving are those that remain low and make mats of tough substance that won't notice being trodden on or kicked around. Like a good wife, in fact, but they're a bit boring when it comes to it. The unromantically named *Cotula squalida* is typical: dense mats of bronzy green serrated leaves; no flowers to speak of. Actually this is quite a pretty little plant but it doesn't make for exciting gardening. Pearlworts and mat-forming thymes are good; rock phloxes stay low but aubrietias are rather humpy and might trip you up after a drink or two while the sun roses, *Helianthemum*, are on the brittle side. Although mat forming, they are shrubs and the underfoot crunch of their branches is not a healthy sound.

I believe that paving provides an ideal opportunity for revelling in the third dimension, not just length and breadth but height as well. But you must adjust your ideas. Where you actually set the tables and chairs should, in the name of common sense and dry feet, be kept clear of all vegetation, but make your terrace or patio or what have you, large enough to include mat formers and taller plants among them. Spiky leaves contrast well with the unfussed flatness of paving stones.

There's a hummocky grass, *Helictotrichon sempervirens* (*Avena candida*), for instance, that makes porcupine humps of blue needle leaves, some 18 in tall and that's how it looks for most of the year. The better the drainage (and drainage is usually excellent in paved areas) the bluer its leaves. In May the plant suddenly changes its habit and throws up 3 to 4 ft sprays of diaphanous flowers. Their elegance can scarcely be appreciated in a border context where they are surrounded and backed by others as tall as or taller than themselves, but where flatness is the rule, a plant or two of this, swaying in the breeze, will make you blink.

Fit in a clump of *Stipa gigantea*, too. The corner of a stone can always be chipped away to make room for planting it. The leaves of this grass are less noticeable than the last's, but the inflorescence, which rises to 6 ft, is

76. The wand flower, *Dierama pulcherrimum*, provides the contrast of height on this paved sitting-out area at Great Dixter.

dreamy. A mosaic gauze that shimmers in the softest tones of pinky beige gradually bleaching. It holds its shape for many weeks.

And then there is the wand flower or angel's fishing rods, *Dierama pulcherrimum*, a plant that looks as though it was created to bow over an expanse of water, but as its fleshy roots demand the sharpest drainage, this is not, unless artificially contrived, a practical proposition.

The wand flower has tough, evergreen, iris-like leaves and from these sends up its steely yet flexible rods to 5 or 6ft, by which time the bell-shaped flowers start opening in series. Their weight arches the stems into parabolic curves and you can appreciate their structure in the uncluttered medium of paving (76) whereas in a border they can only dip their noses into other plants. One is constantly amazed by the strength of those rod stems, which are as restless as a mobile in the lightest air, yet never break or flatten, even in a storm.

Shrubs look well in paving, too. Surprisingly often their seedlings will appear uninvited; such discoveries are among the joys of handweeding. I have a young *Daphne tangutica* brought me by a blackbird, no doubt, its red berries being caviare to this bird. The shrub's stem or trunk would quickly become constricted in a crack, so we enlarged its growing space with a cold chisel.

The general medium of paving is particularly congenial to many plants and you may succeed with them here when, particularly if your soil is heavy, you have failed in more conventional sites. For not only is the drainage good but the root-run beneath stone slabs remains cool and moist in the most parching summer's weather.

Garden your gravel

Gravel is not to be despised. When composed of beach, with rounded, yellowish pebbles, it can look a bit raw but stone chippings from a quarry will look well right from the start and any kind of gravel will pack down and weather in due course.

Where it has to take the disturbance of wheeled traffic, whether a barrow or a motorcar, there's nothing to be done except to keep it clean with weedkiller or flame gun, but where it can be left alone in some quiet bay, there is considerable scope for gardening.

The area is likely to be hot and, given perfect drainage, it will be ideal for plants from climates like California's or for seaside plants like our own blue viper's bugloss or the horned poppy. Poppies, indeed, would be among my first thoughts. Eschscholzias are called Californian poppies. Normally treated as annuals for direct sowing *in situ*, they may often survive the winter in a place like this and will then start flowering in earliest May. The prickly poppies of the genus *Argemone* are excellent. *A. mexicanum* is the one most often offered, with small yellow flowers and leaves attractively blotched white, but my favourite is *A. alba*, carrying larger blooms with translucent white petals and dark stamens. The primrose yellow *Platystemon californicus* is a poppy-like annual, sometimes offered by Thompson & Morgan. Once established it will sow itself. Then, perhaps best of all in this group and hailing from Mexico there is *Hunnemannia fumariifolia*, with quite large yellow poppies on a foot-tall plant above marvellous glaucous, deeply cut foliage. If direct sowing into gravel is difficult or wasteful you'd better raise plants singly in the smallest pots you have and plant them out. These poppies all have tap roots and are extremely sensitive to any kind of disturbance.

At Crathes Castle, the National Trust for Scotland property some twenty miles from Aberdeen, you see how effective are the clumps of *Kniphofia caulescens*, at intervals along the gravelled terrace walk. The leaves of this poker are its chief asset. Anything with a bluish, waxy leaf is likely to be adapted to hot spots and poor soil. But it also flowers handsomely; pale orange and cream yellow, in September. *Eryngium pandanifolium* would also be suited to such a position if you didn't mind a height of 8 ft during its autumn flowering. It is an evergreen species from Uruguay, with long, saw-edged leaves and a beautifully structured inflorescence of tiny flowers.

Yuccas are excellent in gravel, too, and will flower freely in such a position. They range in size according to species from the 6 ft *Yucca gloriosa* to dwarfs like *Y. flaccida* and *Y. filamentosa*. There are also some good variegated forms but if your gravel is at all yellowish they'll not show up well against it.

In the picture (**77**) you see a foot-tall alpine thistle, *Carlina acaulis*, that flowers in August, opening and closing according to the weather. A bold and handsome plant it also dries well for winter decoration. My photograph is a cheat because this particular plant was growing in the front of a

77. An alpine thistle, *Carlina acaulis*, is the sort of plant that will enliven an area of gravel while benefiting from the free drainage that it provides.

border and leaning forward over a gravel path, but it would actually be an ideal gravel inmate.

Stonecrops such as I mentioned in respect of roof plants, would all be good, especially the brilliant yellow *Sedum acre*. Try this with the tiny magenta-flowered maiden pink, *Dianthus deltoides*. It sounds reckless but it works a treat.

The only drawback to this sort of gardening is that it will involve you in some handweeding, but the weeds will be starved and easily extracted. It's well worth the occasional effort.

Scents where you sit

When you take a seat in the garden the probability is that, even if you're shucking peas or stoning plums, your mind will be relaxed, receptive. Plant and flower scents that drift to you on the air will be particularly welcome. So your planting should ensure that they are there, at these key stations, when you want them.

The 'when' of it is important. All the different species of *Sarcococca* (neat evergreen shrubs) waft a delicious smell, but they flower in January and February, so it'll be a question of sniffing as you walk past rather than of sitting near them. For that, you'll bring some sprigs indoors. It's the same with the aromatic winter sweet, *Chimonanthus praecox*, the witch hazel, *Hamamelis mollis* and several others, for the winter garden is surprisingly rich in scented shrubs. Even in early May, when *Daphne pontica* (78) is in full bloom, you'll seldom be sitting near it at the right moment because it doesn't switch on till sunset and May evenings are generally chilly. Near to where you walk in and out is the place for this.

The time factor, with scents, is crucial. Those that switch on when summer evenings are balmy will be specially welcome if you've been out all day. Such are the honeysuckles; our native *Lonicera periclymenum* is less cloying than *L. japonica*, which is popular because evergreen. I would plant it at a distance and so I would a balsam poplar, whose sticky sweetness can be too insistent. In any case this is a tree with roots that disrupt wall and building foundations, so you wouldn't consider it for a town garden at all.

The summer jasmine, *Jasminum officinale*, is a night performer. You might find it excessively sweet. I don't. It grows on our sitting-out terrace and I should add that most of these night-scenteds give good value by continuing into the following morning, until the dew has dried. Not so *Cestrum parqui*, which gives very short commons but is definitely an ideal shrub for the enclosed sitting-out area in a town garden, where heat is long retained and you are tempted to linger till bedtime. This cestrum carries panicles of small, lime green, tubular blossoms from July to October on a shrub that you can train against a wall, where it will reach quite high; or else plant in an open, sunny border and cut to the ground each spring, in which case it will achieve only 3 or 4 ft in a season and start flowering a month later. It gives off a funny little sour smell if you put your nose to it by day or in the early evening. Not till 10 p.m. does it start wafting a most exotic perfume that you can hardly believe to originate from the same plant. If you keep missing it in the garden, cut a spray to put in water indoors.

Another night scent is the nicotiana's and the nearer its colour, or non-colour, to white, the better its scent. Modern bedding-out nicotianas are in a gay assortment of pinks and reds as well as green and white and they are advertised as remaining open all day. In fact they do wilt in the heat of the day and they have scarcely any scent at night. Look for the white *Nicotiana affinis* in the catalogues or, an even more imposing plant, for *N. sylvestris* (offered by Chiltern Seeds and Thompson & Morgan). This grows to 6 ft

78. May-flowering *Daphne pontica* outside the entrance at Coldham (the home of a plantsman), in Kent, is well placed so that its delicious evening and night fragrance can assail those who go in and out when the evenings are still too chilly to sit nearby.

and is a statuesque plant, crowned late summer and autumn by columns of long-tubed white flowers with an exquisite smooth scent, lacking the roughness of *N. affinis*. The already mentioned *Datura suaveolens* or angels' trumpets is a relation of *Nicotiana* and *Solanum*, which can be moved in its pot into and out of key positions and so can pot-grown lilies of which the trumpet varieties (*Lilium speciosum* apart) generally have the strongest night scent.

Speaking for myself as a countryman who is as likely to be at home all day as in the evening, day scents are of as great or greater moment. I seldom sit out after sunset. It usually turns chilly enough to be pleasanter indoors. Anyway mosquitoes and midges are mainly night fliers for whom I'm not anxious to offer myself as a meal.

Grow mignonette in an unimproved form for the best scent and if there's nowhere near to a seat to plant it out, it makes an excellent pot plant, but needs a full quota of sun. *Choisya ternata*, the Mexican orange, wafts with a will, day and night, in its May season; and again, not infrequently, if the summer was warm, in the autumn.

Far and away my favourite of all shrubs to sit near at any time of the clock, when it is flowering in August and September, is the common myrtle, *Myrtus communis* (**79**). Its pouffes of white blossom are sweet but also aromatic in its own special way – an etherealized version of its leaves when crushed. Bees adore it and it is pleasant to see and hear them working while you take your ease. A myrtle needs a warm southerly wall behind it for safety. Once truly established, the severest winter will never kill it, merely cut it back to the ground. It will spring to vigorous life again and you'll miss only a year's blossom.

Flowers, however, are seasonal, and their season is fairly circumscribed in many cases. Foliage plants with an aroma that they are generous with on the air can be much better value, near to those garden seats, whether fixed or mobile that we are giving thought to.

Some aromatic plants, let it first be remarked, are not free with their favours. *Lippia citriodora*, the lemon-scented verbena, is worth growing where you brush past it and can put out a hand so as to pinch one of its glandular leaves, but the effort must always be yours. It will never come to meet you like your spaniel. Neither will rosemary nor bay laurel, except when flowering.

Yet there are many other shrubs with an unsuspected and seldom advertised friendliness. They insinuate themselves into your subconscious

79. One of the best of many scented plants sited around our sitting-out terrace at Dixter is the August–September-flowering myrtle, *Myrtus communis*, seen against the windows.

until you suddenly wake up to their prodding and exclaim 'Hullo old pal' or else (in a strange garden) 'who goes there?', while you start searching. Scents are notoriously elusive and the source will not always be easily pin-pointed. A scent may only begin to develop when it oxidizes on leaving the plant, in which case you gain nothing by plunging your face into it.

I have not mentioned roses and yet, of course, there are many in flower that smell delightfully on the air. Especially free are pale-flowered hybrid musks like 'Penelope' and 'Felicia' and also those enormously vigorous white-flowered climbers like *Rosa filipes*. But when it comes to the plant itself, then the sweet briar, *Rosa rubiginosa*, with its odour of stewed apples, will recommend itself powerfully to our baser senses. The Penzance Briars have the same aroma and are prettier in flower but they are martyrs to black spot so I would always give preference to the healthy sweet briar itself. It is beautiful in fruit in the autumn with swags of sealing-wax red hips. The way I treat a bush is to cut out some of its oldest branches (up to a third of the plant) every year. This stimulates masses of new growth which will continue elongating right into the autumn. That's just what you want for scent, as the young foliage gives it off most freely. But the branches you leave unpruned will flower and fruit to satisfy the eye.

R. serafinii is another aromatic species to grow near a seat, as they do in the white garden at Sissinghurst Castle in Kent and then there is *R. primula* with its remarkable fragrance on the air (but scantly when handled) of incense. Some people express an intense dislike of this aroma but that can only be on account of childhood associations. You couldn't otherwise object to it in the ambience of a garden. It is strongest after warm rain.

Another shrub scent I love to catch on the air is that of the more glandular, clammy members of the *Cistus* tribe. *C. cyprius* is one of the very best and generous even in winter. Then there is that remarkable *Hebe*, *H. cupressoides*, which not only looks like a conifer but smells like a newly opened box of old-fashioned cedarwood pencils.

There is a demure-looking *Olearia*, *O. solandrii*, making an upright bush to 6 ft or more with tiny leaves, golden on their undersides, and young stems the same colour. This has a scent (the flower as well as the bush) which seems to be close to lime blossom. Elusive it may be, but always ready with a friendly nudge at every season of the year.

It would be tempting to have a lime tree near where you sit for the scent of its blossom but they are large and powerful neighbours. Perhaps the drawbacks might be too great. Intoxicated bees crawling around under-neath them is one hazard and the drip of honeydew from the leaves of some species is another. Still, coming to you on the air from a distance, it would be nice. I should choose either the weeping *Tilia petiolaris* or the species of which this is probably only a variety, the European white lime, *T. tomentosa*. Both have a silvery underside to their leaves which they are as ready to display as the top. They flower in August and present no honeydew problems but drugged bees can be a worry.

Dry-wall commune

Dry walling is the best (if also the most expensive) way of catering for a change of levels so that flat terracing alternates with a near-vertical face. This uncemented vertical surface makes an ideal home for many plants requiring sharp drainage and of a rosette-forming habit. Rosettes tend to rot, in our climate, if water lodges at the centre. Vertically orientated, all water is thrown off. Here the alpine gardening enthusiast will grow his treasured saxifrages, drabas and lewisias or, if shady, his ramondas and haberleas. He will plant these as he builds the wall and he will be able to pack a great many species into quite a small space.

But this isn't my style of gardening at all, and perhaps not yours. It may be one day, when I'm reduced by old age and taxation to living on a tiny property. But in the meantime, there are the walls, and the setting is a large garden. No time for *petit point*. The plants in it must look after themselves and if they know how to get the bit between their teeth and spread as though they owned the place, so much the better.

Establishing them in the first place may be a problem because planting into the cracks of a ready-made wall, although by no means impossible, is distinctly tricky: spreading the roots out, packing soil around them, ensuring that they receive adequate moisture until established. All too often the soil you packed in shrinks, and the plant falls out or takes on a distressed semi-stranded look.

At Sissinghurst Castle they have devised a successful method for establishing *Erysimum* 'Bowles's Mauve' by raising the cuttings in Jiffy No. 7s, which are a sort of net bag, and then squashing this (its shape will change under pressure) into the desired cracks. With luck (and there are failures) the erysimum's roots will find their way back into something they like in due course. This is the only possible way to establish such a plant, as it doesn't set seed and it hasn't a running rootstock.

Other plants have. If you site one such as *Campanula portenschlagiana* (syn. *C. muralis*, the wall campanula) on top of a dry wall or, for that matter, of a cemented wall in which the mortar is old and rotten, its thin rhizomes will work their way through the cracks so that it gradually extends its range down the wall face. *C. poscharskyana*, with stars instead of bells, will do the same thing, even more aggressively. As I remarked in my 'Shade' chapter, I recommend obtaining the darker-flowered clone called 'Stella', which is not only a more definite colour but less of a thug. It is also rather nice when planted at the bottom of a wall because its annual flowering shoots, which are a foot or more long, plaster themselves against the wall and climb it.

The hardy, pink-flowered cranesbill, *Geranium dalmaticum*, is a good doer but not so forceful as the campanulas and this will slowly extend its range through wall cracks from an original planting on top.

Euphorbia robbiae is an aggressive spurge useful as ground cover in dry shade (see p. 87), but it is a beautiful plant, too. Mine started itself in a piece of dry walling by seeding into it and is quite a colony, now. *Ceratostigma plumbaginoides* is particularly good on a shady wall face and

80. The June-flowering broom, *Genista lydia*, makes a humpy bracket over the edge of a retaining wall. The Mexican daisy, *Erigeron mucronatus*, is colonizing its face.

will creep through the cracks once happily established but I have not succeeded with this so far and am having another try. It makes a loose mat of growth and carries clusters of dark blue plumbago flowers in autumn. But even more effective are the fiery autumn colours of its leaves.

Some plants you'll site on a dry wall top so that they project like a bracket or hang down like a curtain. *Cotoneaster horizontalis* makes a stiff bracket. Its tiny pink flowers are adored by bees (and by queen wasps) for their nectar in May while its abundant crop of crimson berries in the autumn is even further enlivened when, in late November, the leaves turn carmine before shedding. New foliage is already expanding by February.

Genista lydia (80) makes more of a humpy bracket because its shoots are not straight but arch over like a sickle. It is dazzling in its June season and will live for seven or eight years on average, which isn't bad for a broom. Some of the prostrate conifers, mainly junipers, are excellent for making a curtain down a wall, having been planted on top.

But the most prolific colonizers of walls are those plants that will self-sow into its cracks. More effective than pushing seeds in and hoping for the best is to plant your desired colonizer either at the top or at the foot of the wall. Sooner or later its seeds, abundantly produced year after year, will find their way into the wall face and from then on your task will be to retain control.

Red valerian, *Centranthus ruber* (81), is really quite a dangerous plant because its roots are so long and strong that they are adept at breaking up masonry. One can understand why the guardians of ancient monuments refuse to allow such plants to take over, however decoratively, on ruins. But it seems to me they carry their policy too sweepingly and far, as is the way of large, impersonal institutions wherein there is little scope for the exercise of individual judgement.

Anyway, I can't resist valerian, though I try not to let it seed itself too freely. In fact the most rewarding policy, here, is to cut the plants hard back in July, immediately after their first summer flowering and before they have had a chance to seed. They will then grow and flower again in September. The commonest colour variant is a rather dirty pinkish red. Far more attractive are the true red and white forms seen here. There is also a good pink, which seems to be quite common on the Kircudbrightshire coast of Scotland. Although not a native, red valerian has made itself very much at home on cliffs, and railway cuttings, particularly on chalk.

The antirrhinum is another splendid wall colonizer and more flatteringly displayed than in any bedding scheme. More perennial, too, for the situation promotes hardiness. You'd never think that wallflowers were not native, to see them on some of our cliffs. It's wonderful to stand on top of a cliff on which wallflowers are blooming and to have their scent wafted up to you.

Their cousins, the aubrietias, will have to be planted in or on top of a wall for a start, but these self sow. Eventually most of the fancy shades in carmine and purple disappear and you are left with a range of mauves, but these are varied enough in their own way and they are unpretentious, especially when allowed to make pendulous great mats. The walls along our back drive are thick with aubrietias; and primroses, some of them coloured, have seeded in among them.

Small shrubs may not be inappropriate, especially herbs from the Mediterranean which love hot, dry places: thyme, savory, lavender and best of all, rosemary. The last will hang down a wall face and attain a great age so that its gnarled and twisted stems become quite a feature.

I haven't yet mentioned my most prolific wall colonizer by self-sown seedlings, which is the little Mexican daisy, *Erigeron mucronatus*. It sidles into more than one of my pictures. It is not hardy everywhere but if once established you'll always have seedling replacements even if the old plants are killed by winter frosts. The daisies open white and change to pink as they age, flowering without pause from May till the frosts. If there are no frosts it will flower through the winter. But after such a long flowering season the plants become dishevelled and they should be shorn back each spring. If there are any precious, weaker plants in your wall, they will need rescuing from invading seedlings while you're on the cutting back job.

This daisy will thrive even in the shade and another particularly happy sun or shade colonizer is *Erinus alpinus*, a small rosette-forming plant (wonderful on the walls at Haddon Hall in Derbyshire) either carmine or white. Ferns are delightful in the cracks of shady walls and will spread once established (see p. 89).

A plant to avoid, if you can, is the ultra-invasive *Helxine solierolii*. Particularly in moist shady places it makes dense green mats with which few plants can compete. And it is the devil to get rid of. Mind-your-own-business is its somewhat equivocal common name.

81. Red valerian, *Centranthus ruber*, seen here, also in its albino form, is a handsome dry-wall colonizer but its thick roots are destructive of masonry.

Raised bed

The raised bed has many of the advantages and attributes of the dry wall, with the difference that most of its plants will be growing in the normal horizontal plane. Its particular advantage is that drainage is so good and this will enable you to grow many plants (including bulbs) whose hardiness is increased when there is no danger of water collecting around them. And as raised beds consist principally of made-up soil anyway, you can choose what goes into them. I recommend a strong leavening of grit and if you also surface with an inch-deep layer of stone chippings this not only looks neat and businesslike but makes sure that your plants keep dry around their necks, which is where they are most vulnerable to rotting.

The raised bed makes an admirable alternative to the rock garden. In most settings, rock gardens look pretty horrible. Not only are they difficult to make well, so that the rocks are all of the same material, running in the same strata and appearing as though they really could be natural outcrops but the whole of lowland Britain, where most of our gardening goes on, loudly proclaims by its verdant lushness that rocks are a nonsense. If you have the serious object of growing alpine plants, then the raised bed will happily accommodate the majority, while looking plain and unpretentious itself. The rock garden is often pretentious, shouting to the world that its owner is wealthy enough to make one; while the poor man's rockery is a plum pudding heap of all sorts of stones which his object must be to conceal with vegetation as quickly as he can. He might just as well start with the vegetation and forget the rocks.

In large parts of Scotland, however, and in other similarly mountainous country, rock gardens can look and, indeed, can *be* perfectly natural. Rocks are so numerous and easily procured that the very prevalence of rocky country disposes you to accepting a rocky garden formula. And, of course, the sort of tough alpine plants that benefit from rocky terrain are also the ones best suited to the Scottish climate. For it is a fact that alpine plants which grow wild at high altitudes in low latitudes come down to sea level in Scotland, if, indeed, they grow there at all. *Dryas octopetala*, an evergreen mat-former with white, anemone-like flowers, is a typical example.

My photograph of a cottager's raised bed was taken at Smeaton, a village in East Lothian, not very far from Edinburgh (**82**). I thought how satisfying and dignified it looked in its simple conception, as also is the single storey building behind it, so typical of this region.

The pale stone chippings are a pleasing feature and the balance between them and the plants is just right. You'd lose something if there were complete plant coverage. The balance between plants of different sizes is good too and between those of a low and of a more upright habit.

Is there such a gift as natural good taste or must it all be acquired? All learnt or acquired, I suspect, and most of us pick it up by example but also by a sharp and critical power of observation. To many this never comes.

It could be said that large containers are a form of raised bed – they are higher than ground level and have good drainage. Such 'raised beds'

82. The simple dignity of a raised bed outside a traditional single-storey building in east Scotland.

83. A roof garden outside the refectory at the Pollock Halls of Residence, Edinburgh University. Bottomless hexagonal containers stand on a gravel-filled trough kept supplied with water. Conifers, heathers, ornamental grasses and a sword-leaved *Phormium tenax* are seen in this grouping.

would make a good feature on a flat roof, provided it is strong enough to bear their weight. So I was interested in the refectory roof garden at Edinburgh University's Pollock Halls of Residence (83). The containers are bottomless hexagonals standing on a gravel-filled trough into which water is easily sloshed by anyone intelligent enough to follow a routine. The site is very exposed and windy but drainage is perfect and that beautiful foliage shrub, *Senecio reinoldii*, with thick rounded leaves, survived the 1981–2 winter. Here also are bergenias, heathers, *Phormium tenax*, conifers, hebes, cordylines (which break from the bottom after a hard winter), dianthus and ivies to trail over the rims. The containers are fed three times during the summer with granules of slow-release fertilizer applied on the surface.

Taking in herbs

It is unfortunate that herbs have become a cult, signalling a return to the supposedly better old days when our forebears were closer to Nature and the soil, and knew which plants to turn to that would keep them in or restore them to good health. This ignores the fact that our wretched forebears could only fall back on superstition and desperate measures because they were ignorant of how our bodies work and the real causes of our ailments. Modern medicine, with its reliance on the panacea of drugs, has its ugly side but we have only to remind ourselves of our vastly increased expectation of life to realize that medicine hasn't done too badly. When I read in my morning's newspaper: 'Health Department officials warned that a brand of comfrey tea, sold loose or in packets by Cotswold Health Products, had been found to contain the poison belladonna – deadly nightshade', I can only marvel at the gullibility which lays us open to disastrous health hazards whether we put our uncritical trust in doctors or in unaccountable cranks.

The chief reasons for growing herbs in our gardens should be either because they are beautiful or in other ways attractive plants, or because they add spice to our diet; preferably the two combined. There is also a fun element in growing a plant like *Atropa belladonna* with a long, romantic history. Deadly poisonous plants quite frequently look deadly poisonous and there may be a certain relish in owning them and imagining whom we should like to finish off with their help. That's a fairly harmless way for the beast in us to show its claws.

The only two thoroughly poisonous plant-weeds that I allow to maintain themselves when they appear in my garden are henbane (*Hyoscyamus niger*) and thorn apple (*Datura stramonium*), both of them members of the nightshade family Solanaceae. Quite simply, they are beautifully constructed plants that I love to contemplate. They make such handsome skeletons that if I were an enthusiast for dead flower arrangements I should certainly include these.

Neither henbane nor thorn apple are plants that are ever likely to take your garden over, but that is more than can be said for the majority of herbs. Most of them are weeds at heart and ferociously aggressive colonizers either by underground rhizomes, like the mints, or by billions of seeds, like balm and fennel. Furthermore, a great many herbs, after a brief period of youthful freshness, become weedy in their appearance. Thus a herb garden, unless minded by the strictest custodians – the one at Sissinghurst Castle is the only example that comes to mind – quickly dissolves into an uncontrolled mess. This is made the more likely from the fact that the majority of herbs enthusiasts are congenitally untidy people anyway!

An unpretentious herb patch near to the kitchen has a lot to be said for it. I admired the raised manger in the kitchen yard at Childerley Hall, Dry Drayton, Cambridgeshire (**84**), although its most picturesque element, the crimson bee balm, is more for looks than general use.

84. Raised manger, planted with herbs, in the kitchen area of a Cambridgeshire house. Herbs generally look a mess by late summer but are well contained here.

Whatever it is grown near, a runner like mint should be planted in a container which can be sunk out of sight to its rim. After two or three years it will become over-congested and starved, and will need replanting – just a few pieces – in fresh soil.

And you'll need to prevent other herbs from seeding. Cut them down as soon as they have flowered. A vigorous and persistent flowerer like giant chives will need cutting down three times in a season but this also has the advantage of ensuring new crops of tender young foliage. Neither will the plants leave a noticeable gap for longer than a week, so quickly do they refurnish themselves.

For this reason I believe in accommodating as many herbs as I can into various parts of the flower garden, choosing those forms with the most decorative flowers or foliage. Thus, common chives is a small and squinny plant with miserable flowers but the giant form, here supporting the cranesbill (85), *Geranium* 'Russell Prichard', carries numerous scabious-like flower heads, varying slightly in colour between pink and mauve, as from seedling to seedling. It is an excellent border perennial. You might just as well grow marjoram in its golden-leaved form, as in John Treasure's garden at Burford House, Tenbury Wells, where it hobnobs with pink gypsophila and (pulling an otherwise amorphous scene together) the strong, firm lines both in foliage and flowers of a yucca.

The form of cooking sage that was common when I was young was desperately dull. I now grow a narrow-leaved clone that is covered with purple blossom in its season. Alternatively there are coloured-foliage variants like the yellow-variegated 'Icterina' seen in the Childerley Hall trough. There are also purple-leaved and tri-coloured forms.

I admit that scattering herbs through the garden entails a bit of a walk when a bouquet garni is required, but that won't hurt you much. And anyway you can't expect every herb to be suited to the same situation, to wit that bed outside your kitchen. My bay tree, 25 ft high and just as wide, would be most unsuited. Some herbs, given my heavy clay soil, are happiest perched on the edge of a dry wall; rosemary and winter savory, for instance, while common thyme looks delightful in this situation next to a mat of the rock phlox, *Phlox douglasii*, whose mauve flowers with a darker ring at the centre, look like an old-fashioned cotton print and exactly match the mauve of the thyme's flowers in their May season. Your basil is an annual and will have to be grown under glass anyway, while lovage, a tall, ungainly plant, will need tucking away somewhere out of the general view.

You can always keep your herbs fresh for a few days in water on the windowsill, especially if you change the water, and a few of them, notably tarragon and basil, even retain a high proportion of their flavour when dried. In winter you'll have to resort to the dried equivalent, where a herbaceous plant is in question, unless you can go without for a few months. Why not? A change is as good as a rest. There are other ways of cooking chicken than with tarragon, and tomatoes are not worth eating in winter and spring anyway, which lets the basil off its hook.

85. Giant chives, in a mixed border with *Geranium* 'Russell Prichard'. Choose the handsomest forms of edible herbs and accommodate them in various parts of the flower garden whenever possible.

House walls

The extra protection afforded by house walls (and, indeed, by other walls and solid fences) offers a god-sent opportunity for growing shrubs that would be too tender in an open position. Walls also provide support to plants of a lanky habit that won't stand on their own legs. Further they sometimes provide an effective method of display, even to perfectly hardy material, that entails a different kind of training and end product from what would be normal out in the open. This may be unnatural, but gardening is unnatural anyway and it can be entertaining.

Let us first take a look at the pyracantha. These are vigorous, woody members of the rose family carrying white blossom in spring and yellow, orange or scarlet berries in autumn. And they are evergreen. You can grow them in the open (though a hard winter will hit them back), but they take up a lot of space that way. So they are among the most popular house wall shrubs and will cope as well with a north aspect as with any other.

A pyracantha in fruit against a white-washed wall can be spectacular and all the better if it is only secured to the wall here and there but is otherwise free to grow away from it. But this, because of space limitation and the demand for light through windows, can seldom be. The pyracantha is trimmed back annually. Being vigorous, a lot of trimming becomes necessary and the rub is that the wood on which it should flower and fruit most freely is perforce being removed. So, young pyracanthas that have not yet been subjected to this restrictive treatment are a lot more productive than old ones, which develop into a sombre green, lumpy excrescence on which little fruit is borne.

In the long run, then, pyracanthas are often not a happy choice for a house wall, especially as their foliage is particularly dull. But I have to eat my words in admitting that you *can* make an amusing topiary feature of this dark growth against a light wall by trimming your pyracantha both horizontally and upwards, between every window, perhaps to a height of three storeys, on a large house. Some would say this was a grotesque treatment but it is fun, too. I know of two examples. One is on the Ullapool road from Braemore junction in Wester Ross (northwest Scotland). The house is only a one-storey building but its pyracantha always attracts comment. (Come to think of it, I believe it is a *Cotoneaster simonsii*, but the effect is the same.) The other is on the late Robin Spencer's house at York Gate, on the northern outskirts of Leeds in Yorkshire. Here the wall is a considerable height and Robin obviously enjoyed himself. Enjoyment is contagious.

Laburnums are nearly always seen as trees and they are exceptionally hardy. But what a delightful change it makes to see one treated as a wall shrub, with all those golden chains decorating Jack Drake's house near Aviemore in the cold region of the Scottish Cairngorm hills (**86**).

On walls more than one storey high, self-clinging climbers are the most popular choice. No apparatus is required for the climber to get a grip. There are not many examples of these do-it-yourself climbers, the

86. An unusual way of displaying laburnum by treating it as a wall shrub.

commonest being ivy (*Hedera*), what are loosely termed Virginia creepers (*Parthenocissus*), and the climbing hydrangea. It is easy to cut them away, annually, from window frames and if the walls are ugly it will be a relief to see them disappear. But if they are, for instance, of a pleasing old brick, this should not be allowed. A partial cover of wall shrubs of limited growth will be quite enough.

Ivy has a bad reputation for destroying walls but if the pointing is sound there is no danger. Like wisterias, *Clematis montana* and *Hydrangea petiolaris*, it can do a lot of damage if allowed to push in under roof tiles. Forewarned is forearmed.

There is a great choice of beautiful ivies, many of them with variegated foliage and if they become too dense, as they do in maturity when they start to flower and fruit, they can be cut hard back to the wall face, or even cut off the wall to a low level and made to start again, for there is no disputing that young ivy shoots and leaves are generally the prettiest. My main objection to ivy or any other dense evergreen on a house is that it provides a summer nesting site and a winter roost for sparrows. They make an infernal mess and a terrible noise of squabbling. You'll have far less such trouble from a deciduous creeper.

If house walls have to be repainted from time to time, a self-clinging creeper may be a nuisance but on the other hand ivy, in particular, does protect a wall from the weather and keeps it remarkably dry.

87, 88. Shrubs on house walls can give pleasure from inside, where they frame the view, as well as from without. Here the climbing form of rose 'Shot Silk' is seen trained around a kitchen window. Looking out it makes a frieze along the sill.

The main delight of house walls is to be able to grow on them rather tender exotics that wouldn't survive or, at any rate, ripen their wood sufficiently to flower well, anywhere else. But do beware planting something with immense vigour that you'll almost immediately have to start hacking back. Such are the evergreen ceanothus. They are crowded with blue flowers in spring and this is a rare and precious colour in a shrub. Some (like 'Trewithen Blue') are much more vigorous than others (*Ceanothus impressus*, say), so you should ask around before deciding which to plant. Don't let it grow so much too large that you are obliged to cut it hard back. Ceanothus generally resent being cut back into old wood and it looks dreadful if the stumps you cut back to just remain stumps and don't break into growth again. If you know that space trouble will be inevitable, start your pruning almost from the word go. Any shoots that are not required for training to cover the prescribed area should be shortened back immediately after flowering. Thus you retain control. If the situation has been allowed to get out of hand it's really more sensible to grub out the old shrub and plant a youngster. Ceanothus, after all, develop very fast.

Shrubs of a lanky habit whose cultivation against walls would be particularly suitable would include the winter jasmine and the trailing *Forsythia suspensa*, both of which are happy on north walls and can be trimmed back to the wall immediately after flowering. On sunnier aspects, climbing roses are the most obvious example. The pruning and training of heavily armed roses like 'Mermaid', 'Albertine', or 'Easlea's Golden Rambler', when you are perched on a ladder and trying to tie in one long young cane while another attacks you in the back or grabs your neck or scalp, is a slice of living whose character-forming value has yet to be assessed.

There are less hostile roses. My two pictures (**87, 88**) show Climbing 'Shot Silk' on the front of Allangrange on the Black Isle, north of Inverness in Scotland and as seen from their kitchen window in front of which their breakfast table is sited. You could hardly wish for a nicer prospect and it reminds us that house climbers are seen from inside as well as out.

Sometimes you are faced, at the start of a new season, with a huge gap on your wall, usually because some tender occupant like a ceanothus has been killed in the winter. There are rapid annual or herbaceous gap fillers for such critical occasions. The convolvulus called *Ipomaea* (correctly *Pharbitis*) *purpurea*, with purple, pink or white trumpets, is one such. The canary creeper, *Tropaeolum peregrinum*, with yellow, insect-like flowers, is only slightly less vigorous. *Eccremocarpus scaber*, with clusters of small tubular flowers in orange, yellow or red, usually turns out to be a persistent perennial.

One of the handsomest and most efficient is *Cobaea scandens*, an annual climber with sizeable green bells that change to purple. Its 'white' form 'Alba' is really pale green. This needs a long growing season before it starts flowering so it is best to sow the seeds early in a heated propagator.

Climbers need not climb

If shrubs that we normally grow as free-standing specimens can alternatively be trained against walls, the converse is also true. Ivy is scarcely less popular in a ground covering role than it is as a climber. Less well known is the method of growing it as a free standing bush. In maturity, ivies cease to climb; they produce woody branches on which the leaves are of a simple, unlobed outline and on these branches they carry their rounded umbels of flowers and fruits. The flowers open in October and November. Being green and generally well above head height, they seldom attract attention unless by the hum of visiting insects – wasps, flies, bluebottles and hover flies as well as bees.

If an ivy is propagated from this mature wood, it makes a rounded shrub showing no propensity to climb and this is particularly attractive in variegated clones such as *Hedera colchica*'Dentata Variegata' and *H. canariensis*'Variegata'. The inflorescences in autumn are another charming feature, now viewed at or below eye level. So, in those that mature them, are the berries, which ripen in spring. They are generally black but an attractive shade of crocus yellow in *H. nepalensis*.

The climbing *Hydrangea petiolaris*makes an excellent bush in the open and can take its place near the front of any shrubbery or mixed border. The twining climber, *Actinidia kolomikta*, is effective when treated in the same way and makes a good lawn specimen. It is absolutely hardy, as I first realized when I saw this treatment accorded it in Sweden. The young leaves in spring are banded with white and pink.

When wisterias are grown without a support on which they can climb, they make beautiful features but need quite a bit of attention. As their flower racemes hang vertically, the shrub must first be encouraged to reach head height, at least, so that the flowers can be properly presented. So you train the plant to a stout stake, or to several stakes if you prefer it to have a multiple branch system. Then you will continually spur back to the main framework all its questing shoots.

Climbers look beautiful hanging over low parapets or retaining walls at the edge of terracing. The large-leaved vine, *Vitis coignetiae*, which colours so excitingly in autumn, can be seen doing just that in my picture (**89**). This species is so vigorous that it can climb to the top of a tall tree, if the circumstances are right, but in a position like this, it is merely required to trail and will be pruned back to a basic framework each winter.

89. The vine, *Vitis coignetiae*, entwining and hanging over a terrace parapet. Climbers need not climb.

Clematis without walls

This leads me easily to the subject of clematis. They are an under-exploited genus not because they lack popularity or general appeal but because most gardeners have such a limited concept of how they can be used. The fact to remember about them is that they don't need a special place to themselves. They are an extra, the gilt on the gingerbread (which has always seemed a rather indigestible bonne-bouche to me, but I suppose a gilded ginger-bread would look pretty even if you couldn't eat it, any more than we want to eat clematis or, for that matter, than I want to eat gingerbread). And so, to find a place for a clematis requires no more effort than to find an established shrub on which a clematis is not growing. Clematis vary greatly in vigour and in the size to which they will grow, so you merely need to match the vigour of your shrub with the vigour of the clematis that is to run through and over it. A clematis with a rose is a particularly happy match because both plants are greedy and enjoy the good things in life. And if you have to treat the rose against black spot or mildew, the same treatment will protect the clematis against its own fungus diseases, caused by the wilt fungus and, again, by mildew in sheltered situations.

In gardens where heathers are a feature (not mine), clematis can be allowed to ramble over them at no height to speak of and indeed this is the method they often adopt in the wild. You far less often see *Clematis alpina* growing up a shrub than you do weaving among quite low scrub-like alpine rhododendrons or draping itself over a rock. For us it is a convenience to have them masking a tree stump or, where those of luxuriant growth are in question, simply covering the ground on or over the edge of a bank, for instance. If you had a bed of herbaceous peonies it would be a good plan not only to interplant them with bulbs like hyacinths for the spring but to include a *Clematis flammula* or two, which will produce a foam of white, scented blossom in the autumn. You'll be looking down on them (which always promotes a sense of benevolent superiority) and they, with their countless little cruciform flowers, will be looking (devo-tedly) up at you.

One trouble, often complained about in respect of clematis, on walls is that they will rush up to the top, where a greater supply of light is the lure, there to flower where you can't see them and (greatest insult) only the people in the flat above, can.

Such frustrations and undeserved rewards are avoided when your clematis is creeping around at a low level and works best of all when its blooms, instead of hanging, as they do in *C. alpina* and *C. viticella*, look upwards to the sky.

As, for instance, do the *C. texensis* hybrids of which 'Sir Trevor Lawrence' (**90**) is an example. It is growing over a *Cotoneaster horizontalis*, which had seeded itself into a crack on top of a low wall. I mentioned the stiff bracketing habit of this cotoneaster in my chapter on dry walls, and a stiff shrubby support is just what suits a clematis. It can easily catch hold of it, whereas a shrub that is always moving in the wind is difficult to grasp.

90. 'Sir Trevor Lawrence', a hybrid of *Clematis texensis* with upward-facing flowers, looks well when scrambling over a low shrub, in this case the stiff-branched *Cotoneaster horizontalis*.

91. *(opposite) Clematis viticella* filters through the August–September-flowering *Hydrangea villosa*. In colour and season they are matched but the clematis lanterns contrast with the hydrangea's lacecaps.

'Sir Trevor Lawrence' is only one example of the great variation and range in flower form of which clematis are capable.

Clematis montana is the most vigorous species of all but it can be tamed by pruning hard back immediately it has flowered, which will be in late May or early June. This was the limited treatment given at Dixter to a specimen, again growing over a self-sown cotoneaster, this time at the edge of some Lutyens-designed steps. Here again we have upwards facing blossom which it is nice to look down upon.

However, I'm particularly fond of one link-up that I have achieved where the lanterns of *C. viticella* are spangled through the framework of the most beautiful of all hydrangeas, *Hydrangea villosa* (**91**). They flower simultaneously, in August–September, and their purplish mauve colouring harmonizes. Furthermore you don't want to look into the centre of this clematis, whose colouring tends to be a little washed out, here. It looks prettiest when seen on the lantern's outside, at or below eye level.

There are a few clematis which ramble but do not climb. They lack the usual twisting faculty in their leaf stalks. So it is really perverse to try and make them climb when they can make such satisfying trailers. *C.* × *jouiniana* is an uncommonly vigorous hybrid between our native traveller's

joy or old man's beard, *C. vitalba*, which does climb, and *C. heracleifolia*, which does not. It owes its non-climbing habit and its pale blue colouring to the latter. But its long annual trails make excellent ground cover (for its leaves are lush) and they flower along their entire length from July to early October, in the early-flowering clone called 'Praecox'.

The very individual *C. × durandii* was an early cross between *C. × jackmanii* and the herbaceous, non-climbing *C. integrifolia*. It does not climb but makes annual shoots several feet long so it looks good when hoisting itself through and over the top of a 3 to 4 ft shrub of stiffish habit such as the Jerusalem sage, *Phlomis fruticosa*. I have it over *Senecio* 'Sunshine', the popular grey-leaved shrub widely known as *S. greyi* or *S. laxifolius*. In early June its indigo blue flowers contrast with the senecio's prodigious crops of silvery flower buds (**92**). A few weeks later it is an indigo and yellow set-up, when the shrub covers itself with a gay assemblage of daisies. After the show I cut all the flowered trusses quite hard back and this keeps the shrub from sprawling, as it is naturally inclined to do.

92. The indigo flowers of *Clematis × durandii* are well set off by the grey foliage and buds of *Senecio* 'Sunshine'; later by the latter's yellow daisies. The clematis has no climbing apparatus but its growth is lifted and supported by a 4 to 5 ft shrub of this kind.

Lawn features

When you plant something in a lawn it becomes a specimen. Its isolation will pin-point its whereabouts, constantly drawing the eye. You'll come to love or loathe it, so it matters that the choice is right. It is always possible, of course, that you'll quickly stop noticing and hence totally ignore it, but that is rather a criticism of you than of the plant.

A lawn is generally supposed to be a restful feature across which your eye can travel, relatively unhindered, and come to rest on what lies beyond. So if you are wondering whether the lawn really requires an interruption to its expanse, the answer is probably no. Yet too great an expanse of shorn grass also becomes exhausting.

Overplanting a lawn, especially with conifers, some slim, some spreading, some rotund, suggests that you believe in the wee folk. You're not planting so much as populating your lawn. That tells us something about you but I find that sort of planting fidgety.

I do enjoy topiary, very often, even if it's just one specimen, but that of a comfortable size, in a cottage front garden. Topiary is not as frequent in ordinary (as against show) gardens as it used to be, probably because the best specimens take fifteen or twenty years to develop and most people are on the move again before that time has elapsed. But many of us derive considerable satisfaction from well-designed and well-kept topiary pieces, whether in abstract or geometrical shapes or representational figures. My father was keen on them and created many in the garden at Dixter but when they falter and fail, I'm afraid I don't replace them. I just haven't that kink in me that wants to. And yet I enjoy topiary around me. When its shadows slant across the lawn on summer's evenings, it does create a special atmosphere, a homely spookiness.

Where space allows, a group effect will often look better than a singleton. The single pampas grass that you so often see in the middle of a suburban front garden's lawn always looks self-conscious and silly. A group would be an improvement but best of all not to have pampas as a central feature at all but to one side or at the bottom of the garden with a dark background.

Bamboos, with their many canes, each an individual, automatically create a group effect. A clump can gradually be allowed to enlarge until it is as big as the scale will allow. If new canes push up outside the prescribed perimeter, it'll be no trouble to shave them off with the mower (unless you stay too long away on your summer holiday). Our front lawn had in it a topiary ball-and-saucer specimen in yew. It wasn't objectionable but it was boring. Eventually my family allowed me to replace it with a Chilean bamboo, *Chusquea culeou*, which is a strange-looking plant but gives me pleasure every time I look that way, and that is frequently each day. Quite a test to survive.

A group of smoke bushes, *Cotinus coggygria*, looks nice for a large part of the summer and autumn though it is nothing in winter. Mine (**93**) is a singleton, but I might do better to increase its area and make it up to three.

Soon after it has borne its tiny flowers in June–July, the inflorescence enlarges and a mass of tiny, thread-like stalks turn pink; then, after many weeks, grey, which gives the plant its other name, wig bush. In some autumns, early in November, the foliage changes to dramatically fiery tints but not at all in others, when the weather is against it.

Cotinus (once called *Rhus cotinus*) is an example of a plant that benefits from the restriction to its growth imposed by a surrounding of grass turf. In a border it can grow inconveniently large and lush and if you cut it back its soft young shoots may be torn out by the wind (a lot, of course, depends on your soil and situation). But the competition of turf, which is itself greedy, cuts down its vigour. In other cases turf will cut down a lawn

93. The smoke bush, *Cotinus coggygria*, makes a particularly appropriate lawn specimen or group because its vigour, which can be excessive in a cultivated border, is automatically curbed by the turf.

specimen's vigour too much, so that it hardly moves at all. You have to find out about these things.

Before I finish with *Cotinus*, there's another point that its purple-leaved form raises. The very deep purple kinds like 'Notcutt's Purple' do not smoke, but their translucent foliage glows like rubies when the sun shines through it, particularly at the start and the end of the day. You need to be on the opposite side to the sun and one good point about the lawn specimen is that you can so easily walk around it so as to place yourself in the right position. Another shrub that contributes in the same way is *Rosa sericea pteracantha*, which has huge translucent red thorns on its young wood. You may not want it to project too widely over your lawn turf because it is not a friendly object to brush against when you're mowing, but the plant is more productive of young thorn-clad shoots for being pruned quite hard each year which will automatically curtail its spread.

The colour and texture of tree trunks and the outline of deciduous branches against the sky are flatteringly displayed when set apart in a lawn, but again a group will often be an improvement on a singleton. A group of birch trunks, for instance, or of the paper bark maple, *Acer griseum*. There is no more exquisite tracery against the sky than the outline of our own native birch, *Betula pendula*.

I know it is a temptation to plant a flowering cherry. The abundance and freshness of its blossom is a great excitement in the spring, but few cherries and especially of the largest-flowered and most popular hybrids, make beautiful trees; as I remarked when writing of dry shade, their foliage is often plain and heavy and the flowers only last a few days. Purple-leaved crabs tend to look terribly dim and dirty in summer, especially when their foliage is attacked by scab. But some fruiting trees, especially pears and apples, make delightful specimens. Their fallen fruit may be a nuisance to the mower but it looks pretty. We have an old wild pear tree which sheds quantities of fruit on the lawn each autumn, whenever there has been a wind, and for most of the time we pick it up before mowing or sweep it into the gutter between the lawn and a yew hedge. But finally, in November, when the fruit is pure yellow and quite ripe and lawn mowing is no longer urgent, we let the pear crop lie in a huge informal sweep, just as it fell. It looks right in its season and the blackbirds and thrushes gobble it all up delightedly within a very short while. In spring, for five days in early May, the tree is a towering marvel of white blossom, wafting the typically sickly pear scent which I relish.

When you plant shrubs in lawns you'll generally need to maintain a cultivated area immediately beneath them where mowing and edging would be inconvenient. And anyway most shrubs will need a feed from time to time. But a modest underplanting in this area of small spring bulbs like squills and chionodoxas will extend its season of interest. We have for long grown a tree peony in one lawn, and at its feet is a self-sown violet. It flowers before the peony and makes its own endearing contribution.

Meadow gardening

The community of flowers and grasses that you find in an unimproved meadow is rich and colourful and so are the butterflies, moths, grasshoppers and other fauna that go with it. To see such a meadow in bloom is a great delight but from the farmer's point of view it is a dead loss. Short-term leys produce the best feed and so, except on marginal land, no piece of ground is left unvisited by the plough. Permanent pasture has largely ceased to exist and a great many plants and creatures have disappeared with it.

This partly accounts for the attraction won by the concept of meadow gardening of recent years. It aims at a replica, with discreet and appropriate additions, of an undisturbed meadow community where the plants will find conditions so much to their liking that, having been given an initial push in the right direction, they will look after themselves and increase of their own accord.

To prevent coarser elements from gaining the upper hand, and shrub and tree seedlings from taking over, the turf will need to be cut at least once a year; preferably two or three times, to keep its texture fine. And the mowings must be removed, not only because you don't want to pick them up on your shoes and bring them indoors, or on your clothes when you

94. Disturbed waste ground is quickly and naturally taken over by 'weeds' but many are extremely colourful, like these field poppies and yellow stonecrops, which I photographed in front of a petrol station. A little encouragement by sowing appropriate seeds could help.

recline on the turf, nor only because the windrows of mown grass shade out and kill the turf beneath them, but because you should be attempting to reduce the ground's fertility, not to build it up. High fertility encourages coarse plants like docks, nettles, bracken and cow parsley at the expense of the rest. A low nutrient status enables the widest possible flora to take over. By the same token you must never use manure or fertilizers on your meadow.

In practice, the grass will remain uncut until July at earliest, so as to allow as many of its contents as possible to ripen and shed their seeds. Early August would be an even better date. There'll be a second little season of flowers in September–October, when the colchicums and autumn crocuses (in particular *Crocus speciosus* and *C. nudiflorus*) are contributing. If you can fit in a cut before they start up, they will stand forth and present themselves so much the better. That'll be in late August. Your third and last cut will be made as late as you dare in November before new bulb shoots are pushing up and before the ground anyway becomes too soggy, as it easily can in badly drained areas, to manipulate a machine over it. The turf will now be as tight as it can be for ushering in the season of small things like snowdrops, aconites and crocuses.

It is the June–July season, when the grass becomes long and, in places, untidy through being tossed by wind and beaten by rain and trampled by the heedless, that will test your nerves and sort out those who feel that a garden of all places should be at all times neat and orderly from those who have no objection to a certain periodic disorderliness if they know that the situation is basically under control and that the cause is a good one.

I don't find the July scene in the least trying to my nerves, apart from the visitors who commiserate with me over the difficulty in finding labour these days, or those others who enquire of my staff whether Mr Lloyd has died recently. There are many flowers still at the peak of their glory in July, the blue cascades of tufted vetch (*Vicia cracca*), the similarly coloured meadow cranesbill (*Geranium pratense*), the soft pink haze of common bent grass (*Agrostis tenuis*), the purple clumps of lesser knapweed (*Centaurea nigra*) and the creamy foam of meadowsweet (*Filipendula ulmaria*). I am in no hurry to sweep these aside, especially as there'll be a wealth of butterflies feeding among them.

There are, I am glad to say, many visitors, especially in the younger generation, who see eye to eye with me over this and are delighted with the adjacent contrasts in this garden between organized mixed borders of cultivated plants and other areas where business is at a standstill.

Some of these pieces of meadow, and especially the first you meet on either side of the path on entering our front gate, seem from their proximity to the house as though they might have once been mown, but this is not in fact the case. They were there from the time the garden was first laid out for my parents, around 1910 to 1912, for my mother was ahead of her time in loving this kind of gardening and it was she who got it going.

But there must, I am certain, by many cases where a garden lawn has ceased to have any necessary function as a place for children to romp or bitches to do their jobs (or both!), and where permission to cease shaving can readily be granted.

The inbuilt advantage of turning a lawn into a meadow is that its grasses will already be those fine kinds that make the best substrate for meadow gardening. The flowering and flourishing of red and white clovers will now be welcomed and other flowers like hawk's-beards, hawkweeds and moon daisies that would once have been regarded as weeds will now become welcome interlopers.

You, the owner, can add to their numbers and variety as and when you feel inclined. Equip yourself with a narrow-gauge bulb-planting tool. It is a most efficient implement with which to make places for all sorts of plants, not just bulbs. It needs to have a long shaft so that you can extract 50 or 100 soil plugs from a standing position before getting down on your comfortable kneeling mat to the actual planting. Consult Bentley's, the tool retailers, whose address is given on p. 172. A telephone call will provide you with helpful advice. Bentley's also have a comprehensive illustrated catalogue but specifications of the bulb planters listed in it (three kinds) are not altogether clear (to me, anyway).

The next questions to arise are which plants should you introduce to your meadow and how shall you obtain stock?

The year starts with snowdrops and winter aconites, both of which, once established, will increase by self sowing. They prefer the slightly thinner turf that you find in the partial shade of a tree; so do the dog's tooth violets, *Erythronium dens-canis*, and primroses, in March and April. Don't try to create a lot of shade in your meadow, however, with trees and shrubs but keep the whole of the centre of it open, because your finest turf and most colourful inmates will always be found in an open situation.

If you think that, in an intimate setting, small flowers (looking as though they could be wild) rather than big, make the most satisfying tapestry, then concentrate on these in your turf. When it comes to crocuses, therefore, you'll plant the species like *Crocus chrysanthus* (which has colour variants), the brilliant orange *C. aureus*, the mauve *C. tomasinianus* and *C. sieberi*, rather than the well-fed Dutch hybrids. And when choosing daffodils or narcissi, go for our native lent lily, *Narcissus pseudonarcissus*, the similar miniature trumpet *N. asturiensis* and other species such as the hoop petticoat, *N. bulbocodium*, which makes such a wonderful drift in the 'alpine' meadow at Wisley, and *N. cyclamineus* which is established in its thousands in the Savill Gardens at Windsor Great Park.

Cowslips are easily raised from seed. My picture (**95**) shows them with dandelions, which don't usually need to be introduced. When opened by sunshine they are among the brightest of spring flowers, only underrated because a nuisance where unwanted. It was these cowslips' first season. You wouldn't think so; they look so permanently ensconced, but only time

95. Into a natural crop of dandelions, these cowslips, first raised from seed and grown-on under cultivation, have been planted in the hope that they will naturalize and self-sow.

will tell whether their permanence is more apparent than real. Even if the original clumps weaken, they could carry on by self-sowing.

Some plants are better suited to certain soils than to others. Snake's-head fritillaries figure prominently in the heavy, water-retentive turf at Dixter. They grow wild in water meadows and do not fancy too acid a soil either. My mother started our colonies off from seed, patiently pricking out the seedlings and eventually planting them. If you prefer a short cut and buy your bulbs in the first instance, don't expect an immediate and ravishing display. They'll take time to settle down; many will come blind in the first season. They may eventually decide they do not like you after all, or that they do. One has to be a little phlegmatic about the possibility of disappointments when living material is involved.

Pamla Toler's photograph (96) shows in the foreground (with an aubrietia wall behind) the bank of a piece of moat that we drained on coming to Dixter. This was the first area where my mother established snake's-heads and old-fashioned polyanthus that have proved remarkably tenacious, here. Early orchis, *Orchis mascula*, and *Anemone appenina* also appear, as well as celandines and lady's smock, already in occupation. She called it the Botticelli garden, with his *Primavera* in mind.

Our greatest success in May has been with *Camassia esculenta*, a North American bulb closely related to our bluebells but with spikes of star-shaped blue flowers. They clump up and self sow. The introduction of blue into a meadow tapestry is particularly telling because there is so much contrasting green and pink (clover) and yellow (buttercups, hawk's-beards etc.) there already. Bluebells themselves will establish, especially in slight shade, but even easier, I fancy, are the Spanish bluebells usually listed as *Scilla campanulatus*. These may be pale blue, pink or white and all mix well together. Old-fashioned columbines (*Aquilegia vulgaris*) also do well in grass; you may be able to introduce some from the garden proper, where they self-sow too freely. These are in shades of campanula blue, purple, old rose and white.

Moon or ox-eye daisies really get into their stride towards the end of the month and are at their peak in June, a sea of yellow and white if they like you, and following the sun with their moons. Sorrel makes a soft reddish haze. The magenta spikes of *Gladiolus byzantinus* look marvellous in grass and this is another plant that will provide you with abundant material from an original colony in one of your borders. *Campanula latifolia* grows naturally in roadside verges and *C. lactiflora* is easily introduced. Which brings us to July and the flowers I originally mentioned. But this is only a sample of what you can try out; the whole field is, literally, open to experiment.

Where the turf is rather rough you can often establish coarser plants like oriental poppies and, as at Allangrange, lupins (97). Highly selected Russell lupins would look artificial. Try and collect seed, perhaps from a cottage garden, of something more elegant. But whatever you start off

96. The grassed-over slopes of a piece of drained moat at Great Dixter. In addition to the natural turf flowers that came in, snake's-head fritillaries, polyanthus, early orchis and *Anemone appenina* are naturalized.

with, the seedlings will anyway gradually hark back to the long spikes and soft lavender or pink colours that come naturally to them.

If your meadow area has very poor soil or, indeed, nothing better than sub-soil as often happens where earth has been shifted around for constructional reasons, you may have difficulty in establishing even the grasses. But there are brilliant flowers which love these poverty-stricken conditions, notably field poppies and yellow stonecrop (**94**). Also the pink starry-flowered centaury (*Centaurium*), which opens in the sun; blue viper's bugloss and yellow horned-poppy.

Wild flower and grass mixtures for sowing direct on to cleared ground are available from John Chambers, and likewise from Suffolk Herbs (addresses on p. 172). They also market packets of most of the individual flower seeds that you may require. If you are good at handling seed, the cheapest way is to sow it in a pot or box or as you would a vegetable seedbed in the garden, initially. Prick-out or line-out the seedlings, growing them on until strong and sizeable and then plant them into your turf. This is far more certain and less wasteful than sowing direct on to the final site.

Bulbs will mostly be obtainable from the usual bulb firms but albeit in a restricted range they'll be much cheaper, where quantities are required, from a wholesale merchant prepared to do retail trade. Such is Peter Nyssen (address on p. 172), with whom I have done business for many years.

When it comes to introducing native plants from the wild, you are on trickier ground because this is just the way in which wild species are so easily exterminated. Hence the Conservation of Wild Creatures and Wild Plants Act of 1975, which makes it an offence for anyone without permission of the owner or occupier to dig up any wild plant. So if you know of an abundance of moon daisies, let us say, along a disused railway siding or alongside the municipal rubbish tip, you must apply to the relevant authority for permission to take a clump to start you off in your meadow. Would you get any reply, let alone an affirmative? I shouldn't blame you for taking the law into your hands but don't get caught. Rather unlikely that you would be, when you come to think of it.

97. In some kinds of rough, tumbled-down turf, lupins establish and colonize very easily. They soon revert, as here at Allangrange in Scotland, to the pinks and purples that come naturally to them and that suit a wild setting.

Daffodils

We have a daffodil orchard. In it we mainly grow those hybrids which were fashionable for general planting in the early years of this century (**98**). They make a lovely show and they don't look gross. The mood they create is quite different (more self-consciously opulent) from the drifts of little species and other similarly 'unimproved' wild flowers that I have just been describing and I think it is wise to keep the two kinds of planting separate; to restrict one kind of meadow to wildings and to splash about more ostentatiously in another. All the same I do rebel against many of the modern daffodil cultivars. In any but the most artificial setting they are so overpowering, coarse and muscular. Furthermore, larger flowers mean larger leaves and there'll be all the more evidence of their season of decay.

Still, there are fleeter-footed varieties about, especially among the small-cupped narcissi and jonquils. If you can afford to, plant drifts in single varieties rather than mixtures (you should be able to get a special quotation for quantities anyway). Mixtures are tempting because they are offered in cheap lots 'for naturalizing'. Tempting, too, because their wide-spreading net might include the daffodil of your dreams. But in the mass, mixtures look confused. They make a far less definite and positive impact than single varieties. Furthermore you can alternate trumpets with narcissi, yellows with whites (as was done here), if you have control over what you are planting, and this again will please the eye.

A mistake often made by wealthy enthusiasts (most of them public authorities, these days), keen to do a thorough job and to have an immediate knock-out display, is to overplant. You should leave wide gangways of turf between your groups, planting up no more than one-third of the total area. It is axiomatic not to plant at even distances, otherwise all will turn out in straight lines, from whatever viewpoint. Thickest in the centre of a group and thinnest at the margins with a few outliers, is the recipe. Never plant too thickly. A foot between daffodil bulbs would be a minimum. After all, unless conditions are very disagreeable, each bulb will make up into a clump, over the years, and it is nice to see spaces between the clumps. It is easy to become over-daffodilled, so that the end of their season comes as a relief.

When you consider all the varieties, the season is a long one but weakened, in a big planting, by the inclusion of those that are very early or very late. They are passengers for too much of the time. The May-flowering pheasant's eyes *Narcissus poeticus* 'Recurvus', should have a place to themselves near to where you pass and can breathe their delicious scent. Their flowering is irregular.

Daffodil foliage is really far too great a worry in borders or shrubberies. Tying it into knots aggravates by drawing attention to your battlefield of drunks and additionally prevents the green leaf from functioning properly and building up next year's bulbs for another season of blooms. The beauty of growing them in grass is that their foliage is entirely masked as the surrounding sward engulfs it in May.

98. The daffodil orchard at Great Dixter. Trumpets alternate with small-cupped narcissi; yellow groups with white. Drifts of one variety are more effective than mixtures and there is space for relief.

In the margins of your plantings and the gaps between them – even in the plantings themselves – you can grow the large-flowered Dutch crocuses. All but the yellow ones will self sow and make a carpet each March such as I find even more enlivening than the daffodils. Crocuses sulk in dull, cold or wet weather but open exultantly to the sun which is just as infectious to us.

Pond side

The most relaxing of all places to be in a garden is by the side of a pond. That there should additionally be the sound of tinkling water seems quite unnecessary to me, but I may be in a minority. It merely irritates me to know that the tinkle depends on a circulating pump. Fountains have the further disadvantage of splashing your waterlilies foliage, which they loathe. If you have a natural stream in your garden, that's different, but it is also unlikely and I, for one, don't want it. Streams are liable to inconvenient flooding. Also they tend to locate themselves where frost accumulates, which is bad for the gunneras and arums.

A still piece of water produces its own sounds from its own community, particularly when fish are rising. They have diversity rather than continuity and are music enough for me.

There's always a great deal going on around a pond, except when it is frozen; birds come to drink and may even nest, if there is cover. There are dragonflies and many other insects on the wing. And there is the tangy smell of watermint as you approach the margin, but that will be by a 'natural' pond, by which I mean a pond with a clay or mud bottom, and not a concrete, butyl (polyethylene) or fibreglass lining.

'Natural' ponds have many advantages, even if the puddling of a clay bottom has involved a deal of skill and effort. Your marginal plants will then be able to draw moisture from the water, while the emergent plants will easily be established in the water itself.

Where the pond is lined with heavy-grade butyl, it is difficult to conceal its surfacing at the margins, thus losing the feel of a natural pond. In a more formal setting it can be done by the use of overhanging rock or paving, but where you want plants or turf to come right up to the pond's margin, there nearly always seem to be places where the butyl shows, and this is deplorable. So my pictures are of 'natural' pond plantings.

That taken in Beth Chatto's garden shows large features (**99**): a weeping willow and a swamp cypress (*Taxodium distichum*) on the far bank. Beth admits that the willow was possibly a mistake, yet a handsome feature in this setting. These are trees that quickly grow large and they require a large-scale setting like Kew Gardens or St James's Park. In any but the most extensive private gardens they are a nuisance. Yet what a lot of them there are. They are evidently irresistible.

Trees by a pond are generally troublesome, if you aim at a varied plant and animal community in and around the water. Their leaves collect in the pond bottom and make it disagreeable to fish. The shade they cast makes it difficult for the greatest proportion of water-loving plants, including waterlilies, to flourish and flower freely. And, worst of all, they lap up an enormous amount of water in the growing season, so that your pond's level falls disastrously leaving the marginal plants high and dry.

The horse pond at Dixter (where the farm horses were led in to drink) is entirely open to the sun and has nothing taller round its margin than pollarded dogwoods (*Cornus alba*) and willows. There is no more than two

99. An effective pondside planting in Beth Chatto's garden with ornamental grasses (*Miscanthus*) to the right, *Eupatorium purpureum*, left. The background weeping willow is a handsome feature but possibly a mistake by a pond rather than a lakeside.

or three years' growth on these. Trees we have – oaks, aspens and birches – but they are well in the background.

But whereas sunlight needs to reach the surface of your pond, too much of it does not want to penetrate beyond that, otherwise you will eternally be plagued by unsightly green algae in the water. This is where the role of waterlily pads comes in and of the oxygenating plants that live most or all of their lives underwater. By manufacturing oxygen they create a favourable environment for fish and other aquatic fauna. A balance is reached and the water clears.

For heaven's sake don't choose the wrong oxygenator. Avoid the elodeas, particularly *Elodea crispa* (readily purchasable, however). It was somehow introduced to my horse pond, eight or ten years ago, I don't know by whom, and had before long so choked it that the water disappeared. Birds could walk over the entire surface. I am still conducting a long and expensive fight against it, during which I have lost many of the aquatics that I most value.

The pond was previously invested by the water violet, *Hottonia palustris*, whose deep green clouds of lacy foliage look marvellous at the water's lower levels in winter, especially when goldfish swim into the foreground. It makes candelabrums of delightful, pale mauve primula-like flowers in May. Hottonia grows wild extensively but is not always easily established by casting it upon the waters, so water-plant specialists tend to fight shy of it. The water soldier, *Stratiotes aloides*, is nice, with bronzed underwater rosettes.

Waterlilies can also be tiresome if over-vigorous. You don't want them to take up more than a third of the pond's surface with their pads. After all, to see the water and its reflections is the main point in having a pond. Beware the white and pale yellow varieties of *Nymphaea*. Apart from two or three dwarfs in this category (suitable for miniature pools), they are ultra-vigorous. After midsummer their leaves will stand out of the water, instead of lying flat on the surface, and this is an ugly arrangement, especially as it tends to conceal the flowers. Any nursery specializing in aquatics will advise on the relative vigour of different nymphaeas and recommend depths for planting.

Next we come to the emergent plants: those that live with their crowns permanently under water but flower and make most of their leaves above it. I find these the easiest to manage because you never have to worry about whether they're too wet or too dry as you do the bank-side marginals.

There are two emergent plants in the foreground of my horse pond (**100**): the pale, rush-like *Scirpus albescens* and a handsome, if somewhat invasive, aquatic buttercup, *Ranunculus lingua* 'Grandiflora'. Just visible, to right, are the white blooms of my underwater colony of arum lilies, *Zantedeschia aethiopica*, while a golden patch under the far bank is made by Bowles's golden sedge, *Carex stricta* 'Aurea', whose full colouring only develops in the sun, but is then long retained.

Some aquatics are inconveniently vigorous in a 'natural' pond and may be difficult to pull out. In a lined pool, your plants will be grown in containers and are then easily controlled but even then you may find that the most vigorous sulk and do not give of their best when confined.

The flowering rush, *Butomus umbellatus*, with umbels of pink flowers, is a pretty thing but flowers too sparsely to be worthy of space and, when confined, scarcely at all after the first year. Other plants that I should be inclined to warn you off are arrowhead, *Sagittaria*, and the plants universally known as bullrushes, *Typha latifolia* and *T. angustifolia*, although correctly reedmace. Only *T. minima* is fit for polite society. *Glyceria maxima* 'Variegata', with its cream and green ribbon leaves, flushed pink in spring, is too pretty to disparage and the way its foliage rises a foot or two out of the water contrasts nicely with the flatness of waterlilies. But it wants watching (water voles will destroy a colony in double quick time, however).

Our native *Iris pseudacorus*, with elegant sprays of yellow buds and flowers, is too vigorous and large-scale except for fair-sized ponds, but it is a good plant, contrasting effectively with the blue or white forms of *I. laevigata*. *I. p.* 'Variegata' is less vigorous and therefore suited to a small pond. Its leaves are butter yellow in spring, deepening to green later on. Another iris to sink under water that I have so far only grown in a border is *I. versicolor*, reddish purple and white. 'Gerald Darby' is attractive in a water setting too, its bluish purple flowers offset by purple stems. You may find that *I. sibirica* will live with its crown submerged; it is anyway an excellent marginal, but the glamorous cultivars of *I. kaempferi* must be well drained in winter when they are dormant.

100. Trees, which cast shade, shed leaves and lap up tons of water, are kept well back from the horse pond at Great Dixter, which is entirely open to the sun. This allows the most varied assortment of marginal and emergent plants to flourish. *Ranunculus lingua* 'Grandiflora' is seen in the foreground with the rush-like *Scirpus albescens*.

101. Planting in and around a small pond at Inverewe in north-west Scotland. Blue *Iris laevigata* rises from the water. The scarlet candelabra *Primula* 'Inverewe' enjoys the moisture.

The little pond at Inverewe (the famous National Trust for Scotland's garden way up in the northwest) can be seen (**101**) to have large colonies in it of *Iris laevigata*, which is typically blue-flowered, as here, but there are other colour variants and a ravishingly fresh green-and-white-leaved one (*I. laevigata* 'Variegata'). Obviously in a small pond like this, frequent thinning out is necessary but they have the 'advantage' of a very heavy rainfall. Drying out is infrequent.

The 3 ft-tall *Cyperus longus* and the 2 ft *C. vegetus* are related to the Egyptian papyrus and to the umbrella plant which we grow indoors on window ledges. Their leaves form a ring of spokes, which is a distinctive arrangement structurally. Another pleasing foliage plant is the variegated form of the sweet rush, *Acorus calamus*. It looks more like an iris than a rush but belongs, in fact, to the Araceae. So does the golden club, *Orontium aquaticum*, which makes thick clumps, flowering in spring: golden-tipped clubs that are white lower down.

The Canadian pickerel weed, *Pontederia cordata*, is particularly useful in July and August, with its spikes of blue flowers and this builds into big colonies without ever becoming difficult to control. I have lost all mine in our efforts to get rid of *Elodea crispa* with weedkillers.

A kingcup that is more inclined to grow underwater than above is the vigorous *Caltha polypetala*. Its large buttercup-like blooms start expanding in April. Another yellow flower that I have in water is *Cotula coronopifolia*, with tight yellow buttons (rather like a *Santolina*) over a very long season. The first touch of frost to which it is exposed kills it, but if the water is deepish, its submerged foliage will survive and reappear at the surface in spring. It also sets seed freely.

The first obvious point that still needs making about the banks above your pond is that if the latter is lined, then the soil behind the lining will be as dry as any in the garden. You cannot expect moisture-loving marginals to flourish just because they can see the water they long for.

Second point: there is a bit of a trap, as with our horse pond, when the banks are steep and a planting made on top of them will remain dry until firmly enough established to put roots down to the water. So you'll need to be ready with help.

Third point: water level. Marginal plants need to be moist but will not stand being drowned for any length of time. Your pond's upper limit must be controlled by an overflow.

Point four: maintaining marginal plantings in good condition can be extremely tiresome. I have discussed gunneras, and these grow large enough to look after themselves. But smaller plantings as of primulas (**50**), astilbes and *Iris kaempferi* are readily invaded by weeds and every time you go to pull one of them out, you find a pound or two of wet soil coming with it. This is why, on the whole, I prefer to have turf coming up to the pond's margin and to grow in this position only such plants as will cope with grass. Larger invaders like nettles and brambles will have to be poisoned.

I have not found the yellow, spring-flowering aroid, *Lysichitum americanum*, whose large, glossy summer foliage you can see on the left of the Inverewe photograph, at all easy or quick to establish, but once it feels at home, even in a ditch, it'll never look back. This is one plant that does give a good account of itself in shade. So will our native kingcup, *Caltha palustris*, which is a clump-forming species. Although I generally prefer single flowers in a comparatively natural setting, I do approve in many garden settings of the added flower power that the double kingcup provides.

Houttuynia cordata, whether single or in its double form 'Plena', can be a menace in the garden but a pleasure where it can spread harmlessly. Its long flowering season is in late summer when one is glad to see it, and I find the common montbretias, like *Crocosmia pottsii* and *C.* × *crocosmiiflora*, whose orange and red flowers open in August, cope very well with rough pondside conditions. Some of the more invasive polygonums, with sprays of pink or white flowers, are good here too, though you should generally, except in the grandest settings, avoid the largest and least controllable of them, like *Polygonum cuspidatum*. But *P. molle*, at 4 ft, can be lovely, its later flowers coinciding in the same panicles with black seeds from the early ones. *P. campanulatum* and *P.* 'Reynoutria' would also be suitable.

You can see in the Inverewe photograph how well a bamboo looks at the water's margin while Beth Chatto uses tall grasses, *Miscanthus floridulus* (*sacchariflorus*) and *M. sinensis* 'Zebrinus' (zebra grass) in the same way, while pampas grass looks splendid in autumn sunshine, reflected in the water. On the left, a fine planting of *Eupatorium purpureum*, which stands erect without support at 6 ft plus. Another moisture-loving perennial, one of the latest to flower, that she grows so well is *Chrysanthemum uliginosum*. Six and more feet tall it covers itself with white marguerite daisies but I rather doubt whether this would cope with turf.

The water saxifrage is excellent, however, and will suppress nearly all competitors. This is *Peltiphyllum peltatum*, pink flowered in spring before the umbrella leaves appear. Think of the ornamental rhubarbs in this context, too.

It is nice, just behind the marginals, if there is room for a stand of dogwoods, green-stemmed and red. Their colouring is marvellously vital in winter sunshine and reflects into the water in most weathers. Ice and snow are not that common in Britain.

Road frontage

Villages have become much more conscious of their appearance, of recent years, particularly in the south of England. In and around the townships in the north of Scotland and particularly in the Outer Hebrides, all kinds of rubbish, from old refrigerators to motor cars, are dumped just anywhere; immediately outside their own houses, more often than not.

But affluence is evident in southern villages which are now largely populated by commuters and the reasonably well-to-do retired. We don't yet go in for open planning to any extent, like the Germans. The Englishman's home is still his castle, enclosed by wall, hedge or fence, but he is now concerned about the area between his boundary and the road or footpath. Not so long ago, vagrant or driven sheep and cows would have grabbed anything edible in passing, but you rarely see them on the hoof in public places these days. Except over the shortest distances vans are used.

So the road frontage becomes an extension of the garden. Indeed, the whole village becomes a garden and although that sounds delightful it is often repelling; a suburbanization of the countryside.

There is an annual Best Kept Village competition and in many ways this does a great deal of good, making people aware of how their self-presentation appears to the world. It eliminates rubbish and general slovenliness. But enthusiasm can be carried to excess.

My neighbouring village of Ewhurst Green won the competition in two successive years, but do you want to see a country signpost (**102**) with double daisies or petunias bedded round its foot? The trouble here started, I can readily appreciate, when it was felt that the broad grass verge by the roadside at this point was too rough and untidy when allowed to grow long. It would therefore be an improvement to keep it mown. As you cannot mow right up to a signpost with the same tool as copes with the main area, unsightly grass whiskers will grow around it. (No one would dream of finishing the job off by hand.) To prevent this, a cultivated gap is made around the post. Why let a gap remain unused? Why not pop a few bedding plants into it to cheer things up?

It is an urban mentality which thinks along these lines. For the reasons given in my chapter on 'Meadow Gardening', I believe that the grass, which is full of delightful plants, should be allowed to grow long, to flower and run to seed before it is cut. It will not then appear as wisps around the bottom of the signpost and you will be allowing a home to a community which will not easily be found on farmland. I realize that grass which has been allowed to grow long is a business to cut and carry but it can be done and it will only happen once a year, so the overall labour involved will be no more and probably less than under the permanently mown system. Long grass can be composted (which is what we do at Dixter) or fed to animals. Where there's a will there's a way.

The suburban outlook also shows itself in villages where the house owner has public-spiritedly planted a strip at the front of his boundary hedge or fence with a row of alternating marigolds and lobelias. A hedge

102. In a countryside setting it is inappropriate to practise bedding out, witness the double *Bellis* and daffodils at the foot of this signpost. Grass verges should not be kept like lawns but mown infrequently – twice annually at most – so as to afford a sanctuary for native flora and fauna.

bottom is the ideal place for violets, herb-robert, greater stitchwort and perhaps a clump of primrose followed by cow parsley. Why not? When the cow parsley becomes stemmy, after flowering, you can cut it back and some late-flowering summer wild flower will appear of its own accord. The tufted vetch loves climbing up hedges and is a glorious sight.

And yet the gardener's hand can show itself, outside his wall or fence, with bedding that doesn't look like bedding but rather as something gay and carefree that spilt out of his garden. Not 150 yards from the Ewhurst Green signpost was just such an example (103): annual candytuft outside a garden fence. Whether the candytuft was direct sown that spring or was self sown from a previous year's planting, I cannot say, but there it was enjoying itself and a joy to see.

103. Outside a garden fence, not far from the signpost picture, annual candytuft looking carefree, as though it had simply spilt over its owner's boundary.

Fun with bedding

To see the routines that are practised in municipal parks and gardens, you'd think there was no fun, no interest to be derived from bedding-out at all. Just blocks and strips of colour; nothing more subtle than that. But this is merely because the municipal gardener is not interested in gardening except that it's a secure and cushy job and brings him a living. Which is an awful waste of opportunity. The production line in a factory really may be soul destroying but in gardening, no less for the public than in private, there is infinite scope for skill and experiment.

Especially is this true of bedding out, where there's a change of plants twice yearly and never any need to repeat yourself. The kinds of plants you are handling are fresh and lively. It is certainly one of the branches in gardening that has given me greatest pleasure. But there is always the danger of splashing about for splashing's sake.

Bedding is no longer as popular as it was in the public sector because it is labour intensive. Institutions like the National Trust and the owners of large private properties have also been obliged to cut down drastically on their bedding but in small private gardens where the owner is keenly interested, there is no reason whatever why bedding shouldn't play an important role. It doesn't need to be expensive.

Carpet bedding, scarcely if ever practised in private today, is the most costly and the formal parterre the next most. In carpet bedding the plants are more important as units in a pattern than they are as individuals. In fact, it can just as well, in a slightly different way, be executed with coloured earth and stones instead of plants and this is by no means objectionable. It has a long tradition in France.

I'm sure carpet bedding will never go out completely and will always find a place in holiday resorts, because people enjoy it, but it is usually a lamentable failure, witness the example (**104**) which I photographed in France many years ago. Everything about it looks uncomfortable. The railing is too high. The statue needs its own stone plinth. Then the plants, instead of being tilted at a ridiculous angle, could make a more or less horizontal carpet round its feet but not in that hectic combination of colours.

104. *(below left)* An example of the worst kind of carpet bedding.

105. *(below right)* Formal bedding at the Grand Trianon, Versailles, entirely appropriate to its setting, the begonias set off by grey foliage and themselves picking up the colour in the buildings' pink marble.

Compare this with the bedding which I photographed in the Grand Trianon at Versailles (**105**). Not carpet bedding at all, in this case, but formal, as befits the setting. The pink begonias with their silver outline perfectly harmonize with the pink marble of the palace pillars. A few dark green vertical accents forestall incipient flatness but there is no plethora of uprights, nothing fussy. All is restful and yet lively, too.

A first lesson in bedding is not to be fussy. Don't cram in too many different kinds of plants, nor too many colours. Think out a simple colour scheme, say with orange, yellow and green, as it was one year outside the Palm House at Kew (**106**), and work it out with a few varieties of plants. You constantly see an undigested stew in tropical bedding, in conservatories for display and in private front gardens, but it is restless and confusing.

Variations in height will be necessary but let plants of varying stature do this work for you. Don't heap up the soil towards the centre or back of the bed. Keep it the same level as are the surrounding lawns, paving or whatever. This is much more comfortable to look at.

Kew, at the time I am writing, has an assistant curator in charge of the bedding out who is really interested in what he is doing and in experiment.

106. Summer bedding outside Decimus Burton's early Victorian Palm House at The Royal Botanic Gardens, Kew. A simple colour scheme in orange, yellow and green is worked without fuss.

An interesting point in the orange/yellow/green scheme here is that the marginal marigolds form, as it were, a lip to the saucer of bedding in which the central yellow-green *Coleus* 'Dairy Maid' is at a lower level. Normally the lowest plants are at the margin, but this is unnecessary and, indeed, may be undesirable where there is a grass surround on to which no plants can be allowed to spread.

The oblong bed which I photographed in the Cambridge Botanic Gardens (**107**) has paths all round it, which makes bedding simpler and allows it to be more relaxed because the plants, in this case the inestimable *Helichrysum petiolatum*, can spread out over them. They are here interplanted with modern gerbera hybrids – big South African daisies with gleaming rays. Their dandelion-like leaves are coarse and unprepossessing but the helichrysum conceals them.

This is the simple kind of bed that I should recommend for a private front garden rather than circles (what my mother called open jam tarts), squares, kidneys or half moons cut uncomfortably out of lawns and bearing no relation to the design of their surroundings.

Actually, bedding out does not need to be practised in purpose-made beds at all. It can just be a part of borders that otherwise have permanent contents. To have your annuals or bedding plants backed by shrubs or plants of firmer consistency helps set them off. You won't have to worry about contrasting dot plants, which so often look like a fit of the fidgets.

Keep to single-colour groupings rather than mixtures, as far as you can. They make more impact and you can choose your colours, whereas in most mixtures they are chosen for you, like them or not. Unfortunately the demand, nowadays, is mainly for mixtures and few retail seed houses are

107. A simple oblong bed near the glasshouse range in the Cambridge Botanic Garden where the grey foliage plant, *Helichrysum petiolatum*, is not cabined by a lawn surround but can lap over on to a hard path. The modern gerbera hybrids provide both colour and excitement.

offering separate colours. They are obtainable from wholesale sources only by public and institutional gardens and this is a little frustrating.

You can still obtain wallflowers in a range of separate colours. I like to juxtapose two or three of these in blocks (**108**) and if I'm growing tulips with them, rather than dot them among the wallflowers, I mass them behind, again in their separate colours. It looks stronger this way. It also enables you to set your wallflowers so that the plants are touching, which is much more effective than seeing them separately, for they are scraggy individuals, easily blown on to their sides, when solitary. It's nonsense, really, to buy wallflower plants. For the price that people are prepared to pay for them, the plants can never be other than runts. You must grow them properly yourself, lining them out individually in June or early July to make fat, bushy units.

Do visit the Royal Botanic Gardens at Kew in spring and summer to give you ideas on unusual combinations that you might like to try yourself. It's surprising how much there is in a big garden that is easily applicable to a small one. An idea that I picked up and have twice used was of interplanting the pale yellow tulip 'Niphetos' with the feathery young foliage of the bronze form of common fennel, *Foeniculum vulgare*. For a start you need a stock plant of the fennel which you then allow to seed all around itself in a spare corner, and its seedlings will provide you with your underplanting.

Another smashing, yet simple, idea is to use *Anthemis cupaniana* (with dazzling white daisies over grey foliage and a loosely mat forming habit) as a carpet for red or yellow May-flowering tulips. You probably have a plant

108. Wallflowers are more telling in large groups of single colours than in mixtures. Tulips are better grouped themselves, rather than dotted over the carpet.

of the anthemis already. It provides masses of cuttings and you don't need to take these till early August, striking them in a box in a cold frame or greenhouse. Pot the young plants off individually and plant them out, a foot apart, in the autumn with tulips between. The planting will look thin at first but makes up surprisingly by the time spring arrives.

Yellow doronicums look well with white tulips in a shady bed; the blue *Brunnera macrophylla* (another hardy perennial, stock of which you increase by splitting and lining out for the summer) with pink lily-flowered tulips; the pale blue, starry flowered bulb, *Camassia cusickii* looks good above London pride; double red pomponette daisies with *Muscari* 'Blue Spike' (a delightful edging in front of lavender).

It is the same varied story with summer bedding, only here you will be using tender rather than hardy perennials with your annuals. It is quick, from a stock plant or two, to work up quantities of a tender bedder like the shiny, green-and-yellow-variegated *Coprosma repens* 'Variegata', taking your cuttings in late summer. They can be overwintered in the pots in which you struck them in a greenhouse kept only warm enough to exclude frost; potted off singly to grow on under cold glass in the spring and then bedded out with, for example, *Verbena rigida*, which you'll have raised from spring-sown seed (**109**).

Once you come to feel that all this experimenting is fun and sometimes a great success (failures are soon forgotten) you'll be eyeing every plant in your garden and greenhouse with the ulterior thought in your mind: 'I wonder how you would look as a bedder.'

Tired routines are for mindless hacks.

109. From a single stock plant, any gardener with a small frost-free greenhouse can quickly work up plants of unusual tender perennials like the variegated *Coprosma repens*, seen here, for bedding out in summer. *Verbena rigida*, from South America, can be treated as an annual and raised from March-sown seed.

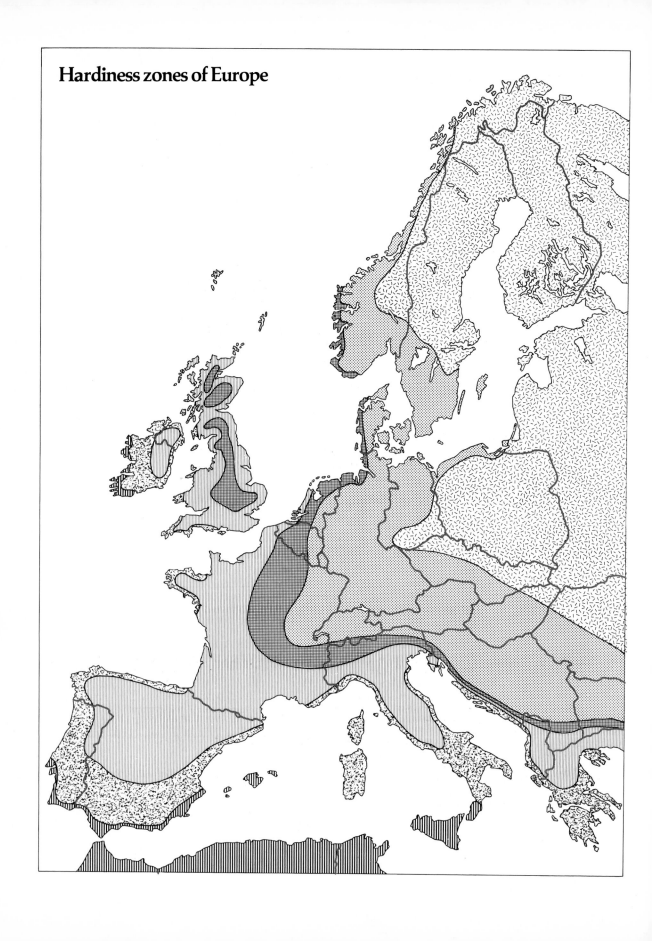

Hardiness zones of Europe

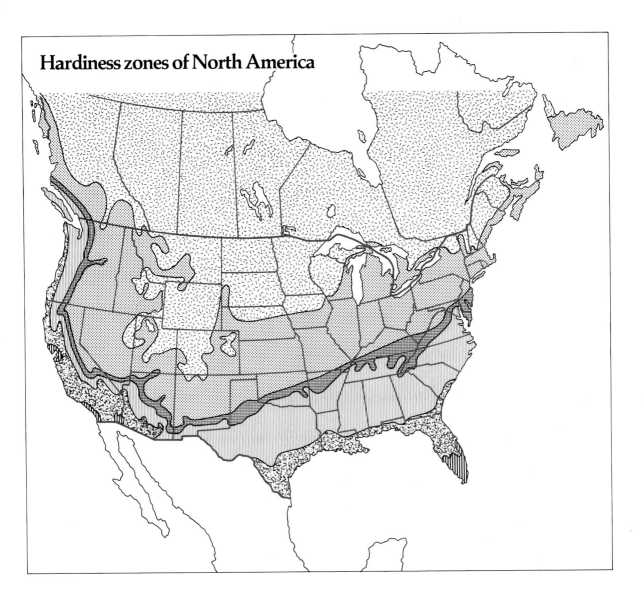

Hardiness zones of North America

Hardiness: The plants listed on pp. 156–72 have been given six hardiness ratings such as 'very hardy', 'tender' etc. These are based on the minimum temperature the plants will stand according to general experience, and assumes a normal gardening environment and no special winter protection given. Gardens, even in the same area, can have quite different physical characteristics: altitude, exposure, moisture and type of soil. Thus, a less-hardy plant grown on a south-facing slope in a free-draining soil is more likely to survive than if planted in an ill-draining one on a north-facing position. The ratings and zones shown on the maps should, therefore, be looked upon only as a rough guide on which to build and to experiment further.

Maps drawn by Eugene Fleury

KEY

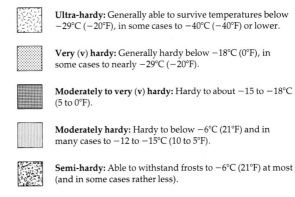

Ultra-hardy: Generally able to survive temperatures below −29°C (−20°F), in some cases to −40°C (−40°F) or lower.

Very (v) hardy: Generally hardy below −18°C (0°F), in some cases to nearly −29°C (−20°F).

Moderately to very (v) hardy: Hardy to about −15 to −18°C (5 to 0°F).

Moderately hardy: Hardy to below −6°C (21°F) and in many cases to −12 to −15°C (10 to 5°F).

Semi-hardy: Able to withstand frosts to −6°C (21°F) at most (and in some cases rather less).

Tender: Not hardy below −1°C (30°F), thus needing to be moved under frost-free cover.

A-Z of plants

It should be noted that the characters given after a generic name apply only to those species and cultivars listed thereafter, not necessarily to the genus as a whole.

Abies koreana (Korean fir)
Small evergreen coniferous tree or bush to 15 ft; small blunt dark green leaves, silvery beneath; blue-purple to brown 2½ in barrel-like cones, even on quite young plants; prefers a cool, moist, sheltered site; v hardy.

Acaena affinis
Prostrate, woody plant of rambling habit; leaves pinnate, strikingly glaucous, deciduous; young stems pink; v hardy.

Acer (maples)
Deciduous trees, often with strongly coloured and/or compound/palmate leaves, or with beautiful autumn colour; v hardy unless stated below. *A. griseum* (paperbark maple): leaves green, compound with three leaflets, bright crimson in autumn; bark peeling, cinnamon-brown, shiny mahogany wood beneath; to 20 ft. *A. japonicum* 'Aureum' (golden Japanese maple): leaves compound with 7–11 leaflets, bright yellow-green; horizontal branches; to 15 ft. *A. palmatum* (Japanese maple): brilliant autumn colouring, many varieties with variously coloured leaves, often much divided; 'Dissectum Purpureum' (cut-leaved Japanese maple) has dark maroon-purple, much-divided leaves, crimson in autumn; usually small hummocky bush. *A. platanoides* 'Crimson King' ('Goldsworth Purple'): yellow flowers in clusters in spring followed by large purple-maroon three-lobed leaves; to 50 ft; ultra-hardy.

Achillea (yarrow)
Minute petalless yellow flowers in large flat heads on upright sturdy stems with feathery leaves; best in hot sunny position in any soil; v hardy. *A. filipendulina* (fernleaf yarrow): mustard-yellow flowers in 3–4 in wide heads in summer; 3 ft; leaves grey-green, very feathery, toothed and hairy; hybrids include 'Coronation Gold' (2½–3½ ft), 'Gold Plate' (golden-yellow, 4 ft). *A.* 'Moonshine': bright yellow flowers in 3–4 in wide heads in late spring to midsummer; 2 ft; leaves silver-grey. *A. taygetea*: pale yellow flowers in 4 in wide heads in summer; 18 ins; leaves slightly silvery, evergreen.

Achnatherum (*Stipa*) *calamagrostis*
Perennial grass with tufts of grey-green leaves and arching feathery 1 ft long inflorescences of silvery to gold-brown flowers in summer to early autumn; 3–4 ft; full sun; moderately hardy.

Acorus calamus 'Variegatus' (sweet flag)
Rhizomatous arum relative, grown for its iris-like leaves which are striped creamy-gold; 2–3 ft; best in shallow water; ultra-hardy.

Actinidia kolomikta
Twining deciduous climber up to 20 ft; can be grown as non-climbing specimen without support; leaves ovate-oblong, partly suffused pink from tip, then through white to green, often in 3 distinct stripes; v hardy; best in full sun.

Adiantum venustum
Carpet forming rhizomatous rooted dainty perennial fern with bright green filigree fronds consisting of triangular pinnules, pinkish when young, on wiry black stems; 10 in; for moist soil in shade; v hardy.

Agapanthus
Tuberous plants with strap leaves to 2 ft long and umbels 6–12 in wide of deep blue or white bell-shaped flowers on erect stems in late summer; 2–3 ft; mostly moderately hardy; 'Headbourne Hybrids' selected for hardiness (v hardy). *A. campanulatus* 'Isis' has deep blue flowers; moderately hardy.

Ajuga reptans (common bugle)
Flowers deep blue in a compact spike; mat-forming; good ground cover in partial shade; ultra-hardy; many coloured-leaved forms, including 'Atropurpurea' (purple).

Alchemilla mollis (lady's mantle)
Yellowish-green flowers in summer; leaves kidney-shaped, 2–6 in, palmate lobes toothed at margins; 12–18 in; v to ultra-hardy.

Allium (ornamental onions)
Bulbs bearing small starry flowers in umbels on erect leafless stems; leaves mostly narrow, smelling of onions when touched; tolerant of any soil, in sun or shade; v hardy unless stated below. *A. aflatunense*: purple flowers in 3–4 in wide round heads in late spring; 2½–4 ft. *A. christophii* (*A. albopilosum*): silver-lilac flowers in 6–10 in wide round heads in early summer; 1½–3 ft. *A. giganteum*: very large dense spherical heads to 6 in wide of mauve flowers in summer; 3–5 ft. *A. murrayanum*: rose flowers in large heads; 1 ft. *A. neapolitanum*: white flowers in small heads in late spring; 12–18 in; moderately hardy. *A. tuberosum* (Chinese chives): white flowers with dark eye in flattish heads in late summer; 20 in.

Alstroemeria aurantiaca (Peruvian lily)
Flowers orange, trumpet-shaped, in loose umbels in summer; rootstock invasive; 3 ft; best in south-facing border with well-drained deep sandy soil; protect young growth from frost in exposed areas; 'Dover Orange' has orange flowers; moderately hardy. Ligtu Hybrids (*A. ligtu* × *A. haemantha*) are similar, but with flowers in shades of pink, flame, apricot or beige.

Anemone appenina
Rhizomatous low-growing plant with deep blue 1½ in wide solitary starry flowers in spring, above deeply cut basal leaves; 8 in; good for naturalising; likes lime; v hardy. *A. blanda* 'White Splendour': similar to above with profuse white 1½ in wide flowers in early spring; 6 in; best in warm sheltered site; v hardy. *A. hortensis*: tuberous rooted plant similar to above with solitary pinkish starry 1–2 in wide flowers in spring, above palmately lobed leaves; 8 in; v hardy. *A. × hybrida* (*A. hupehensis*, *A. japonica*, Japanese anemone): herbaceous perennial of garden origin with dark green lobed leaves and rose-pink 3 in wide flattish flowers with a central ring of stamens; 3–5 ft; numerous named varieties in range of pinks and pinkish-reds, also white; best in moist soil in sun; v hardy.

Anthemis cupaniana
Loosely mat-forming sub-shrub with evergreen silvery-grey, finely divided leaves and white daisies 1½–2 in across borne singly on 6 in stems over a long period, principally in May; 6–10 in; propagate annually in late summer by cuttings, moderately hardy. *A. tinctoria*: deep or pale yellow daisies up to 3 in across in summer; leaves feathery; 3–6 ft; perennial, very large with age, requiring support; best propagated annually (division in spring or autumn, or

cuttings in summer) and treated as a bedding plant (then shorter and self-supporting); ultra-hardy.

Argemone (prickly poppies)
Hardy annuals with prickly stems and leaves, and showy poppy flowers in summer; for sunny site. *A. alba*: white 3 in wide flowers with dark stamens; leaves pinnately lobed and spiny; 1–3 ft. *A. mexicana*: bright lemon-yellow 2 in wide flowers; leaves light green with white veins and blotches, spiny; 1½–2 ft.

Aronia arbutifolia 'Erecta'
Narrow, fastigiate form of the red chokeberry; deciduous shrub with 3 in lance leaves, turning brilliant red in autumn; white or pinkish flowers in corymbs in late spring, followed by dull red fruits; v hardy.

Artemisia arborescens (shrubby wormwood)
Shrub to 6 ft but usually less; finely divided very silvery-grey foliage, aromatic; flowers inconspicuous; for any soil (even poor) in full sun; best propagated by cuttings in summer annually; moderately hardy.

Arum italicum 'Pictum'
Tuberous rooted perennial grown for its decorative highly marbled leaves which appear in late autumn; fleshy orange-scarlet berries in prominent heads in autumn; 10 in; moderately to v hardy.

Arundinaria
Woody stemmed bamboos with evergreen lance-shaped leaves borne on sturdy erect characteristically jointed canes; for moist fertile soils. *A. falconeri*; olive green canes to 12 ft, slender with purplish staining at joints; leaves to 4 in long, pale green with hairy margins; moderately hardy. *A. viridi-striata* (*A. auricoma*): dwarf bamboo to 4 ft; leaves 3–8 in long, narrow-pointed, dark green, striped gold; less vigorous than above, and clump-forming; moderately to v hardy.

Arundo donax
Tall perennial reedy grass; stems to 12 ft with glaucous arching leaves; for moist soil; moderately hardy.

Asperula odorata (sweet woodruff)
Mat-forming, rhizomatous perennial herb; deep green narrow leaves in whorls, 1½ in long with bristly tips; heads of small white starry flowers in late spring; to 10 in; plants smell of new mown hay when dried; stems and leaves dried for herbal sachets; for moist light soil in semi-shade; v hardy.

Asphodeline liburnica (yellow asphodel)
Clump-forming perennial with grassy glaucous leaves and erect spikes of closely-spaced yellow, green-striped starry flowers which open at random up the spike at around 4 p.m. in midsummer; to 3 ft; v hardy.

Asplenium (spleenworts)
Evergreen ferns for all soils; good in rock/wall crevices; self seed. *A. adiantum-nigrum* (black spleenwort): erect leathery fronds borne on blackish stalks, bipinnate, to 9 in long; v hardy. *A. ruta-muraria* (wall rue): small sparsely clad fronds to 2 in long with serrated and incut pinnae; ideal in small wall cracks and crevices; v hardy. *A. scolopendrium* (hart's-tongue fern): undivided strap-shaped fronds to 2 ft long, bright green; wavy, crisped or crested in selected varieties; ultra-hardy. *A. trichomanes* (maidenhair spleenwort): pinnate bright green fronds with oval pinnae and curving glossy black stalks, in tufts; 10 in; ultra-hardy.

Aster
Perennials which include the Michaelmas daisies of late summer/autumn; soil should not dry out when plants are in flower; taller spp may need staking; ultra-hardy. *A. amellus* 'Violet Queen' ('Veilchenkönigin'): woody stems; rough, grey-green leaves and violet daisies, 2½ in wide; 2 ft. *A. divaricatus* (*A. corymbosus*): corymbs of white 1 in wide flowers on lax stems; 2 ft; useful in shade. *A. ericoides* 'Esther': Pale green foliage and pinkish ½ in wide flowers in panicles; 2 ft. *A.* × *frikartii*: garden hybrid derived from *A. amellus* × *A. thomsonii*; lavender-blue 2 in wide flowers over a long season from midsummer to autumn; to 2½ ft; 'Mönch' is the best cultivar. *A. sedifolius* (*A. acris*): bushy species with spidery lavender-blue 1 in wide flowers in dense corymbs; to 3 ft; needs support.

Astilbe
Herbaceous perennials with rich green, deeply cut compound leaves (often suffused reddish in red flowering varieties), usually bronze when young, in a basal clump; tall fluffy spires of tiny flowers in summer; 1–4 ft; best in moist or boggy soil; v hardy. *A. tacquetii* 'Superba': crimped leaves and long spires of bright mauve flowers in summer; to 4 ft.

Astrantia major (masterwort)
Clump-forming perennial with whitish, sometimes pink-tinged bracts forming a ruff around pincushion flowers; 3 ft; v hardy.

Athyrium filix-femina (lady fern)
Delicately cut fern with bright green bipinnate fronds in tufts; plumed and crested varieties available; 1½–3 ft; for moist soils; tolerant of sun, but best in partial shade; ultra-hardy.

Aucuba japonica
Sizeable shrub; leaves leathery, evergreen; bright scarlet berries in clusters on females; plants are unisexual with male and female flowers on separate bushes; at least one male bush must be interspersed with females to ensure berries set; good in shade; 'Crotonifolia' has leaves heavily spotted yellow, 'Lance Leaf' has narrow tapering glossy green leaves; moderately hardy.

Berberis (barberries)
Dense, spiny shrubs; leaves small, evergreen or deciduous; flowers small in clusters in spring; prefer sun, and tolerant of lime; v hardy. *B.* × *ottawensis* 'Purpurea': deciduous purple leaves to 1 in long; to 7 ft. *B. thunbergii*: deciduous oval leaves to 1¼ in long turn brilliant red in autumn; red berries; 5–6 ft; numerous purple leaved clones such as 'Atropurpurea' and its dwarf form 'Atropurpurea Nana'.

Bergenia (formerly *Megasea*)
Mostly evergreen plants with distinctive large rounded, leathery leaves on stout stalks; white to magenta or purplish bell-shaped 2 in flowers in large inflorescences on fleshy stems from early spring; 12 in; good ground cover plants, tolerant of quite moist soils; ultra-hardy. *B. ciliata* has deciduous slightly heart-shaped, toothed and hairy leaves with forked inflorescences of pink flowers. *B. cordifolia* has deep green leaves and mauve-pink flowers.

Blechnum (hard ferns)
Evergreen ferns with leathery fronds, some fertile, some sterile; lime-hating. *B. chilense* has ovate fronds to 4 ft; rather sparse growth in shade, but dense, though shorter in sun;

coppery tints on young fronds when grown in sun; best cut down to ground in March. *B. penna-marina* is a creeping species with dark green fronds comprising narrow pinnae; 6 in. *B. spicant* (common hard fern) has narrow pinnatifid fronds which become pinnate on older plants; evergreen sterile fronds spread, whilst fertile deciduous fronds stand upright and are longer; 1–2 ft.

Brunnera macrophylla
Forget-me-not-like blue flowers in spring; leaves heart-shaped, up to 6 in across, rough; 12–18 in; for moist, ordinary soil and partial shade; propagate by division in eary autumn or spring; 'Variegata' has white splashed leaves (best in partial shade); ultra-hardy.

Buphthalum speciosum
Large herbaceous perennial; all parts hairy; leaves large, heart-shaped; golden-yellow daisies in July; for moist soil; v hardy.

Bupleurum fruticosum
Evergreen shrub up to 5 ft, sometimes more; dark shiny blue-green leaves; pale greenish-yellow flowers in umbels in summer and autumn; moderately hardy.

Caltha palustris (marsh marigold, kingcup)
Clump-forming perennial for stream or pond margins; heart-shaped leaves with fleshy stalks; flowers cup-shaped, pale to golden-yellow, 2 in across in spring; the double flowered variety, 'Plena', has more solid flowers. *C. poly-petala* (giant kingcup) is larger and more sprawling with 3 in flowers. Both ultra-hardy.

Camassia
Bulbous plants closely related to bluebells with strap-shaped leaves and star-shaped flowers in spikes; best in full sun; v hardy. *C. cusickii*: pale lilac-blue flowers up to 1½ in across in summer; 1½–2 ft. *C. esculenta*: deep blue stars on 4 in spikes in May; 2 ft; naturalises well in grass; bulb eaten by N. American Indians.

Campanula
Mostly herbaceous perennials with characteristic bell- or saucer-shaped flowers in shades of mauve-blue, white or rarely pink, mostly borne in spikes; v hardy unless stated below. *C. lactiflora*: bell-shaped lavender-blue to whitish 1½ in flowers in dense panicles in summer; 3 ft. *C. latifolia*: grey or purplish-blue 2½ in long bell-shaped flowers in tapering spikes in midsummer; 4–5 ft; ultra-hardy. *C. persicifolia*: evergreen basal rosette of narrow leaves; racemes of blue or white 2 in wide bell-shaped flowers in midsummer; to 3 ft; ultra-hardy. *C. portenschlagiana* (*C. muralis*): mat-forming species with semi-evergreen leaves; mid-blue ¾ in long bell-shaped flowers in midsummer; 6 in, spreading up to 2 ft across. *C. poscharskyana* (Serbian bellflower): rather rampant species with lax stems forming a dense carpet; lavender-blue starry 1 in flowers in long sprays; useful ground cover over banks and walls; 1 ft, spreading to 3 ft across; ultra-hardy.

Canna (Indian shot)
Rhizomatous plants with broad green or bronze-purple leaves; stems crowned with racemes of flaring, bright flowers to 4 in across from summer to autumn; colour range from reds and pinks, through orange to yellow. *C. indica* 'Purpurea' has purple-red leaves and small reddish flowers. Treat rather like tuberous begonias, for summer bedding or container planting; semi-hardy.

Carex stricta 'Aurea'
Evergreen sedge with grass-like arching golden-yellow leaves in tufts; flowers insignificant; useful foliage plant; to 2 ft, usually less; most vigorous in moist soil or shallow water; v hardy.

Carlina acaulis
Low-growing perennial thistle with rosettes of spiny leaves to 6 in long and whitish thistle-flowers with silvery bracts, 2–5 in across in late summer; 4 in; for dryish soils; v hardy.

Ceanothus (Californian lilacs)
Fast-growing wall shrubs generally, though can be grown free-standing; tiny blue flowers in tight and profuse panicles in spring to early summer; semi- to fully-evergreen; best not pruned. *C. arboreus* 'Trewithen Blue': small tree or large shrub, vigorous, flowers pale china blue or deep blue in large panicles in early spring; leaves dark green, grey beneath; semi-hardy. *C. impressus*: very free-flowering wall shrub with deep blue flowers; leaves small; to 15 ft on a wall; moderately hardy.

Centranthus ruber (*Kentranthus ruber*, red valerian)
Woody herbaceous perennial with small deep pink to red flowers in domed heads in summer, often repeating later; leaves ovate, slightly toothed, rather fleshy to 4 in long; happy in hot, dry position such as wall crevice; vigorous and can become a pest; strong roots easily damage masonry; v hardy.

Ceratostigma plumbaginoides
Dwarf sub-shrubby perennial up to 1 ft, spreading to make ground cover; flowers blue in clusters in autumn; valuable also for autumn foliage colour; moderately hardy. *C. will-mottianum*: taller and more shrubby than the last, though often cut to the ground in winter; can reach 3 ft or more in sheltered sunny position; flowers rotate, bright blue in clusters, plumbago-like from early August to first frosts if old growth survives previous winter, but starting a month or more later otherwise; moderately hardy.

Cestrum parqui
Deciduous shrub to 8 ft, usually less; willow-like narrow leaves to 5 in long; flowers yellowish lime-green tubular, 1 in long in large clusters in summer to autumn, very fragrant at night; best against a wall; elsewhere cut down in spring; moderately hardy.

Ceterach officinarum (rusty back)
Tufted evergreen fern with sage-green pinnatifid fronds forming scalloped margins thickly coated with brown scales beneath; 6 in; for rock/wall crevices; tolerates full sun; likes lime; v hardy.

Chamaecyparis (false cypresses)
Evergreen conifers with dense foliage in sprays or plumes; adult leaves are scaly, juvenile leaves are needle-like; golden-leaved varieties are best grown in full sun, but may scorch if too hot and dry. Numerous dwarf forms have been selected from the species, which are ideal for specimen planting or amongst rock garden plants etc; these include *C. lawsoniana* 'Ellwood's Gold', a golden leaved Lawson's cypress of upright habit, slow-growing to 6 ft, but eventu-ally forming a small tree, v hardy; *C. obtusa* 'Tetragona Aurea', a dense and irregular, golden leaved Hinoki cypress with scale leaves like mossy encrustations, to 5 ft, v hardy; *C. thyoides* 'Ericoides', a compact very slow-growing bush

with blue-green heather-like juvenile foliage turning purple in winter, to 3 ft, ultra-hardy.

Chimonanthus praecox (*C. fragrans, Calycanthus praecox,* wintersweet)
Shrub up to 10 ft, usually spreading; flowers pale waxy-yellow with crimson-purple centre appearing on leafless branches in winter; strong aromatic scent: needs plenty of sun to flower freely; moderately hardy.

Choisya ternata (Mexican orange)
Evergreen shrub up to 5 ft, widely spreading; flowers white, in clusters in early summer, sometimes again in autumn, sweetly scented; leaves shiny and conspicuous throughout the year; tolerates shade in warmer climates; moderately hardy.

Chysanthemum
Herbaceous perennials with daisy flowers; leaves much-divided and incut, somewhat aromatic when crushed. *C. leucanthemum* (ox-eye/moon daisy): small white flowers with yellow disc, in branched sprays in early summer; to 2 ft; beautiful wayside plant; ultra-hardy. *C. uliginosum* (*C. serotinum*); white flowers with greenish-yellow disc, in October; likes moist, fertile soil; 6 ft; ultra-hardy.

Chusquea culeou
Evergreen bamboo up to 20 ft, usually less, with green or yellowish, thick, short jointed canes standing erect or somewhat spreading; leaves deep green, sharp-pointed, narrow, to 2½ in long on characteristically dense, tufted branches; best in moist fertile soil; moderately hardy.

Cistus (rock/sun roses)
Evergreen shrubs, usually gummy and aromatic; showy single rose-like flowers in shades of pink, magenta, mauve-purple and white, often with dark blotches in centre, consisting of 5 papery and rather crumpled petals, and a central boss of stamens (each flower lasts only a day, opening at sunrise but replaced by a succession of new ones over a quite long season from late spring to midsummer); best in hot, dry sunny sites; moderately hardy. *C. cyprius* has lance-shaped dark leaves, lead-grey in winter, and white 3 in flowers with maroon blotches around central boss; to 6 ft.

Clematis
Popular deciduous woody climbing plants with showy flowers; leaves often pinnate with twining petioles; best with roots in shade but top growth in sun; need support; v hardy. *C. alpina*: bell-shaped blue flowers to 1½ in long with white stamens in spring; silky seed-heads; climbs to 8 ft. *C. × durandii*: indigo-blue flowers to 4½ in across with ribbed sepals, all summer; non-climbing, spreading to 10 ft. *C. flammula*: white 1 in wide cruciform flowers in loose panicles in autumn, fragrant; climbs to 10 ft. *C. × jackmanii*: violet-purple flowers to 5 in wide in late summer to autumn; very vigorous. *C. × jouiniana*: white flowers with lilac-blue tint, 1 in, in panicles in autumn; non-twining, best allowed to trail rather than climb; very vigorous, spreading to 12 ft or more; var 'Praecox' comes into bloom in early July. *C. montana*: profuse white 2–2½ in flowers in May, rose-pink in var *rubens* and certain named cultivars; very vigorous, climbing up to 40 ft. *C. texensis*: glaucous pinnate leaves and nodding urn-shaped 1 in long flowers in summer; climbs to 6–12 ft; usually represented in cultivation by pink and carmine hybrids. *C. viticella*: profuse violet 1½ in wide flowers in late summer, climbs to 12 ft; varieties in range of colours including double types.

Large-flowered clematis hybrids with flattish flowers to 6 in across cover a range of colours from white, through pinks reds and mauves, to deep purple; these generally climb 8–15 ft.

Some species are herbaceous, non-climbing sub-shrubs for the border, 2–3 ft by 3–5 ft, including *C. heracleifolia*, a sprawling plant with bell-shaped, purple-blue, 1 in long flowers in late summer, and *C. integrifolia*, with small violet-blue, bell-shaped, nodding, 1½ in long flowers in summer.

Cobaea scandens (Cathedral bells)
Vigorous climber, perennial when grown as greenhouse plant, but often grown as half-hardy annual for planting out of doors in April–May; flowers pendulous, violet and green (pale greenish-white in var 'Alba'), bell-shaped with prominent green calyx, up to 3 in long, peduncles long up to 6 in; leaves pinnate, about 4 in long.

Colchicum
Autumn-flowering corms with showy, goblet-shaped or starry, somewhat crocus-like flowers in shades of pink, lilac and reddish-purple, borne directly from ground without leaves; glossy leaves appear in profusion in spring, then die down in early summer; v hardy. *C. speciosum* 'The Giant' has very large rosy-mauve flowers with a white throat, to 4 in wide.

Convolvulus althaeoides
Prostrate or climbing herb; rounded pink flowers up to 2 in across in spring and summer; leaves much divided, hairy, silvery; young stems twining; up to 1½ ft; plant in warm, sunny position; moderately to v hardy. *C. mauritanicus*: trailing; flowers clear blue-mauve, 1 in across freely produced over a long period of summer and spreading freely; up to 1 ft; semi-hardy, more so once established in a warm, well-drained site.

Coprosma repens 'Variegata'
Evergreen shrub to 3 ft, usually much less; leaves glossy, oval, to 3 in long, strongly marked yellow-green; semi-hardy.

Cornus alba (red-barked dogwood)
Deciduous wide-spreading shrub grown mainly for the crimson or carmine colour of young stems, so best pruned to one third of bush each spring; 6 ft; small yellowish-white flowers and white fruits; v hardy.

Cortaderia selloana (pampas grass)
Flowers in silky cream plumes 1½–3 ft long in late summer to autumn; leaves narrow, glaucous, arching to 9 ft long; best in sun and well-drained soil; most effective near water; moderately to v hardy. *C. argentea* 'Pumila' is dwarf, to 6 ft; upright, brush-like inflorescensces, densely set.

Corylus maxima 'Purpurea' (purple-leaved filbert/hazel)
Suckering deciduous shrub to 18 ft; rounded dark purple leaves 4–6 in long; purple catkins to 2½ in long in spring; responds well to stooling; v hardy.

Cotinus coggygria (*Rhus cotinus,* smoke tree/bush)
Large bushy deciduous shrub to 10 ft; rounded leaves, light green, to 3 in long, turning brilliant yellow-red in autumn; flowers minute in showy, plumose panicles, pink in summer, changing to grey in autumn (hence alternative name of 'wig bush'); for poorish soils in sun; v hardy; 'Foliis

Purpureis' has purple leaves, turning with age through green to reddish; 'Notcutt's Variety' has deep purple leaves, but less effective flowers; 'Royal Purple' is similar.

Cotoneaster
Evergreen or deciduous woody shrubs, noted mainly for their showy, mainly red berries, though many have equally attractive small white or pinkish flowers; best on poor soil in sun. *C. horizontalis*: low, spreading deciduous species, readily trainable against a wall; branches arranged in herringbone fashion with small rounded dark green leaves and bright red berries in autumn; spreads to 8 ft; v hardy. *C. simonsii*: erect bush species with dark rounded deciduous or somewhat evergreen 1 in long leaves and persistent red berries; to 8 ft; often used for hedging; v hardy.

Cotula coronopifolia (brass buttons)
Semi-prostrate aquatic plant suitable for planting in shallow water at pond margin; narrow fleshy leaves to 3 in long and profuse yellow button-like flowers (actually central disc of daisy flower without ray petals); self seeds; semi-hardy.

Crambe cordifolia (giant seakale)
Flowers white, in large loose gypsophila-like panicles, in early summer; leaves heart-shaped, very large; 4–6 ft; v hardy.

Crepis incana
Low-growing perennial rosette-plant, somewhat dandelion-like; flower heads clear pink in summer; leaves greyish, hairy; for sunny site; v hardy.

Crocosmia (*Montbretia*)
South African corms with narrow leaves and arching or upright spikes of bright trumpet-shaped 1–2 in long flowers from midsummer onwards; to 4 ft; for full sun; moderately to v hardy. *C. × crocosmiiflora*: scarlet, orange or yellow flowers; 'Citronella' is lemon-yellow; 'Emberglow' is deep orange; 'Lucifer' is taller to 3½ ft and deep orange-red. *C. masonorum*: broader orange-red flowers, held erect on stems curving to horizontal. *C. pottsii*: broader leaves; crimson-red flowers in erect spikes; 3 ft.

Crocus
Very popular, colourful small corms, flowering between autumn and spring; flowers usually goblet-shaped, often opening out rather starry; leaves grassy, with silver-white streak along centre, usually develop just after, occasionally with flowers; v hardy. *C. aureus* (*C. flavus*): orange-yellow flowers in late winter. *C. chrysanthus*: goblet-shaped flowers in late winter; many named hybrids in range of colours including cream, yellow, bronze, mauve-blue, purple and reddish-purple; also suffused and feathered in contrasting colours. *C. nudiflorus*: large purple flowers with prominent orange style, in early autumn, before leaves develop. *C. sieberi*: white to purple flowers with yellow throat, star-like, from late winter, before leaves develop. *C. speciosus*: large lilac-blue flowers with paler throat and dark veining, in autumn, before leaves develop. *C. tomasinianus*: lavender star-like flowers from narrow buds in mid–late winter. *C.* 'Dutch Hybrids': derived from *C. vernus*; large goblet-shaped flowers in late winter and spring; wide colour range including white, yellow, mauve-blue and purple.

Cuphea cyanea
Herbaceous perennial to 18 in; leaves ovate and hairy; flowers cigar-like, tubular calyx, 1 in long, yellow at mouth, scarlet at base, with protruding violet-blue true petals; brightest colouring in full sun on poor soil or where root growth is restricted; semi-hardy.

Cyclamen
Low-growing tuberous-rooted plants for full or partial shade; leaves rounded, usually marbled or blotched silver-green, forming carpet; flowers nodding with recurved 1 in long petals, commonly in shades of pink and mauve, sometimes white or magenta. *C. coum* (*C. orbiculatum*): pink, crimson or white broad flowers with purple blotches; winter to early spring; to 5 in; leaves sometimes marbled; v hardy. *C. hederifolium* (*C. neapolitanum*): mauve-pink flowers, with deeper blotches, in autumn; quite large, often ivy-like, lobed leaves, marbled silver; v hardy.

Cynara cardunculus (cardoon)
Thistle-like perennial with handsome, deeply cut blue-grey leaves and purple-blue flower heads in late summer; to 8 ft; moderately to v hardy.

Cyperus longus (sweet galingale)
Rhizomatous sedge with narrow rush-like leaves, ribbed dark green; very small red-brown flowers in graceful plumes subtended by glossy green pendant bracts in late summer; 3–4 ft; for wet soil or shallow water at pool margin; v hardy. *C. vegetus* is more compact with pale green glossy leaves and green inflorescences in late summer, turning brownish; 2 ft; moderately to v hardy.

Dactylorhiza foliosa (Madeira orchid)
Hardy orchid; lance-shaped sheathing leaves; erect spikes of lobed and lipped red-purple flowers; 2 ft; for moist soil in semi-shade; moderately hardy.

Danaë racemosa (Alexandrian laurel)
Evergreen sub-shrub to 4 ft; bright shiny green leaf-like phylloclades, tapering, to 4 in long; flowers greenish-yellow followed by ¼ in bright orange berries after a hot summer; for moist soil in semi-shade; moderately hardy.

Daphne
Deciduous or evergreen shrubs; tubular flowers with four flaring lobes borne in clusters, often scented, followed by berry-like fruits; v hardy. *D. pontica*: rounded shrub to 4 ft; shiny 3 in evergreen leaves and yellow-green fragrant flowers in spring. *D. tangutica*: rounded shrub with dark green leathery 2 in leaves and rose-purple scented flowers in spring, and often again in summer; red berries.

Daphniphyllum macropodum
Rounded evergreen shrub to 10 ft; leaves oblong, to 8 in long deep green, glaucous beneath, with slender point; leaf stalks, veins and dormant buds tinted reddish; flowers inconspicuous; moderately to v hardy.

Datura stramonium (thorn apple)
Half-hardy annual to 3 ft; large ovate, toothed leaves; flowers funnel-shaped, white, in July; night-scented; poisonous. *D. suaveolens* (angel's trumpet): evergreen shrub to 10 ft; large trumpet-shaped white flowers in summer, hang downwards, very fragrant in evening; leaves large, coarse, ovate, to 12 in long; tender.

Davallia mariesii (hare's-foot fern)
Semi-evergreen fern with much-divided fronds from a creeping hairy rhizome which resembles a hare's foot; fronds turn coppery in autumn; 8 in; for moist soil in cool shade; moderately hardy.

Dianthus deltoides (maiden pink)
Mat-forming evergreen plant, 6 in with a spread of some 1½ ft; leaves narrow, deep green, sometimes suffused red-purple; flowers profuse, ½–¾ in wide, red, pink or white with crimson centre, on narrow grassy stems in summer; 6–9 in; full sun; ultra-hardy.

Dimorphotheca (Osteospermum) ecklonis **'Prostrata'**
Sub-shrubby prostrate perennial, usually treated as half-hardy annual since it only sometimes survives the winter; white daisy flowers to 3 in across with blue eye and bluish reverse to petals, throughout summer, but only opening in strong light; for light soil in full sun. *D. barberae* is similar, but hardier and flowers have a yellow eye and pinkish-mauve petals; can form a very large carpet.

Dorycnium hirsutum (canary clover)
Short-lived shrub to 2 ft; silver-hairy throughout with clover-like leaves and small heads of blush-white pea-flowers in summer; seed pods bronze and glossy; best in hot site on poor soil; self-seeds; moderately hardy.

Dryopteris wallichianum
Herbaceous fern with large fronds from a central crown arranged like a shuttlecock, to 3 ft; covered with dark brown scales whilst unfurling when young; best in moist soil in shade; v hardy.

Eccremocarpus scaber
Semi-woody but fast growing tendrilled climber; flowers in clusters, narrowly tubular and contracted at mouth, 1 in long, bright orange-red, sometimes yellow or deep red; leaflets doubly pinnate with tendrils at end of main stalks; moderately hardy; may be treated as half-hardy annual.

Elaeagnus pungens **'Maculata'**
Evergreen shrub up to 8 ft grown mainly for variegated leaves, liberally splashed with deep golden-yellow, green at edges; valuable for winter effect; fragrant flowers in autumn but rarely borne in any numbers; red berries ripening in spring; moderately to v hardy.

Eremurus robustus (foxtail lily)
Blush-white flowers in closely packed spike in May, 7–9 ft; leaves bright green, sword-shaped, up to 4 ft long; for well-drained soil in full sun; moderately to v hardy.

Erica carnea (heath)
Dense, mounding evergreen dwarf shrub with very small needle-like leaves; flowers small, bell-shaped, rose-red in species, though variously coloured in named varieties, borne in winter to early spring in short racemes; 6–12 in; heaths and heathers are generally lime-haters, though this species is tolerant; v hardy.

Erigeron mucronatus
Rock plant to 10 in; flowers open white, turning pink with age, small, dainty, daisy-like on rather long stems up to 6 in; leaves lanceolate, small; tends to spread and flower abundantly from May till first frosts; grows well in wall crevices and paving cracks; moderately hardy, but self-sown seeds survive hard winters.

Erinus alpinus
Small tufted rosette-forming, perennial, evergreen plant; leaves spoon-shaped, toothed and hairy; flowers starry, whitish or carmine in 2½ in racemes from spring to mid summer; 3 in; coloniser for sun or shade; especially good in crevices or dry walls; v hardy.

Eryngium (sea-hollies)
Much-branched spiny herbaceous perennials; leaves prickly, in basal cluster, mostly deeply incut; flowers individually small, borne in branched panicles of very tight compound, usually rather globular heads in summer, each subtended by very spiny, often blue- or purple-tinted bracts; tolerant of lime and poor soil. *E. oliverianum* has blue 1½ in flower heads with blue pointed bracts and metallic-blue stems; 3–5 ft; v hardy. *E. pandanifolium* is a massive plant to 8 ft or more, with glaucous leaves and purplish flower heads which lack developed bracts; moderately hardy.

Erythronium dens-canis (dog's-tooth violet)
Bulbous plant with pink, crimson-purple or white flowers in early spring; petals recurved resembling Turks-cap lilies with a ring of orange-red markings around base; lance-shaped basal leaves, mottled brown and bluish-grey; 6–8 in; best in partial shade; dislikes dry heat; ultra-hardy.

Escallonia **'Iveyi'**
Evergreen flowering shrub to 10 ft or more, eventually becoming tree-like; leaves dark glossy green; flowers profuse, white, tubular with 5 flaring petals, in large inflorescences to 6 in long in summer; attracts bees; moderately hardy.

Eschscholzia californica (Californian poppy)
Hardy annual with profuse, crinkled satiny flowers in summer, cup-shaped and bright orange, yellow, carmine or creamy-white; commonly single, but some semi-double; leaves grey-green and finely divided; 9 in–1½ ft; best in sandy dryish soil in full sun.

Eucalyptus gunnii (cider gum)
Evergreen tree up to 70 ft; juvenile foliage, glaucous rounded up to 2½ in, notched and rounded where it joins to stem; adult foliage leathery and narrow lance-shaped to 3 in; flowers white with boss of yellow stamens in autumn; bark greenish-white, peeling; moderately to v hardy.

Euonymus fortunei
Slow-growing bushy and spreading evergreen shrub usually represented in cultivation by its numerous coloured- and variegated-leaved forms; leaves glossy, 1–2 in long; v hardy; 'Emerald 'n' Gold' is low-growing with golden-edged emerald green leaves which acquire a bronzed-pink hue in winter, to 2 ft; 'Silver Queen' has creamy leaves, turning green edged silvery-white with age, to 3 ft.

Eupatorium purpureum (Joe Pye weed)
Tall perennial with purplish-pink flowers in corymbs on erect stiff stems in late summer; leaves slender-pointed, in whorls; 3–6 ft; ultra-hardy.

Euphorbia (spurge)
Shrubs, herbs and succulents with heads of showy bracts surrounding insignificant flowers; leaves and stems exude a milky sap, called latex when cut. *E. griffithii*: bracts brick-red, spring; leaves green; more or less suffused red; 2 ft; 'Dixter' has burnt-orange bracts and heavily suffused leaves; 'Fireglow' has brilliant orange-red fiery bracts and green leaves; moderately hardy. *E. palustris* (fen or bog spurge): lime-green bracts in domed heads, spring; leaves lush green; 3–4 ft; moderately hardy. *E. robbiae*: bracts pale green, spring; leaves evergreen, leathery, dark green, up to 4 in long, borne in rosettes; 2–2½ ft; suckering habit; good ground cover; moderately hardy.

Euryops acraeus (*E. evansii*)
Dense silvery shrublet rarely more than 1 ft high; flower heads of bright yellow daisies on 3 in stems in summer; leaves linear, very brightly silvered with dense short hairs; for a sunny position; dislikes excessive dampness; moderately hardy.

Fatsia japonica (*Aralia japonica*, *A. sieboldii*)
Evergreen shrub up to 12 ft but usually less; flowers creamy-white in globular clusters in autumn; leaves very large, deeply lobed, leathery, shiny up to 15 in across; small black fruits in spring; best in partial shade; moderately hardy.

Felicia
A group of sub-shrubby or annual daisies from South Africa with blue or pinky-mauve flowers (*Aster pappei* belongs here); all are sun-lovers. *F. amelloides* (blue daisy): perennial, but tender usually treated as a half-hardy bedding plant; bright sky-blue flowers, 1¼ in across; to 18 in. *F. bergerana* (kingfisher daisy) is annual with steel-blue ¾ in wide flowers (open only before midday); 6 in.

Festuca cinerea (*F. glauca*, blue fescue)
Evergreen perennial grass forming neat hummocky tufts of bright blue-grey spiky leaves; to 10 in; best on light soil; colour is brightest when clumps are divided and replanted annually in spring; v hardy.

Foeniculum vulgare (fennel)
Tall perennial with yellow flowers borne in umbels in summer; leaves finely cut, bronze in one form; 4–6 ft; aromatic; leaves can be dried or used fresh for flavouring fish, etc; becomes weedy if allowed to self-sow; v hardy.

Forsythia suspensa
Woody deciduous shrub to 10 ft of flexible habit and suitable to train against a wall of any aspect; profuse bright yellow blossom borne on naked branches in early spring; leaves follow flowers, bright green at first, becoming deep green, to 4 in long; v hardy.

Fuchsia
Deciduous shrubs grown usually for their very showy flowers, but occasionally for variegated foliage; flowers nodding, consisting of a tubular or bell-shaped skirt of petals, and a cluster of protruding stamens and long pistil; the whole backed by a star of contrasting or similarly coloured sepals. Vast number of named varieties in shades and combinations of pink, mauve, red, purple and white; some are hardy enough to withstand permanent planting outdoors, others are somewhat tender and require protection in winter, best containerized permanently. 'Tom Thumb' is a dwarf moderately hardy variety with red sepals and violet-purple petals; to 16 in. *F. gracilis* 'Versicolor' has variegated foliage in shades of carmine, pink and grey-green (shoots reverting to plain green should be removed in early summer), with very small narrow, red and purple flowers; v hardy.

Galtonia candicans (*Hyacinthus candicans*, Cape hyacinth)
Late summer flowering bulb with white, pendulous bells numerous on stout stems up to 4 ft; narrow basal leaves, strap-shaped and glaucous; for full sun; moderately to v hardy (more so if mulched in winter, but best lifted for winter in colder areas).

Genista (broom)
Mostly deciduous shrubs with green linear stems and rather sparse narrow leaves; bright yellow profuse and showy pea-flowers, to ⅝ in long; for full sun; tolerant of poorish soils, wind and drought; v hardy unless stated below. *G. aetnensis* (Mount Etna broom): large shrub to 15 ft, often tree-like, with slender arching branches; very sparse leaves; golden-yellow, sweetly scented flowers in midsummer. *G. canariensis* (alias *Cytisus fragrans*, florists' genista): dense evergreen shrub to 8 ft in suitable conditions; bright yellow flowers in elegant racemes in spring and early summer, and again in autumn; usually for pot culture under glass; semi-hardy. *G. cinerea*: fast-growing shrub up to 10 ft, with spreading branches covered in silky hairs; leaves narrow, to ½ in long, also silky below; flowers bright yellow in early summer. *G. lydia*: low-growing shrub with stiffly arching branches; to 2 ft; profuse yellow flowers in late spring to early summer.

Geranium (cranesbill)
Clump-forming, mostly herbaceous perennials with deeply cut palmate leaves and characteristic 5-petalled saucer-shaped flowers; curious long tapering carpels disperse seeds by an explosive mechanism; leaves acquire red and orange tints in autumn; for all soils; v hardy unless stated below. *G. dalmaticum*: small species forming a cushion of glossy leaves with pale pink flowers in early summer; good for rock gardens or in dry walls; 6 in. *G. endressii*: mauve-pink flowers, 1 in wide, May till autumn; to 1½ ft; 'A.T. Johnson' has silvery-pink, 'Wargrave' salmon-pink flowers. *G. pratense* 'Coeruleum Plenum': double-flowered form of the meadow cranesbill with blue flowers in summer; 3 ft. *G. psilostemon* (*G. armenum*): bushy species to 3 ft; magenta flowers with black centre. *G. 'Russell Prichard'*: hybrid derived from *G. endressii* × *G. traversii* with grey-green leaves and rose-magenta flowers throughout summer; prostrate, but climbs into neighbours; moderately hardy. *G. sanguineum* (bloody cranesbill): vigorous low growing species to 10 in with magenta flowers throughout summer. *G. wallichianum* 'Buxton's Blue': rambling species to 1 ft; clear blue flowers with white centre and purple stamens, borne from July to late autumn. *G. wlassovianum*: rambling species to 2 ft; dusky purple flowers with deep purple veining, throughout summer; leaves and stems hairy.

Gladiolus
Summer-flowering corms bearing sword-shaped leaves with ribbed longitudinal veins, and erect one-sided spikes of open trumpet-shaped flowers; semi-hardy generally. *G. byzantinus*: magenta 2½ in long flowers in loose 1½ ft long spikes in early summer; 2 ft; v hardy. *G.* × *colvillei* (*G. nanus*): upward-facing 3 in flowers in loose 10 in long spikes in early summer; flowers vary in colour according to named variety, but most are irregularly blotched; 'Robinette' is cherry red; 2 ft; moderately hardy.

Gloriosa superba (glory lily)
Tuberous-rooted climbing plant from S. Africa; flowers deep orange and red or deep clear yellow, very exotic and conspicuous, the petals being recurved like a Turks-cap lily and crimped or wavy along the margin; leaves to 7 in long with terminal tendril; stem up to 6 ft, requires support; tender; start tubers into growth in a warm greenhouse, planting out for summer; most commonly grown as greenhouse plant. *G. rothschildiana* is similar but with bright crimson-red flowers, yellow at base.

Glyceria maxima **'Variegata'**
The variegated form of reed grass; vigorous perennial grass for moist soils or shallow water with golden-yellow, white and green striped reed-like foliage to 2 ft high, acquiring pink tints in spring and late autumn; v hardy.

Grindelia chiloensis
Sprawling, 2–3 ft evergreen shrub from southern S. America; flower buds capped with white mucus, opening to brilliant yellow daisies, usually borne singly on long stems in July to August; for sunny site; v hardy.

Gunnera manicata
Rhizomatous herbaceous perennial for boggy or waterside planting with enormous, rather rhubarb-like leaves to 7 ft or more across, held roughly horizontally on huge fleshy, densely-spined stalks, also spiny beneath; insignificant flowers in very large cone-like brownish-green inflorescence to 3 ft tall in spring; 10 ft; semi- to moderately hardy, though v hardy if crown is well covered in winter.

Hebe (shrubby veronicas)
Evergreen shrubs mainly from New Zealand, some grown for showy flowers, others for foliage effect; flowers individually small in axillary spikes; often rather bottle-brush-like with protruding fluffy anthers; best on light soils or near a protecting wall; ideal near coasts; those listed below are moderately hardy. *H. cupressoides*: slow-growing foliage shrub, somewhat resembling a conifer and with cedarwood fragrance; leaves bright green, minute and scaly (whipcord); flowers pale blue in clusters; to 8 ft. *H.* 'Midsummer Beauty': leaves to 4 in long, willow-like; profuse racemes, to 5 in long of lavender-purple flowers from midsummer through to early winter, sweetly scented; 6 ft. *H. recurva*: rounded bush to 3 ft with narrow 2 in long glaucous leaves which tend to curl backwards, and profuse 2 in racemes of pure white flowers in midsummer.

Hedera (ivy)
Vigorous evergreen woody-stemmed self-supporting climbers to 30 ft, popular for providing a dense covering of dark green or often variegated foliage over walls, fences etc; can however be grown as non-climbing rounded bushes when propagated from mature wood; two types of foliage are produced: juvenile, often attractively lobed leaves; adult, simple, lance leaves on separate shoots bearing somewhat insignificant globular clusters of greenish flowers which later develop poisonous berries (usually black); for any soil in any aspect and tolerant of quite heavy shade (except coloured leaved forms). *H. canariensis* 'Variegata': leaves to 8 in long, two shades of green edged silvery and creamy-white, on reddish stems; moderately hardy. *H. colchica* 'Dentata Variegata': large heart-shaped leaves up to 10 in across, dark green, splashed cream; v hardy. *H. nepalensis*: rather triangular leaves to 2½ in long, often toothed, greyish-green; berries are bright yellow.

Hedychium gardnerianum (ginger lily)
Rhizomatous 'exotic' plant with bold broad, sheathing leaves to 20 in long and curious irregularly shaped but showy yellow flowers to 3 in wide with red stamens, in large spikes; powerfully sweet scent at night, autumn; tender, requiring winter protection; best containerised.

Helenium autumnale **'Moerheim Beauty'**
Herbaceous perennial with profuse bronze-red daisies 1–1½

in across with conical central disc, in mid- to late summer; smooth lance leaves; 3 ft; for sunny position; ultra-hardy.

Helichrysum petiolatum
Perennial sub-shrub with lax, semi-trailing stems; woolly, grey leaves, 1½ in long; useful foliage effect plant, particularly for hanging baskets, pots and window boxes; semi-hardy. *H. splendidum*: bushy, rounded shrub to 3 ft; covered in woolly white hairs throughout; leaves to 1½ in long, narrow; flowers bright yellow in tight globular clusters to 1½ in across; grown for foliage effect; hard pruning each spring obviates flower production; moderately to v hardy.

Helictotrichon sempervirens (*Avena candida*, blue oat grass)
Perennial grass with blue-grey evergreen narrow leaves in tufts; 15 in; for a sunny position in well-drained soil; v hardy.

Hemerocallis **'Marion Vaughan'** (daylily)
Hybrid of complex parentage; herbaceous lily-like perennial forming a large clump; leaves strap-shaped, arching; flowers pale yellow, trumpet-shaped, slightly upward-facing, 5 in wide, scented, borne in branched clusters on tall stems in summer; ultra-hardy.

Hosta (plantain lily)
Herbaceous perennials, grown chiefly for their leaves, forming dense clumps; leaves mainly rounded or lance-shaped, mid- to deep green, variegated or glaucous in many of the popular varieties, usually somewhat ribbed or veined; flowers often quite showy, mostly trumpet- or lily-like, white, lavender or purplish, in racemes above leaves in summer; ground cover plants for moist soil in sun or shade; mostly ultra-hardy. *H.* 'Buckshaw Blue' has glaucous leaves; dwarf habit, 1 ft. *H. sieboldiana* 'Elegans': large blue-green, rounded, puckered leaves to 1 ft across; flowers whitish; to 3 ft. *H. undulata*: undulating or wavy leaves to 6 in long, broadly lance-shaped, green splashed creamy-white; flowers lavender; to 2 ft; 'Mediovariegata' has more boldly variegated leaves striped yellowish, 1 ft; 'Univittata' is more vigorous with narrow centrally striped, less wavy leaves.

Hottonia palustris (water violet)
Perennial water plant for shallow water; good oxygenator; spongy stems bear rosettes of deep green, much-divided leaves; submerged; flowers lilac-white with a yellow eye in a whorled, primula-like candelabrum in May; 1–2 ft; v hardy.

Houttuynia cordata
An invasive, though attractive rhizomatous perennial for damp places; leaves blue-green, heart-shaped, borne on red branching stems; white flowers with white bracts, in small spikes in late summer; non-invasive in hot, dry positions, where leaves become purple; 'Plena' has double flowers; to 18 in; v hardy.

Hunnemannia fumariifolia (Mexican tulip poppy)
A perennial poppy, most commonly treated as a hardy to half-hardy annual; flowers cup-shaped, yellow, to 3 in across, petals glistening, in summer; leaves blue-green, deeply cut; 2–3 ft; full sun.

Hydrangea
Deciduous woody shrubs, mostly bushy, a few climbing; flowers in summer, borne in panicles or corymbs, sometimes 'lacecap' with sterile ray florets in ring around less showy and very small fertile florets; flower colour varies from pink/red to mauve/blue according to pH of soil

(alkaline to acid respectively), sometimes pure white (on any soil); best on rich, moist soil. *H. arborescens* 'Sterilis' (*H. cinerea* 'Sterilis'): loose bush species with profuse spherical heads of creamy-white flowers 4–7 in across, all sterile; to 6 ft; v hardy. *H. macrophylla* 'Générale Vicomtesse de Vibraye': a very free- early-flowering bush hybrid, producing light pink to clear light blue flowers, according to soil, in hortensia-type (bun-headed) inflorescences 5–8 in across (mostly sterile flowers); moderately hardy. *H. paniculata* 'Floribunda': large bushy species, often almost tree-like unless hard pruned; flowers creamy-white in very large cone-like pyramidal panicles to 1 ft long, consisting of a mixture of sterile and fertile flowers; to 12 ft; v hardy. *H. petiolaris*: a climbing species to 80 ft; leaves to 4 in long, ovate, glossy, turning yellow in autumn; flowers creamy-white in flat corymbs up to 9 in across; v hardy. *H. serrata* 'Preziosa': flowers in hortensia-type inflorescence to 5 in across, pale rose-pink at first, ageing deep crimson or purplish according to soil; young leaves and stems reddish-purple; reddish autumn tints; to 3 ft; moderately hardy. *H. villosa* (*H. aspera villosa*): large shrub; leaves hairy; flowers in 'lacecap'-type flat inflorescences to 10 in across; inner fertile flowers bluish, outer sterile flowers rosy lilac regardless of soil, late summer; tolerant of chalk; moderately hardy, but young shoots frost-tender in spring.

Hypericum 'Hidcote' (shrubby St. John's wort)
Often listed as *H. patulum* 'Hidcote', but probably a hybrid of *H. calycinum × H. forrestii*; compact semi-evergreen shrub with profuse golden-yellow 3 in saucer-shaped flowers in summer; leaves dark green, lance-shaped and aromatic; to 5 ft; for any soil in sun or partial shade; v hardy.

Iberis sempervirens (perennial candytuft)
Profuse white, dense rounded heads of flowers up to 2 in across in spring; leaves dark, evergreen, forming a spreading neat sub-shrubby bush; 9–12 in; for sun; suitable for dry wall planting; tolerant of poor soil; ultra-hardy.

Ilex × altaclarensis 'Golden King'
Beautiful golden-variegated holly; slow-growing to 12 or 15 ft; leaves broadly ovate without spines; female, bearing scarlet berries freely if male pollinator within bee-flight range; moderately to v hardy.

Indigofera heterantha (*I. gerardiana*, Himalayan indigo)
Deciduous shrub to 6 ft, though taller if grown against a wall; leaves pinnate; pea flowers in short racemes in summer, pinky-mauve; moderately hardy; may be cut down by frosts, but base usually survives.

Inula magnifica
Herbaceous perennial of substantial size, often to 8 ft; leaves large, rough-textured; golden daisies with narrow rays, to 6 in across in summer; tolerant of wet soil; ultra-hardy.

Iris
Rhizomatous or bulbous plants with characteristic flowers consisting of three outer segments (falls) and three inner segments (standards); bearded irises have a tuft of fleshy hairs on the haft of the falls; leaves mostly sword-shaped, arranged in a fan. *I. bucharica*: bulbous species of the Juno group; glossy leaves, dying down in summer; flowers cream and gold, to 3 in wide, borne in groups of four or more in spring; to 18 in; for well-drained soil; v hardy. *I. kaempferi* (Japanese iris): rhizomatous beardless species; leaves narrow, deciduous; flowers in midsummer, 4–8 in across, clustered on erect stalks, falls very broad; varieties in shades of blue, violet, purple, pink or white, some double; for moist or even wet soils in full sun, though not tolerant of wet soil in winter; to 3 ft; v hardy. *I. laevigata*: aquatic beardless species for planting in shallow water; flowers blue-purple, 4–6 in across, borne in groups of three; varieties in shades of blue, violet, purple, pink and white, one with variegated leaves; 1½–2½ ft; v hardy. *I. pseudacorus* (yellow flag): vigorous aquatic species; leaves green, creamy-yellow in spring in 'Variegata'; flowers deep yellow, 3 in across, borne on branched stems in early summer; 3–5 ft; v hardy. *I. reticulata*: dwarf bulbous species; leaves tubular and pointed; flowers purple with orange patch on falls, 3 in across, in late winter, scented; 6 in; v hardy. *I. versicolor*: rhizomatous-rooted species; flowers reddish-purple and white in summer; for moist soil, tolerant of being submerged in water in summer only; to 2 ft or more; v hardy.

Jasminum
Deciduous or semi-evergreen lax shrubs or climbers with small yellow or white, often very fragrant trumpet-shaped flowers. *J. nudiflorum* (winter jasmine): lax, green-stemmed species, often trained against a wall; flowers bright yellow with five flaring lobes, borne in winter on leafless branches; leaves trifoliate, 1¼ in long, glossy green, deciduous; to 3 ft, or more if trained; v hardy. *J. officinale* (summer jasmine): vigorous climber often reaching 30 ft; flowers white, 1½ in long in summer, very fragrant at night; leaves pinnate, deciduous to semi-evergreen; needs support; moderately hardy.

Jovibarba, see *Sempervivum*

Juniperus sabina tamariscifolia
Low prostrate juniper, spreading or cascading; juvenile leaves dense, needle-like, blue-green, to 1 in long; adult leaves very small, scale-like; ultra-hardy.

Kniphofia (red-hot pokers)
Mostly herbaceous perennials; leaves grass-like in large tufts, often quite long and strap-shaped; characteristic poker-like terminal spikes of very tightly arranged tubular, downward facing flowers on a sturdy erect fleshy stalk; best dead-headed. *K. caulescens*: very glaucous leaves, evergreen, from a woody base; flowers reddish-salmon fading yellow, in autumn; 4 ft; moderately hardy. *K.* 'Little Maid': dwarf, to 18 in; flowers creamy-white in late summer. *K.* 'Modesta': flowers coral, fading white in summer; 2 ft. *K.* 'Snow Maiden': flowers white in late summer; 3 ft.

Laburnum (golden rain/chain trees)
Small deciduous trees to 20 ft, popular for their very profuse and showy bright yellow pea-flowers, borne in pendant racemes in late spring to early summer; leaves generally in threes; seeds very poisonous. The common laburnum is *L. anagyroides*; v hardy.

Lathraea clandestina
A root parasite particularly of willows and poplars, lacking its own chlorophyll with colourless or pale pink degenerate leaves, but flowers showy, violet, hooded, with a dark-purple lip, to 2 in long in dense tufts up to 6 in tall in March to May; 3 in; grown from seed scattered around host's roots, but can be transplanted; not harmful to host in moderation; v hardy.

Ligularia clivorum (L. dentata)
Robust perennial with orange-yellow daisies on large erect branching 3–5 ft stems in summer; leaves kidney-shaped, to 18 in across, coarsely toothed, flushed deep purple beneath in some cultivars, on long stalks forming a dense mound; best on moist soil or by water but subject to unsightly slug damage; v hardy; 'Hessei' is a tall variety; 'Desdemona' is slightly shorter with orange-yellow flowers, and purple tinted leaves.

Lilium
Very showy bulbs; leaves narrow or lance-shaped on erect stem, alternate or in whorls, crowned with a loose inflorescence of six-lobed trumpet or reflexed cup-shaped flowers in wide range of colours; often heavily scented; v hardy unless stated. *L.* 'African Queen': hybrid strain derived from Asiatic spp; flowers apricot, trumpet-shaped, to 8 in long, heavily scented, in midsummer; to 6 ft. *L. auratum*: deep green leaves to 9 in long; flowers white, crimson-spotted with gold band on each petal, to 1 ft across in heavy racemes, in late summer; rankly scented; 5–8 ft; lime hating; moderately hardy. *L. candidum* (madonna lily): leaves, to 9 in long at base, develop in autumn; flowers white, waxy, open trumpet-shaped, held horizontally, to 3 in long, with golden anthers, in midsummer; very sweetly fragrant; to 5 ft. *L. formosanum*: leaves narrow, deep green, to 8 in long, densely packed on flowering stem; flowers white, funnel-shaped, to 8 in long, petals marked purple on reverse, in late summer and autumn; sweetly night-scented; to 6 ft; moderately hardy. *L. henryi*: leaves glossy, to 6 in long, close-packed; flowers apricot-orange, spotted reddish-brown, to 3½ in long, held horizontally with reflexed petals, in mid–late summer; no scent; to 8 ft; may need support. *L. pardalinum* (leopard lily): leaves in whorls; flowers orange-red, paler in centre and with purple spots, strongly recurved petals (Turks cap), nodding, borne in sparse inflorescence or solitary in June–July; to 7 ft; dislikes lime. *L. regale* (regal lily): leaves to 5 in long, closely packed on stem; flowers funnel-shaped, to 6 in long, white, rose-purple shading on outside, sulphur-yellow in throat, held horizontally in large inflorescence in midsummer; very fragrant; to 6 ft. *L. speciosum*: leaves leathery, broader than most, to 7 in long, sparse; flowers white or pink, often shaded and spotted claret-red, to 6 in wide, waxy textured, Turk's-cap-type with reflexing petals, nodding, in late summer and autumn; very fragrant; to 5 ft; dislikes lime; moderately to v hardy.

Linum (flax)
Herbaceous, generally rather short-lived perennials; leaves small, narrow and densely packed; flowers bright, five-petalled and flattish saucer-shaped; individually short-lived, but borne throughout summer in succession; v hardy. *L. flavum* (golden flax): sub-shrubby species with evergreen leaves and branched clusters of very profuse golden-yellow 1 in wide flowers; 1 ft. *L. narbonense*: wiry-stemmed species bearing narrow grey-green leaves (semi-evergreen) and bright blue 1½ in wide flowers; 1½–2 ft.

Lippia citriodora (lemon-scented verbena)
Deciduous shrub to 10 ft; leaves lance-shaped, pale green, rough-textured, mostly borne in threes, to 4 in long, strongly scented of lemons when touched; flowers tiny, lilac, in clusters, rather insignificant; semi-hardy.

Liriope muscari
Evergreen, tufted perennial; leaves grassy, deep green, dense; flowers mauve, small, rather bead-like in spikes above the leaf tuft in late summer to autumn; good ground cover; cut foliage to ground each spring; 18 in; v hardy.

Lonicera (honeysuckle)
Bushy or climbing shrubs, some grown for their very sweetly scented flowers, others for foliage effect; leaves opposite and short-stalked; flowers tubular or funnel-shaped, two-lipped and five-lobed, borne in whorls or in axillary pairs; fruits are fleshy berries. *L. japonica*: semi- or fully evergreen, vigorous twining climber to 30 ft; flowers white and yellowish, to 1½ in long, very fragrant, in summer and autumn; leaves rounded, to 3 in long (the form described is 'Halliana'); v hardy. *L. nitida* 'Baggesen's Gold' (box honeysuckle): vigorous, dense, bushy species grown for its bright yellow, evergreen ½ in long tiny leaves (turn greenish with age or in shade); to 6 ft; prune to shape each spring; moderately to v hardy. *L. periclymenum* (woodbine): vigorous deciduous climber to 20 ft; flowers creamy-white, sometimes shaded pinkish or red on outside, to 2 in long, in summer, heavily night-scented; v hardy. *L. tragophylla* (Chinese woodbine): vigorous deciduous climber to 20 ft; flowers rich golden-yellow, to 3½ in long, in showy clusters; no scent; best in shade; v hardy.

Lunaria annua (L. biennis, honesty)
Hardy biennial with violet-lilac to purple, or white flowers in broad panicles in spring; leaves heart-shaped, coarsely toothed; variegated silvery-white in 'Variegata'; showy papery silvery seed pods, 1 in across, disc-shaped, useful for drying for winter decor.

Lychnis chalcedonica (Maltese cross)
Herbaceous perennial with brilliant scarlet flowers in domed clusters to 5 in across (white and pink forms also) in summer; 3 ft; ultra-hardy. *L. coronaria* (rose campion): vivid magenta circular flowers on widely branching inflorescence to 1½ in across in summer; leaves oblong, softly woolly, whitish; 2½–3 ft; ultra-hardy; relatively short-lived, but self-sows freely.

Lysichitum americanum (skunk cabbage)
Moisture-loving perennial of the arum family with yellow flower-like spathes before the leaves in April, 1–1½ ft tall; leaves 2–3 ft long, paddle-shaped, somewhat rank smelling if bruised; for waterside or bog garden planting; moderately to v hardy.

Lysimachia nummularia (creeping Jenny)
Creeping herb with overground-trailing stems; flowers deep yellow, cup-shaped, up to ¾ in across, upward facing, in summer; leaves evergreen, roundish on short stalks, deep green ('Aurea' has effective yellow leaves); useful ground cover plant, though may become invasive, for sun or partial shade; prefers moist soil; ultra-hardy. *L. punctata* (yellow loosestrife): somewhat aggressive herbaceous perennial with bright yellow cup-shaped flowers in whorls on erect stems in summer; leaves oval, pointed; 3 ft; for moist soil in sun or partial shade; v hardy.

Mahonia
Evergreen shrubs; leaves pinnate with spiny-margined leaflets, often acquiring rich orange-red to bronze-purple tints in autumn; flowers yellow, barberry-like, bell-shaped,

in clustered racemes between autumn and spring; small grape-like blue-black fruits. *M. japonica*: large shrub, as broad as high; leaves leathery somewhat lustre-less; flowers in spreading 10 in racemes, October–March, lily-of-the-valley-scented; to 10 ft; moderately hardy. *M. lomariifolia*: erect stemmy species; large leaves to 2 ft long each with up to 37 narrow leaflets, exceptionally elegant borne in rosette; flowers in erect 6–10 in long racemes, scent-less; to 10 ft; semi-hardy. *M. 'Undulata'*; handsome bushy shrub; leaves glossy, crimped, turning purple in winter; flowers bright yellow, scented, in dense clusters, March to April; easily controlled by hard pruning immediately after flowering.

Malope grandiflora (*M. trifida* 'Grandiflora')
Hardy annual of branching habit; leaves rounded mallow-like; flowers trumpet-shaped, to 3 in across, deep rose-purple with purple veining, throughout summer; white and rose-red varieties available; 3 ft.

Matteuccia struthiopteris (*Struthiopteris germanica*, ostrich feather/shuttlecock fern).
Herbaceous fern of vigorously rhizomatous and suckering habit; large ostrich-feather-like deciduous fronds arranged in an open-centred vase resembling a shuttlecock; later in season smaller fertile fronds develop in the centre; tends to scorch in summer; 3–5 ft; for moist or boggy soils with some overhead shade; ultra hardy.

Matthiola bicornis (night-scented stock)
Hardy annual of rather untidy habit with greyish leaves; flowers lilac, cruciform, open only in evening/night; not showy, but has a very strong sweet fragrance; 12–16 in.

Meconopsis cambrica (Welsh poppy)
Deep-rooted herbaceous perennial with yellow or orange poppies 2 in across in summer; leaves pinnate; 2 ft; for sun or shade; self-seeds; double flowered forms available – these must be propagated by division; v hardy.

Mesembryanthemum criniflorum (Livingstone daisy)
Half-hardy prostrate annual, with daisy-like flowers in many shades of pink, carmine, yellow, pale mauve, magenta and buff in summer, open only in sunlight; leaves succulent; 3–4 in; for sunny, well-drained site; an excellent bedder for early summer flowering.

Mignonette, *see Reseda odorata*

Mimulus glutinosus (bush monkey flower)
Evergreen shrubby perennial; leaves sticky, lanceolate, to 3 in long; flowers open trumpet-shaped with larger lower petals, to 2 in across, buff-yellow or orange-apricot; 'Puniceus' has deep bronze-red flowers; to 4 ft but weak-stemmed and spreading; best in sun; often grown in containers, or under glass; semi-hardy.

Miscanthus
Vigorous, upright herbaceous perennial grasses; leaves to 1 in across with pale mid-rib, developing rather late; flowers silky, flushed red or purplish, in showy inflorescences from midsummer to autumn, though persistent throughout winter; for moist soil. *M. floridulus* (*M. sacchariflorus*): rhizomatous, clump-forming species with imposing, fountain-like habit; 7–10 ft; v hardy. *M. sinensis*: clump-forming species; 4–10 ft; ultra-hardy; 'Gracillimus' has narrow leaves, 4–5 ft; 'Silver Feather' has showy inflorescences late August onwards which can be cut and dried, to 8 ft; 'Strictus' is very upright with yellow cross-banding on its leaves; 'Variegatus' has yellow and silvery striped leaves, to 4 ft; and 'Zebrinus' (zebra grass) is of rather lax habit, but otherwise similar to, though less impressive and less hardy than 'Strictus', 4 ft.

Molinia caerulea **'Variegata'**
Herbaceous tufted and neatly formed perennial grass; leaves striped creamy-yellow, tapering; flowers purplish-brown in branched inflorescences in autumn; 2 ft; v hardy.

Monarda didyma **'Beauty of Cobham'** (sweet bergamot)
Herbaceous perennial with pink sage-like flowers in 3 in wide heads with purple bracts in summer; leaves aromatic; 2–3 ft; best in moist soil; v hardy, but apt to die out.

Muscari armeniacum **'Blue Spike'** (grape hyacinth)
Dwarf bulb; grassy leaves appear in autumn and over-winter; flowers cobalt-blue, sterile, double, in large, dense, tapering spikes in mid-spring; to 10 in; for full sun; v to ultra-hardy.

Myrtus communis (common myrtle)
Evergreen shrub up to 12 ft; flowers white, up to 1 in across, very fragrant, boss of numerous stamens in centre, August to September; leaves ovate to lanceolate 1½ in long, dark lustrous green and strongly aromatic when bruised; only suitable as a wall shrub except in very mild areas; for full sun; semi- to moderately hardy.

Narcissus
Very familiar spring-flowering small bulbs; v to ultra-hardy. *N. asturiensis*: very small flowered trumpet daffodil with golden-yellow 1 in long flowers in early spring; 3–5 in. *N. bulbocodium* (hoop petticoat daffodil): rush-like leaves; flowers yellow, with enlarged conical trumpet, to 2 in long, perianth segments narrow, diminutive, from late winter; to 9 in. *N. cyclamineus*: flowers nodding with narrow trumpet to 2 in long and reflexed perianth segments resembling a cyclamen flower in shape; 6–8 in; best on moist soils in sun or partial shade. *N. poeticus* 'Recurvus' ('Old Pheasant's Eye'): flowers white, to 3 in across, with very short cup which is fringed with red; late spring; 16–18 in. *N. pseudo-narcissus* (Lent lily, wild daffodil): flowers yellow, trumpet-shaped 2–2½ in long, with perianth paler than trumpet, in early spring; 6–12 in.

Nerine bowdenii
South African bulb with bright pink flowers in autumn, trumpet-shaped with prominent stamens, up to eight to a cluster on 2 ft stem; petals strap-shaped up to 3 in long, wavy and curving back near tips; for warm sunny site; moderately hardy.

Nicotiana
Half-hardy annuals; rather sticky-haired throughout; leaves ovate to lanceolate, to 2 ft long; flowers funnel-shaped with long tube and flaring starry mouth, in many-flowered branching racemes, throughout summer and autumn. *N. affinis*: similar to *N. alata* below, but flowers slightly larger. *N. alata*: flowers white, greenish-yellow outside, each to 3½ in long; open at night, strongly scented; 2 ft. *N. langsdorffii*: flowers pendant yellowish-green, to 1 in long in a nodding, rather one-sided panicle in August; odourless, but open by day as well as night; to 4 ft. *N. sylvestris*: large leaves to 1½ ft long, rough-textured and veined; flowers white, 1 in across with a long tube, borne in a dense panicle in August onwards; very sweetly scented; to 7 ft.

Oenthera (evening primrose)
Biennials or herbaceous perennials usually with yellow saucer-shaped flowers; for any soil. *O. biennis*: hardy biennial; leaves lance-shaped to 6 in long; flowers pale yellow, to 2 in wide, in branched panicles throughout summer; open in evening, scented; to 4 ft. *O. lamarckiana*: hardy biennial; similar to above but larger and taller, to 7 ft. *O. tetragona*: herbaceous perennial with small dark leaves; flowers open during daytime and close at night, to 1½ in across; 9 in, but soon collapses into a prostrate pool of yellow.

Olearia
Evergreen shrubs with daisy flowers; leaf form extremely variable; moderately hardy. *O. macrodonta* (New Zealand holly): leaves holly-like, but soft textured, greyish-green, to 4 in long; flowers small, white in showy clusters, in early summer; to 10 ft or more. *O. solandrii*: leaves tiny, to ½ in long, dark green, felted yellow beneath, on yellow-felted stems; flowers small, off-white, in late summer to autumn; all parts scented like lime blossom; to 6 ft or more.

Omphalodes (navelwort)
Annual or perennial plants with loose recemes of forget-me-not-like flowers. *O. cappadocica*: evergreen perennial forming a low carpet; leaves ovate to lanceolate on long stalks; flowers blue, rather similar but larger than forget-me-not, throughout spring; 8 in; excellent shade plant; moderately to v hardy. *O. linifolia*: hardy annual with branching stems bearing narrow glaucous leaves to 2 in long; flowers white, from late spring onwards according to when sown.

Onoclea sensibilis (sensitive fern)
Widely colonising rhizomatous fern; sterile fronds large, fresh pale green and somewhat triangular with toothed pinnae; fertile fronds narrow with bead-like pinnae (hence alternative common name: bead fern), persist into winter and can be cut and dried; fronds turn bronze-brown in early autumn; for moist soil in sun or shade; 2–5 ft; ultra-hardy.

Origanum vulgare 'Aureum'
Golden form of the common marjoram; perennial herb with yellow leaves fading to lime-green with age but baking brown in hot dry conditions, rounded and aromatic; purplish flowers in clusters in summer, though not showy; 9–12 in; neat tufted habit suitable for edging; ultra-hardy.

Orontium aquaticum (golden club)
Deep-rooting aquatic perennial for shallow water; leaves blue-green to 1 ft long, standing upright in very shallow water, or else floating; arum-like yellow 4 in long spadices borne on long white stalks from late spring; v hardy.

Osmunda regalis (royal fern)
Vigorous herbaceous fern; sterile fronds bright green in summer, coppery at first and golden-brown in autumn, large and borne in tufts; fertile fronds curious, consisting of tufts of pinnae, which, when mature, look like dried flowers; best in moist soil, especially at waterside; hates lime; to 6 ft or more; ultra-hardy.

Osteospermum (*Tripteris*) *hyoseroides*
Half-hardy annual; bright orange daisies with deep violet disc, opening only in mornings; leaves rather variable in shape, to 4 in long, sticky; to 2 ft.

Ozothamnus (*Helichrysum*) *ledifolius*
Evergreen dense rounded shrub to 3 ft; leaves short, blunt-tipped, leathery and with incurved margins, yellowish beneath, aromatic of stewed prunes; flowers in dense corymbs, burnt-orange in bud, opening whitish, daisy-like, from April; v hardy.

Papaver orientale (oriental poppy)
Herbaceous perennial with large bowl-shaped, crepe-textured flowers in late spring to early summer, scarlet in species with black blotch at base of each petal, and central boss of purple-black stamens; leaves grey-green, hairy, deeply cut; 2–3 ft; for deep soil in full sun; ultra-hardy; varieties in numerous colours, including 'Goliath', actually a form of *P. bracteata*, to 4½ ft with blood-red flowers.

Paris polyphylla
Perennial herb, spreading slowly by creeping rhizomes; leaves four to nine in whorls on long stalk, broadly lance-shaped with a narrow point, appear in June; flowers green and yellow with purple pistil, long lasting, followed by scarlet berries; 9 in to 2½ ft; ideal woodland plants; v hardy. *P. quadrifolia* (herb paris) is similar but with whorls of four leaves, and starry yellowish-green solitary flowers with prominent stamens; poisonous; to 12 in.

Parthenocissus quinquefolia (true Virginia creeper)
Vigorous deciduous self-supporting climber to 70 ft; compound, palmate leaves comprising five 2–5 in long leaflets, borne in sprays, developing brilliant warm-red autumn colour; ultra-hardy. *P. tricuspida* (Boston ivy, Virginia creeper) is similar, but coarser with shiny, coarsely toothed leaves held closer to main stem and developing harsh autumn colour.

Pelargonium
Evergreen sub-shrubs, commonly referred to as geraniums, though botanically distinct; stems rather succulent, becoming woody; flowers five-petalled or frequently double in rounded clusters; vast range of colours including pinks, reds, orange, mauves and white; leaves variable in shape, forming part-basis of classification. Regal pelargoniums have lobed, toothed and often rather fluted leaves to 4 in wide, and umbels of large, often frilly flowers, each to 2 in across. Zonal pelargoniums have rounded leaves to 5 in wide with scalloped margins and characteristically with a central ring of bronzy colouring (some with variegated colouring); flowers to 1 in wide in tight umbels to 6 in wide. Ivy-leaved pelargoniums have trailing stems, reaching up to 3 ft, with ivy-like rather fleshy leaves and smaller umbels of 1 in wide flowers (ideal for hanging baskets). Scented-leaved pelargoniums are grown chiefly for their lemon-, nutmeg-, mint-scented etc leaves, fragrant only when touched.

Peltiphyllum peltatum (*Saxifraga peltata*, water saxifrage)
Perennial bog plant with pale pink flowers in large clusters in April, before foliage appears; leaves large, rounded, lobed; 2–3 ft; ground cover for deep moist soil beside water; v hardy.

Pennisetum villosum (*P. longistylum*)
Perennial grass often treated as a half-hardy annual; flowers pale green in feathery plumes up to 6 in long in summer; leaves narrow, arching; 1½–2 ft; best in sheltered sunny site; moderately hardy.

Periwinkles *see Vinca*

Pharbitis (*Ipomoea*) *tricolor* (morning glory)
Half-hardy annual climber to 8 ft; twining slender stems bear heart-shaped leaves to 10 in wide; flowers trumpet-

shaped, sky-blue with a paler throat (pink, white or rose-lavender in some varieties), to 4 in long, from midsummer; for light, but rich soil in sun.

Philadelphus coronarius **'Aureus'**
Yellow-leaved form of the common mock orange; deciduous shrub to 12 ft with bright yellow young leaves, becoming greenish with age, oval to 3 in long; creamy-white cup-shaped flowers with prominent yellow stamens, to 1 in wide, in large clusters in early summer; strong orange-blossom scent; v hardy.

Phlomis fruticosa (Jerusalem sage)
Evergreen shrub up to 4 ft, vigorous grower, spreading widely; branches rather soft and covered with grey hairs; flowers dusky yellow in whorls at ends of branches in early summer, 1¼ in long, two-lipped; leaves grey-green, hairy, rather wrinkled like those of a sage; inedible; for warm sunny site; moderately hardy.

Phlox douglasii
Cushion species with woody stems forming a dense mat, 2–6 in; flowers variable in colour, mostly white, lavender or pink, profuse, small and 5-petalled in late spring to summer; small, hard leaves; v to ultra-hardy. *P. subulata* (moss phlox) is similar but of looser habit; flowers shocking bright magenta-crimson in 'Temiscaming', in spring. *P. paniculata*: herbaceous perennial typically with mauve flowers in summer, in dense terminal leaves oblong, slender-pointed 3–4 in long; 2–4 ft; 'Norah Leigh' has cream and green foliage with small mauve flowers; best in well-cultivated moist soil; v hardy.

Platystemon californicus (cream cups)
Half-hardy annual with cream or pale primrose yellow, saucer-shaped poppy flowers in summer; leaves narrowly oblong, roughly hairy; 6–12 in; for light soil full sun; will self-sow.

Polygonum (knotweed)
Herbaceous perennials ranging from 8 ft to low ground cover; stems have swollen joints or 'knots'; flowers small, mostly in shades of pink and red or white, in profuse densely packed spikes above the foliage. *P. campanulatum*: 3 ft herb; leaves mid-green, broadly lance-shaped, to 6 in long; flowers bell-shaped, pink in branched inflorescences to 3 in long from early summer to autumn; moderately invasive; v hardy. *P. molle*: bushy perennial to 6 ft; flowers white, in large terminal clusters in July to autumn, followed by shiny black berries; v hardy. *P.* 'Reynoutria': sturdy, branched, purple-spotted stems reaching 2 ft high bear rounded leathery, wavy-edged leaves to 3 in long; flowers white and red in erect panicles borne in leaf axils, in late summer; invasive; v hardy.

Polypodium vulgare (polypody)
Evergreen fern with creeping habit, to 1½ ft; fronds leathery, pinnatifid, with alternately arranged pinnae; new fronds appear late in the season giving bright green flush; some varieties such as 'Cornubiense' have much-divided, lacy fronds; in others they are forked or crested; tolerant of lime and poor dryish soils; ultra-hardy.

Polystichum (shield fern)
Clump-forming ferns; tolerant of lime; v hardy. *P. aculeatum* 'Bevis': a curious form of the hard shield fern with evergreen finely-divided glossy deep green fronds of a rather leathery and rigid texture; the tips of the fronds taper into a tail-like appendage; 2–3 ft. *P. setiferum* 'Acutilobum': a narrow, finely-divided form of the soft shield fern; semi- or fully evergreen twisting and arching to 2–4 ft.

Primula
Perennials with leaves usually in basal rosettes; flowers showy, five petalled on erect leafless stalk (scapes). The following enjoy moist rich soil, and are ideal near waterside; v hardy. *P. bulleyana*: leaves toothed, rounded to lance-shaped, to 1 ft long, with reddish centre vein; flowers apricot-orange, each to ¾ in wide, borne in many whorled clusters up a tall erect scape (candelabrum-like) in early summer; to 2½ ft. *P. florindae* (giant cowslip): leaves round-ed and heart-shaped at base, roundly-toothed, to 8 in long, reddish-tinted stalks; flowers pendant, sulphur-yellow, co-vered with a powdery, creamy-yellow farina within, bell-shaped to ⅓ in long, borne in large umbels in midsummer, fragrant; 2–4 ft. *P. japonica*: leaves oblong or somewhat spoon-shaped, toothed, to 1 ft long, on winged stalks; flowers purple-red, pinkish or white, with a yellow eye, each ¾ in wide, borne in a candelabrum as in *P. bulleyana*, May; to 2½ ft.

Quercus rubra (*Q. borealis*, red oak)
Deciduous tree to 60 ft; vigorous and fast-growing with large rounded head and somewhat spreading habit; leaves pale bright green at first, becoming dark green with age, broad and sharply lobed, to 8 in long. 'Aurea' is a golden-leaved form. Both acquire rufous autumn tints; lime-hating; for sheltered sites, branches being rather brittle; v hardy.

Ranunculus lingua **'Grandiflora'** (great spearwort)
Rhizomatous aquatic perennial for shallow water; leaves blue-green, to 8 in long, erect, lance-shaped; bright golden-yellow buttercups, 2 in wide, in branched sprays in mid-summer; to 4 ft; v hardy.

Reseda odorata (mignonette)
Hardy annual of lax habit grown for its sweetly scented, though somewhat insignificant flowers; leaves lance-shaped; flowers yellowish with saffron anthers, and rela-tively large green sepals, in erect racemes in summer; to 18 in.

Rheum palmatum (ornamental rhubarb)
Large herbaceous perennial related to the edible rhubarb; leaves deeply cut, glossy, to 3 ft long, purplish-red when young, ageing deep green; flowers pink to red or white, small, but in large erect panicles in early summer; for moist soil; 5–8 ft; v hardy.

Ricinus communis (castor oil plant)
Half-hardy annual grown for its large palmately-lobed leaves on long stalks, giving tropical effect; flowers green in clusters in midsummer, rather insiginificant; 3–8 ft; 'Gib-sonii' has deep reddish-purple leaves and stems, 4–5 ft; poisonous.

Robinia pseudacacia **'Frisia'** (false acacia)
Deciduous tree up to 40 ft, often less with large pinnate leaves up to 1 ft long, bright golden; thorny branches; flowers white in pendulous racemes, pea-like in early summer, but seldom seen in this variety; ultra-hardy.

Rodgersia pinnata **'Superba'**
Herbaceous perennial with large, long-stalked, pinnate leaves, bronze-purple when young; flowers bright pink in

much-branched panicles to 20 in long fading slowly to dusky red; 3–4 ft; best in sheltered site in moist soil; v hardy.

Romneya coulteri (Californian tree poppy)
Sub-shrubby perennial with tall stems up to 8 ft, wide-spreading by suckers; flowers large, up to 5 in across with broad overlapping white satiny petals with centre boss of golden stamens, in midsummer to early autumn; for light soil in sheltered sunny site; moderately hardy.

Rosa (rose)
Deciduous thorny, woody shrubs, often of lax, spreading or climbing habit; leaves pinnate with toothed oval leaflets; flowers often single and five-petalled or semi-double with a prominent central boss of golden stamens; best in fertile soil in full sun. *R. filipes*: vigorous climber to 40 ft; branches with few thorns; flowers white, to 1 in across in large panicles in midsummer; hips globular, red, to ½ in long; v hardy, but can be cut in severe winters. *R. glauca* (*R. rubrifolia*): arching, generally thornless branches, red-purple when young; leaves glabrous, purplish-grey; flowers single, rose-pink to purplish-red, to 2 in wide in small corymbs in June; hips red-brown, ovoid, ½ in long, showy; to 5–8 ft; ultra-hardy. *R. moyesii*: erect leggy bush to 6–12 ft; flowers single, blood-red, to 2½ in wide in June; hips long, flask-shaped, to 1¼ in long, vermilion-red in August to September; moderately to v hardy. *R. pimpinellifolia*: suckering species to 6 ft, much shorter by pruning; stems bear dense slender thorns interspersed with bristles; flowers solitary, to 2 in wide, creamy-yellow in early summer, but with many sports, often double; hips black, to ¾ in wide; v hardy. *R. primula* (incense rose): upright dense shrub rose to 6 ft; stiff, flattened, paired, red thorns; leaves glaucous and aromatic, especially after rain; flowers pale yellow, single, solitary, 1½ in wide in late May to June; hips globular, maroon-red, to ⅔ in wide. *R. rubiginosa* (*R. eglanteria*, sweet briar): briar rose to 7 ft with dense hooked thorns and bristles; flowers pink to 2 in wide; hips to 1 in long, orange-scarlet, showy, aromatic stewed apple scent; v hardy. *R. rugosa*: thorny, dense and rather vigorous shrub roses with rugose or wrinkled and rough-textured, though glossy leaves, turning pure yellow in autumn; flowers white, pink or red, to 3 in wide, very fragrant, borne over a long period from early summer till autumn; hips globular, orange-red, to 1 in wide, only on single- or semi-double-flowered forms; ultra- to v hardy; variants include 'Alba' (single, white), 'Frau Dagmar Hastrup' (single, soft pink), and 'Scabrosa' (single, magenta). *R. serafinii*: tangled aromatic bush; flowers solitary, pink, quite small but scented in June; hips bright red, to ½ in wide; to 4 ft; v hardy. *R. sericea pteracantha*: shrub rose to 8 ft bearing huge translucent-red broad, flat thorns on young branches; flowers white, four-petalled, 2 in wide in early summer; hips inconspicuous; moderately to v hardy. *R. setipoda*: upright species to 6–10 ft; flowers pink, to 2 in wide, in many-flowered panicles in early summer; hips flask-shaped, bright red, 1 in long; moderately to v hardy.

Rudbeckia (coneflower)
Annuals and herbaceous perennials with daisy flowers having a characteristic conical dark brown or green central disc; moisture-loving. *R. fulgida* 'Goldsturm': perennial with rich yellow, narrow-petalled flowers, 3 in wide, August to October; 2–3 ft; shade tolerant; v to ultra-hardy. *R. hirta*

'Monplaisir' (black-eyed Susan): short-lived perennial, usually grown as a half-hardy annual; flowers deep golden-yellow, 3 in wide, with a nearly black cone, in late summer to autumn; to 3 ft.

Sage see *Salvia officinalis*

Salix (willow)
Deciduous trees, shrubs or prostrate mat-forming plants; leaves mostly lance-shaped; characteristic catkins are borne on many species in spring before the leaves develop; male plants have fluffy 'pussies', females have greenish less showy catkins; best on moist soil. *S. alba argentea*: silver-leaved subspecies of the white willow; tree to 30 ft, but often pollarded for foliage effect and then reaching only up to 10 ft; leaves silver and downy, to 3 in long; ultra-hardy. *S. daphnoides* 'Aglaia': fast-growing tree, eventually to 40 ft, though can be pollarded as above; new wood purple with a white bloom; leaves leathery and dark green; male catkins large and very silky, to 2 in long from late January to March; v hardy. *S. lanata*: slow-growing bushy species, eventually reaching 2 ft or rarely more; young branches hairy; leaves rounded, silvery-haired, to 2½ in long; male catkins with bright golden-yellow pollen; ultra-hardy.

Salvia (sage)
Annuals, herbaceous perennials and sub-shrubby evergreens, mostly with aromatic foliage; leaves often felty or rough textured; flowers two-lipped and tubular, usually borne in whorled spikes. *S. nemerosa* 'Superba': bushy herbaceous perennial with profuse spikes of violet-blue flowers with crimson-purple bracts, from midsummer to autumn; to 3 ft; v hardy. *S. officinalis* (common/culinary sage): semi-woody sub-shrub to 2 ft; shoots covered in greyish down; leaves wrinkled, greyish-green to 3 in long, felted; flowers blue-purple; ultra-hardy. Coloured-leaved forms include 'Icterana' with golden variegated leaves, 'Purpurascens' with purplish-red leaves, and the more tender 'Tricolor' with yellow-white and pink/purple-tinted variegated leaves. *S. patens*: semi-hardy perennial often treated as a half-hardy annual; flowers gentian-blue in summer and autumn. 2–2½ ft.

Sambucus racemosa 'Plumosa Aurea'
Golden-leaved form of the red elder; deciduous shrub to 8 ft, widespreading; slower-growing than parent species; leaves finely divided golden-yellow, deeply toothed; flowers yellowish in large panicles in summer, but hard annual pruning for foliage effect prevents flowering and fruiting; bright scarlet berries; v hardy.

Sanguinaria canadensis 'Flore Pleno' (Canadian bloodroot)
Rhizomatous herbaceous plant; flowers white, double, globular with numerous petals, on very short stems, in April; leaves orbicular with scalloped margins, rather glaucous, after flowers; 6 in; all parts have bright red sap; for peaty soil in cool shade; ultra-hardy.

Santolina chamaecyparissus (lavender cotton)
Evergreen shrub of dense and mounting habit; best pruned hard regularly in spring to maintain a neat bush of about 2 ft; leaves finely divided, aromatic, to 1½ in long, crowded on stems and intensely silvery-white felted; flowers bright yellow, profuse, button-like, avoided by pruning, moderately hardy. *S. neapolitana* is similar but of less dense habit and longer more finely divided leaves.

Saxifraga fortunei
Clump-forming deciduous perennial; leaves in rosettes, deep green, rounded and lobed, red beneath; flowers white, star-like with longer lowest petal 1 in wide, in loose panicles on upright slender stalks, in late autumn; to 1 ft; for cool, moist soil in partial shade; moderately hardy. *S. stolonifera* (mother of thousands) makes evergreen rosettes and spreads by runners which produce small plantlets at their tips; leaves veined and rather marbled, reddish tinted and deep red-purple beneath. *S. cuscutiformis* is probably correctly a subspecies of this, with more strongly marked leaves.

Schizostylis coccinea (Kaffir lily)
South African rhizomatous perennial bearing erect spikes to 2½ ft of numerous starry flowers up to 2 in across in autumn, scarlet, crimson or pink; leaves narrow, iris-like; 'Viscountess Byng' has pure pink flowers; for a damp, sunny site; moderately hardy.

Scilla campanulatus (*Endymion hispanicus*, Spanish bluebell)
Bulbous large-flowered bluebell, to 1½ ft; flowers pendulous, white, pale blue, deep blue, pale rosy-purple or pink in spring; leaves strap-shaped; forms large clumps; good for naturalising; v hardy.

Scirpus albescens
Grassy aquatic perennial of the sedge family with erect narrow spiky leaves longitudinally striped creamy-white and green, to 4 ft tall; flowers insignificant; for planting in shallow water; moderately to v hardy.

Sedum (stonecrop)
Succulent rock garden or herbaceous perennials, with small five-petalled starry flowers, borne singly or more often in flat cymes; generally for any soil, even poor, in sun; v to ultra-hardy. *S. acre*: mat-forming plant; leaves evergreen, yellow-green, small cylindrical and succulent; bright yellow flowers to 1½ in in carpets, early summer; 2 in. *S. anglicum* and *S. dasyphyllum* are of similar habit: the former is a glabrous evergreen with white or pinkish-red tinted flowers; the latter has pink-flushed white flowers and pink-flushed glaucous leaves. *S. album*: creeping mat-forming evergreen with ascending branches; leaves grey-green, narrow, to ½ in long, larger on the pink-tinted flower stems; flowers white, ⅜ in wide, in 3 in corymb-like inflorescences in July; to 6 in high, spreading to 1 ft; very invasive. *S.* 'Autumn Joy': hybrid derived from *S. spectabile* × *S. telephium*: herbaceous perennial forming a compact hummock of upright succulent stems clad with closely set fleshy, stalkless pale grey-green leaves and capped with flat heads to 8 in across of pinkish flowers in late summer to autumn which fade to deep coppery-red; to 2 ft. *S. spectabile*: similar to 'Autumn Joy' but shorter and with clear pink flower heads, popular with butterflies. *S.* 'Ruby Glow': of low decumbent habit; to 10 in, with purple-green leaves and 4 in heads of ruby-red flowers, August to September.

Sempervivum (houseleek, some correctly named *Jovibarba*)
Many species are in cultivation, but all are somewhat similar – hummock-forming plants with tight rosettes of fleshy leaves, ½–6 in or more across; many species having showy red, purple, bronze or silvery coloured/tinted leaves; flowers star-like, pink, red or white, in tight clusters, borne terminally on an elongated leaf rosette; 6–12 in tall, in midsummer; for free-draining soil in full sun; v hardy.

Senecio
A huge genus of annuals, perennials and evergreen shrubs, always with daisy flowers. The following shrubs are moderately hardy. *S. cineraria* (*Cineraria maritima*): sub-shrub to 1–2 ft covered throughout in dense woolly-white felt; leaves pinnately lobed, to 6 in long; flowers in terminal compound corymbs, though best removed for continuity of foliage effect. *S. leucostachys* is similar, but more rambling with pinnately divided leaves and white flower heads. *S. reinoldii* (*S. rotundifolia*): dense, rounded shrub to 10 ft; leaves thick leathery, rounded, deep glossy green above, yellowish below, to 3–4 in long; flowers of no account. *S.* 'Sunshine' (often known as *S. greyi* or *S. laxifolius*): bushy, rather lax shrub with grey-green leaves (very grey at first), white-felted beneath; flowers bright golden-yellow to 1½ in wide, in terminal panicles, from silvery-grey buds in June.

Serratula seoanei (*S. shawii*)
Much-branched plant with mauve-purple somewhat cornflower-like heads of flowers in autumn; leaves deep green, finely cut, 6–9 in long, with a purplish cast; 2 ft; for full sun; v hardy.

Sidalcea 'Sussex Beauty'
Herbaceous perennial related to hollyhocks and mallows; leaves mostly in a basal clump, rounded and lobed; flowers cup-shaped, silky-textured, to 2 in wide, clear pink, in tall branched leafy spikes to 3½ ft, in midsummer; tolerant of poor soils; moderately hardy.

Sisyrinchium angustifolium (blue-eyed grass)
Not a grass, but a tufted iris-like herbaceous perennial with narrow grassy leaves; flowers violet-blue, starry and satiny-textured, ½ in wide, with yellow eyes, borne in elongated clusters on erect stems, opening at noon, early summer; 10 in; ultra-hardy.

Spiraea
Deciduous shrubs; some grown for their small flowers borne in profuse dense corymbs or panicles, a few for coloured foliage; full sun; v hardy. *S.* × *bumalda* 'Goldflame': bushy plant to 3 ft; leaves toothed, to 3 in long, suffused orange-red when young, becoming yellow-green to lime-green; flowers rose-pink in flat corymbs in midsummer; hard pruning in spring improves foliage quality. *S.* × *vanhouttei*: hybrid derived from *S. trilobata* × *S. cantoniensis*; vigorous plant to 7 ft, though best pruned after flowering to maintain smaller size; arching branches bear white flowers in profuse 2 in wide clusters in May.

Stipa gigantea
Semi-evergreen perennial grass reaching quite large proportions and suitable as a specimen plant; leaves narrow, borne in large tufts; flowers in large oat-like inflorescences to 1 ft long on tall stalks to 6 ft, pinkish-beige fading with age to yellowish; plant or divide in spring; moderately hardy.

Stratiotes aloides (water soldier)
Free-floating aquatic perennial; leaves spine-edged and spiky in a rosette, rather like a pineapple top, to 8 in across; flowers seldom seen; v hardy.

Syringa (lilac)
Deciduous upright shrubs; flowers 4-limbed or double in prolific scented panicles; often produce suckers, but can be left on, provided the plant has not been top grafted; v hardy. *S.* × *persica* 'Alba': white flowered form of the Persian

lilac; bushy, rounded plant to 7 ft; leaves lance-shaped, to 2½ in long; relatively small inflorescences of white flowers, to 4 in long in May. *S. vulgaris* (common lilac); suckering vigorous shrub to 12 ft or more, often tree-like; leaves to 6 in long; flowers lilac in large pyramidal inflorescences in late spring; 'Souvenir de Louis Spaeth' has reddish-purple flowers, ultra-hardy.

Tamarix pentandra (tamarisk)
Shrub or small tree up to 15 ft with slender branches; leaflets small but giving plumose effect; flowers pink in short cylindrical racemes, borne in branched clusters, giving a feathery panicle-like spray, in late summer; best in full sun; ultra-hardy.

Tellima grandiflora (fringecup)
Evergreen perennial; leaves lobed, hairy, to 4 in across, becoming purplish in winter; flowers bell-shaped, pale green, in upright sprays in spring and early summer; 2 ft; tolerant of poor soil; for cool shade; v hardy.

Thuja occidentalis 'Rheingold'
A dense pyramidal form of the American arbor-vitae, to 8 ft; leaves golden-yellow, bronzed in winter; full sun; ultra-hardy.

Tiarella cordifolia (foam flower)
Semi-evergreen low-growing perennial, spreading by runners; leaves toothed, lobed and bronze-tinted in winter; flowers star-like, very small, creamy-white, in fluffy racemes in May; to 1 ft; for rich soil in partial shade; ultra-hardy.

Tigridia pavonia (tiger flower)
Mexican bulb with large, spectacular flowers up to 6 in across, orange-red, scarlet, yellow or white with three larger spreading petals and spotted cup-shaped centre, opening in succession, on 1–1½ ft stems, leaves sword-shaped; in colder areas, lift for winter; moderately hardy.

Tilia (lime)
Large and vigorous deciduous trees; leaves mostly heart-shaped; flowers cream in pendant clusters with a long winged bract, scented, attract bees; site carefully as some species become infested with aphids which drip sticky honeydew; v hardy. *T. petiolaris* (weeping silver lime): probably a weeping subspecies of *T. tomentosa*, eventually reaching 100 ft; leaves dark green and white-felted beneath readily displaying their under-surface.

Tithonia rotundifolia (*T. speciosa*, Mexican sunflower)
Half-hardy annual with rich-orange daisies in summer, resembling a zinnia, 2–3 in across; leaves coarse heart-shaped; 4–7 ft; for sunny site in light soil; 'Torch' is a common seed strain.

Tropaeolum
Vigorous annuals or herbaceous perennials, of climbing or trailing habit; leaves usually rounded; flowers trumpet-shaped with a long spur, usually vividly coloured in shades of red, orange or yellow. *T. peregrinum* (*T. canariense*, canary creeper): short-lived perennial, usually cultivated as a half-hardy annual; climber to 12 ft with five-lobed bluish-green leaves; flowers fringed, vivid yellow with green spur, 1 in wide; useful for rapid infill. *T. tuberosum*: tuberous-rooted climbing perennial; leaves palmate; flowers yellow and red in autumn; orange in early-flowering 'Ken Aslet'; moderately hardy and often grown in pots.

Veratrum
Fleshy-rooted herbaceous perennials; leaves pleated and fan-like, to 1 ft long; flowers small and starry, forming erect branched panicles in summer; for moist rich soil in shade; ultra-hardy. *V. album*: flowers greenish in 1–2 ft inflorescences; 4 ft. *V. nigrum*: flowers deep maroon in 3 ft inflorescences; 4 ft; leaves prone to scorch in summer. *V. viride*: flowers bright green in 1–2 ft inflorescences; to 7 ft.

Verbena rigida (*V. venosa*)
Rhizomatous short-lived perennial, often treated as an annual; flowers vivid violet-purple borne on erect, rigid stems in summer; roots tuberous; 1½–2 ft; for sunny site; moderately hardy.

Viburnum
Rather diverse group of evergreen or deciduous shrubs grown for showy and often fragrant white or pink flowers (sometimes borne in winter on naked stems) and/or for often brightly coloured persistent berries; flowers mostly tubular and five-lobed in flat or semi-spherical inflorescences; v hardy. *V. opulus* 'Compactum': compact form of the guelder rose, to 6 ft; leaves palmately lobed; flowers white, lacecap-type having a ring of showy sterile florets surrounding small insignificant fertile flowers, in flat inflorescences resembling those of lacecap hydrangeas; berries bright red and rather translucent, ripening in August and persisting for several months.

Vinca (periwinkle)
Mat-forming low ground-cover evergreen perennials; sub-shrubby and self-rooting; leaves mostly dark green and glossy, rounded, to 2 in long; numerous variegated forms; flowers opening from a tube into five petals, in shades of blue, purple and white, borne in late spring to midsummer except for *V. difformis* which flowers from autumn to spring; tolerant of any soils, even poor, and full shade; v hardy.

Viola (violas, violettas, violets and pansies)
Mostly perennials, though the familiar pansies are annual or biennial; leaves rounded or heart-shaped and toothed; flowers variable in shape, in wide range of colours. Violas are like small pansies with flat 1–1¼ in wide flowers consisting of rounded and overlapping petals, borne on leafy branching stems. Violettas are similar, but smaller-flowered. Violets have smaller nodding flowers with narrower petals, less flat in shape and with often quite prominent spurs; and with broad heart-shaped basal leaves. Violets often spread vigorously by stolons; self-seed. *V. cornuta* 'Alba': a white flowered viola with fresh green leaves; 6–10 in; moisture-loving; moderately to v hardy. *V. labradorica*: a mauve-flowered violet with heavily purple suffused, dark green leaves; 5 in; v hardy. *V.* 'Maggie Mott': hybrid viola having silvery-mauve flowers with a cream centre, to 2 in across; 6 in; v hardy. *V. odorata* (sweet violet); a very sweetly scented violet, spreading vigorously by stolons; flowers deep violet with short-spurs, spring; hybrids in various colours including pink, blue, apricot and white; 6 in; v to ultra-hardy.

Vitis coignetiae (crimson glory vine)
Very vigorous deciduous climber, up to 60 ft, grown partly for its brilliant crimson and scarlet autumn colouring of the large 10 in long roundish ovate, shallowly lobed leaves; v hardy.

Weigela florida 'Variegata'
Deciduous woody shrub to 6 ft; leaves edged white when young, turning to gold and green with age, to 4 in long; flowers funnel-shaped with five lobes and tubular base, pale pink, scented, in clusters in May; moderately hardy.

Wisteria sinensis
Very vigorous deciduous woody climber up to 100 ft, often making large trunk, gnarled at base; flowers lilac-mauve, pea-like up to 1 in long in pendulous racemes in spring, up to 6 in opening together before leaves, very fragrant; leaves pinnate; new shoots should be cut back to two or three buds annually; v hardy. *W. floribunda* is similar but later flowering and with much longer racemes, but little scent; flowers open with the early leaves.

Yucca gloriosa
Shrub with rosette of glaucous leaves on top of short thick woody trunk; flowers in very large panicles up to 4 ft tall, widely bell-shaped, creamy-white, in midsummer to mid-autumn; leaves up to 2 ft long by 3 in wide, stiff, growing erectly and spine tipped, sometimes glaucous; best in full sun; moderately hardy. *Y. filamentosa* and *Y. flaccida* are dwarfer species without trunks. All these have variegated-leaved forms.

Zantedeschia aethiopica (arum lily)
Rhizomatous South African perennial with arum flowers in spring and summer consisting of a very large snow-white spathe up to 10 in long, recurved in upper part, and a creamy-yellow central club-like spadix fading to white at base; stem up to 3 ft but generally less; leaves broad, glossy and somewhat arrow-shaped; best in moist soil or in shallow water; moderately hardy.

Zephyranthes candida (flower of the west wind)
Small bulbous plant with white flowers in autumn, like a crocus, 1½–2 in long; leaves narrow, rush-like; multiplies freely; for warm sheltered site; moderately hardy (lift overwinter in colder areas).

Useful addresses

FOR BRITISH READERS

SEEDSMEN
John Chambers
15 Westleigh Road, Barton Seagrave, Kettering, Northants NN15 5AJ
Chiltern Seeds
Bortree Stile, Ulverston, Cumbria LA12 7PB
Suffolk Herbs
Sawyers Farm, Little Cornard, Sudbury, Suffolk
Thomson & Morgan
London Road, Ipswich, Suffolk IP2 0BA

PLANTS
Hilliers Nurseries (Winchester) Ltd
Ampfield House, Ampfield, nr. Romsey, Hants SO5 9PA
Peter Nyssen Bulbs Ltd
Railway Road, Urmston, Manchester M31 1XW

SOCIETIES
Alpine Garden Society
The Secretary, Lye End Link, St John's, Woking, Surrey GU21 1SW
The Hardy Plant Society
Miss Barbara White, 10 St Barnabas Road, Emmer Green, Caversham, Reading, Berks RG4 8RA

TOOLS
Joseph Bentley Ltd
Chemical Works, Barrow-on-Humber, South Humberside DN19 7AQ

FOR NORTH AMERICAN READERS

SEEDSMEN
Geo. W. Park Seed Co.
Greenwood, South Carolina 29647
W. Atlee Burpee Co.
Parks Avenue, Warminster, Pennsylvania 18974
Thompson & Morgan
P.O. Box 100, Farmingdale, New Jersey 07727
Stokes Seed Inc.
Main Street, Box 548, Buffalo, New York 14240

PLANTS
Wayside Gardens Co.
Hodges, South Carolina 29645
White Flower Farm
Litchfield, Connecticut 06759

SOCIETIES
Hardy Plant Society
Pacific Northwest Group, 124 N. 181st Street, Seattle, Washington 98133
American Rock Garden Society
Norman Singer, Norfolk Road, S. Sandisfield, Massachusetts 01255
American Hosta Society
Olive Langdon, 5605 11th Avenue South, Birmingham, Alabama 35222
American Hemerocallis Society
William E. Monroe, 2244 Cloverdale Avenue, Baton Rouge, Louisiana 70808

Index